D1152543

# REACHING AND KEEPING TEENAGERS

*With grateful thanks for the support of:*

All Saints Educational Trust
Alpha/Youthwork
Baptist Union of Great Britain
The Boys' Brigade
Christian Herald
Church of England Youth Office
Dulverton Trust
Frontier Youth Trust
The Girls' Brigade
Diocese of Liverpool
Methodist Association of Youth Clubs
Mulberry Trust
Salvation Army
Scripture Union
Shaftesbury Society
United Reformed Church
Youth Alive Ministries
Youth for Christ
and others


All royalties from this book will go towards
the cost of further research on the church

# *Reaching and Keeping Teenagers*

**PETER BRIERLEY**

MARC

Tunbridge Wells

First published 1993

ISBNs
1 85424 221 0 (MARC)
1 85321 118 4 (CRA)

Published jointly with the Christian Research Association,
Vision Building, 4 Footscray Road, Eltham,
London SE9 2TZ.
For details please see end of book.

Also co-published with:
The Church Pastoral Aid Society, Athena Drive,
Tachbrook Park, Warwick CV34 6NG. CPAS is a mission agency which exists to
strengthen churches to evangelise, teach and pastor people of all ages. It seeks through
people and resources to stimulate evangelism, equip and train leaders, advise about
ministry and make grants for mission and training.

And the British Church Growth Association.
The BCGA acknowledges the financial assistance received from the Drummond
Trust, 3 Pitt Terrace, Stirling, in the co-publication of this book.
For details please see end of book.

Produced by Bookprint Creative Services
P.O. Box 827, BN23 6NX, England for
MARC an imprint of Monarch Publications
P.O. Box 163, Tunbridge Wells, Kent TN3 0NZ
Printed in England by Clays Ltd, St Ives plc

To Lindsey Mansfield and Boyd Myers
who, over two and a half years,
made the MARC Europe
Research Team
respected and well-known,
and gave it
commitment, effectiveness and fun

# Contents

# *Acknowledgements*

This book, and the research that lies behind it, is the result of team work. In the opening stages that was very much through the commitment of the Steering Committee and the enthusiasm of its Chairman, Gordon Holloway of the Shaftesbury Society. I would especially like to acknowledge my thanks to him. His organization helped in many practical ways to ensure that the project went ahead. Humanly speaking, without his help, it would have failed.

But others also contributed much: John Buckeridge of *Alpha/Youthwork,* Danny Brierley (no relation) of Chawn Hill Christian Centre, Sylvia Bunting of the Girls' Brigade, Martin Hardwidge of Frontier Youth Trust, Sydney Jones of the Boys' Brigade, Colin Reeves of Herald House, and Andy Wilson of the Baptist Union.

We are grateful too for others who contributed to the planning discussions: Nick Aiken and Ruth Ward of the Church of England Youth Office, and Richard Turner of the Diocese of Liverpool. Others attended the initial exploratory meeting: Tony Barker of the Baptist Union, Sheila Brain of the YWCA, Kevin Braund of Ichthus Christian Fellowship, Sandra Kimber of the Evangelical Missionary Alliance and Pradip Sudra formerly of Youth for Christ.

I would like to record my warm thanks to the representatives of the Frontier Youth Trust and the Shaftesbury Society who undertook the majority of face-to-face interviews. Other Christian organizations like the Girls' Brigade and churches in the Diocese of Liverpool and elsewhere were kind enough to help too. These interviewers were Jennie Appleby, Samuel Asaolu, Catherine Bardsley, Arkle Bell, Peter Birch, Dave Botterill, Chris Bristow, Andy Gilroy, Phil Harper, Nathan Jones, Sylvia Kennell, Tim Lovejoy, Ned McWhirter, Matthew Newstead, Nick Rowark and Connie Sardo.

We are grateful too to the six people who gave time to being personally interviewed: Nick Aiken, Youth Minister of the Diocese of Guildford; Steve Chalke, National Director of Oasis Trust; Patrick Harrison, Youth Officer of the Diocese of Arundel and Brighton; Andy Hickford, Youth Pastor at Stopsley Baptist Church; Mark Landreth-Smith, Youth Worker with Coign Church (New Frontiers) and Ian Valance, a Scripture Union Schools Worker.

Thanks are due too to the heads and RE teachers of many schools who gave permission and organized the distribution of questionnaires in their schools, and to many individual church youth leaders who did the same with their youth groups. It was the input from all these which has made the information available.

Warm thanks are due to Lindsey Mansfield, formerly the Research and Information Officer at MARC Europe, who organized, minuted, drafted questionnaires, and generally made the surveys and the whole project happen. Were it not for the demise of MARC Europe she would undoubtedly also have been involved in writing this book. Her efficiency and incisive thinking made a great contribution. The detailed work of computerizing 2,022 questionnaires was admirably handled by Boyd Myers, formerly Research Officer at MARC Europe, and also John Mortimer. Boyd also interviewed three Youth Officers.

Finally, I would like to thank Valerie Passmore very much indeed for her superbly efficient editing, Mary Lawson for typing and re-typing the manuscript, and our publisher, Tony Collins, whose enthusiasm for this project, especially in the early stages, gave it a significant push towards final agreement to go ahead. I am also most grateful to Barbara Kohl, Sydney Jones, John Buckeridge, Gordon Holloway, Andy Hickford and my wife Cherry who made most helpful comments on an early draft of the text.

Any in-depth study like this depends on teamwork, and while all the faults and failings of this book are my responsibility, without the support, help and energy of so many it simply would not have happened. For all who have made it possible, thank you.

*Peter Brierley*
June 1993

# *Preface*

How often have you come away exasperated from hearing an ageing Christian 'guru' pontificating on the decadence of British youth? The older we get the greater the gap between our knowledge and our opinion, between our experience and our prejudice. And yet it is we ageing Christian leaders who are making decisions about the allocation of money and people resources in youth evangelism and outreach. Where, apart from the sensation-picking media, is the hard evidence?

This is the question which several UK Christian organizations involved in bringing the Gospel to young people asked themselves as they came together last year. We needed an up-to-date piece of market research work which commanded 'street cred' through a representative and colloquial approach to both churched and unchurched youngsters. Partial studies were available both at home and overseas but we all wanted something which would give us fresh high-quality and relevant data on which to build an action programme for reaching and keeping teenagers in the Church—and I speak collectively of the Church of Christ. Not so much your wayout and marginalized youngster who is a 'problem in society' but the two-thirds of our total sample questioned who had a notional or vestigial belief in a Creator God of Love.

I don't think any of us expected anything very startling or

new to come out of the research that we commissioned MARC Europe to carry out. At that time last year we little realised it would be the last piece of work that Peter Brierley and his team would be undertaking under that name, but we rightly (as it has turned out) believed that he would come up with a reliably professional and factual guide to the way the average English teenager is thinking today about Christianity.

As you would expect there is a wide gulf between those whom the Spirit of God has truly called to the service of Jesus, and those who have dipped their toes or heads into 'churchianity' and found it, for a variety of reasons, not worth total immersion. What we must try to pick out from the reasons they offer for giving up on the Church, is how much our inflexible and adult-orientated systems and methods have contributed to the 'turn-off'. We have to remember Jesus' awful warning about 'offending against one of these little ones'.

One particular hobby-horse of mine is our approach to Bible study. Much of our teenage (and adult) Bible teaching is still geared to secular classroom methods that I grew up with forty years ago—except we even do without the help of a blackboard! My wife as a secondary school teacher spends far more of her time these days setting, supervising, and marking individual and group projects (inside and outside the school) than she does in conventional up-front teaching—and the youngsters respond well to it . . . particularly the less academic. How much project work (both Bible-based *and* community-based) is tried out with our 'fringe' teenagers or is it too much like hard work?

I think you will find some pointers to this approach towards the end of this book which I can thoroughly recommend to those who really want both to understand and to reach those young people who we pray will soon be sharing with us in church leadership and growth into 'Dawn 2000'.

*Gordon Holloway*
Chief Executive
The Shaftesbury Society

# *Foreword*

Lucy stepped tentatively into the wardrobe. She started to walk through the hanging coats, at any moment expecting to feel the woodwork against the tips of her fingers . . . but it never came. Slowly the floor turned to snow, the coats to trees and before she knew it she had entered a whole new world where nymphs live in wells, dryads dance with fauns and huge lions even talk with children.

So begin the famous Lewis chronicles. But having read this book I find myself praying for a similar 'Narnia' like experience for all those who read its pages. That as people come to what at first appears simply to be some research on youth work, they will quickly find themselves stepping into a much larger world with far bigger questions.

For make no mistake. This is not just a book on youth work. It is not simply addressing some side issue on the Church's wider agenda. This book is a doorway that leads right to the heart of God's intentions for human history and the Church's mission to the world.

For young people are a sensitive barometer to an ice-age Church, however much youth leaders might try and warm things up. They are often the first to feel the chill of cultural irrelevance. The first to feel left out in the cold by a Church obsessed with looking inward. And so they leave . . . sadly in their droves. But when they do, it is a symptom of the cancer in Church life not the tumour itself. Fundamentally the Church does not have a problem with young people, it has a problem with the Gospel.

When Jesus calls us to be a lifeboat station and the Church insists on being a yacht club; when Christians so twist their calling that instead of being selfless they become self-seeking, a generation of young people is betrayed and the Church has no future. The current Christian climate in this country is literally that stark.

Despite the Biblical mandate for the Church to pass on its faith to the next generation (Ps 78, Deut 6, etc.), by 1979 only 13% of English teenagers attended Church and worse was to come. By 1989 this had declined still further to only 9%.

Once again 'a generation has grown up that does not know God' (Judges 2:10) and just as surely as moral, social and political collapse was to follow in Israel's history when that happened, so thousands of years later we have today, mirrored on our TV screens, similar evidence of society imploding on itself. It is the inevitable result of a spiritual vacuum at the centre of community life.

Whatever advances have been made in British Churches over the last thirty years (and there have been many), these statistics are a damning indictment. With 91% of teenagers having no contact with organized Christianity in this country, the Church's response to its primary task has clearly been weighed in the scales and found wanting. Now is the time to pronounce old approaches as having failed and urgently seek a new strategy for the future. That is the heart of this book.

Peter Brierley resists the temptation to apportion blame and in a workmanlike manner simply gets on with the task of researching why young people have been leaving the Church and what we can do to reverse the trend.

The pages of this book will fascinate all youth specialists. The results of the carefully conducted survey will intrigue the reader and raise as many questions as it answers. But this book is more than just tables and graphs. Contained within it are clues and suggestions as to how the Church might respond to the crisis. One of those clues is a better understanding of culture.

In this 'Decade of Evangelism', the issue of cultural communication is one of the biggest issues facing the Church. As the former Bishop of Southwark is quoted as saying 'We have moved from where Christianity is culture to where Christianity is choice.' For the Church to communicate with young people today is clearly an exercise in cross-cultural communication and for the Gospel to be understood by this 'Walkman' generation, it is clear the Church will need to do more than just shout.

My mind is taken to Acts 17 with Paul at the Areopagus. He acknowledges the religious orientation of his listeners and then goes on to explain the Gospel using terms that they could understand. A knowledge of Old Testament scripture could no longer be assumed of his audience and so he quoted from the Greek poets. He never once compromised the Gospel message, but rather made the unpalatable understandable. A skilled piece of cross-cultural communication if ever there was one.

But we so easily forget that the road to the Areopagus was a difficult one for the early Church to walk. They struggled with the question of Gospel and culture. It was a journey of considerable personal discomfort (as Peter showed in Acts 10) and corporate trauma (as the Council of Jerusalem proved in Acts 15). Readers of this book, therefore, will need to be warned at the outset, that if you take Brierley's work seriously, Acts 17 is your undoubted destination, but similar struggles along the way will not easily be avoided.

This is the journey that thousands of youth leaders are labouring along every week. Now is the time for the Church in Britain to walk with them on this road and to recognize that the Church's outreach to young people is critical in what we call the 'Decade of Evangelism'. Read properly, this book will bring us to our senses, then bring us to our knees and then help bring us into the twenty-first century, having recaptured God's heart for mission.

Finally, I am reminded of David Pawson speaking on the story of Samson. The once mighty judge of Israel was now an impotent stumbling shadow of his former self. At last trusting in God alone, he asked a young boy to guide him to the centre of the Philistine temple and in one final incredible display of strength, God's enemies were defeated. Possibly God will do it again, Pawson ventured. This time the slumbering giant of the Church, stripped of every security save its faith in God, will be brought to the centre of our nation's life to display His power . . . and perhaps again He will use young people to do it.

*Andy Hickford*
**Youth Minister**
**Stopsley Baptist Church**

# *Introduction*

In 1974 I set up a research project into the attitudes of secondary school pupils towards Christianity. Data were collected from 500 pupils in East Anglia. I selected fifty boys and fifty girls from five consecutive age bands: years seven, eight, nine, ten and eleven.[1]

It would have been good to have had a larger sample and a wider geographical area, but the resources were not available. Nevertheless, the data clearly confirmed the ways in which teenage attitudes were hardening against the church and Christianity over this five year age span. For example, while 46% of the year seven pupils were confident that they experienced help from God, the proportion had fallen to 27% among the year eleven pupils.

In 1978 I went back to the next generation of pupils sitting in the same school desks as those who had taken part in my 1974 study. Four years later the same age trend was clearly identified. Now, however, it was also possible to chart how alienation from the churches had accelerated between 1974 and 1978.[2] For example, whereas in 1974 47% believed that God listened to their prayers, in 1978 only 38% believed this.

By returning again to the same school desks at four yearly intervals, in 1982, 1986 and 1990, I began to map how teenagers' views of the church were continuing to change. After the 1986 data were collected, I wrote a short paper under the title 'Drift from the Churches'.[3] The drift was illustrated by the following statistics.

Only 25% of the pupils in 1986 felt that God helps them in their personal lives, compared with 27% in 1982, 34% in 1978 and 42% in 1974. Only 19% of the pupils in 1986 felt that prayer helps them a lot, compared with 22% in 1982, 29% in 1978 and 36% in 1974. Only 29% of the pupils in 1986 believed that God listens to prayers, compared with 33% in 1982, 37% in 1978 and 47% in 1974. Similarly, 56% of the pupils in 1986 dismissed church services as boring, compared with 53% in 1982, 49% in 1978 and 39% in 1974.

These statistics confirmed that there has been a consistent, widespread drift away from the churches among secondary school pupils during the twelve year period between 1974 and 1986.

The 1990 study introduced the first glimpse of hope[4]. Three apparent trends emerged from comparison between the 1980 data and the earlier studies.

First, there seemed to be a clear improvement between 1986 and 1990 in some aspects of pupils' attitudes towards God and towards the Bible. For example, in 1982 43% of the pupils reported that they found it hard to believe in God and the proportion grew to 50% in 1986. In 1990, however, the proportion of pupils who reported that they found it hard to believe in God fell to 41%. Such trends seemed to imply a greater openness to the possibilities of the religious dimension.

Second, there seemed to be little real change between 1986 and 1990 in some aspects of the pupils' attitude towards prayer and the church. For example, the proportion of pupils who felt that saying their prayers helped them a lot, having fallen from 24% in 1982 to 18% in 1986, remained at 20% in 1990. Similarly, the proportion of pupils who dismissed church services as boring stood at 53% in 1982, 56% in 1986 and 54% in 1990. These figures also seemed to imply that the greater openness to the possibility of the religious dimension apparent in the 1990 sample does not necessarily involve increased commitment to personal religious practice, like prayer, or to public religious practice, like church attendance.

Third, there seemed to be a clear continued decline into the 1990s in some aspects of the pupils' attitudes towards Jesus and the religious education given in school. For example, the proportion of pupils who claimed commitment to the central figure of the Christian tradition by agreeing that they wanted to love Jesus fell from 39% in 1974 to 34% in 1978, 26% in 1982, 23% in 1986 and 18% in 1990. Similarly, the proportion of pupils who agreed that they like school lessons about God very much fell from 32% in 1974, to 28% in 1978, 23% in 1982, 21% in 1986 and 13% in 1990. These trends seemed to imply that the greater openness to the possibility of the religious dimension apparent in the 1990 sample may be operating contrary to the greater interest either in the Christian faith or the specifically religious aspects of the school curriculum.

Placed alongside studies conducted in 1974, 1978, 1982 and 1986, these new data from the 1990 replication study suggests that the progressive hardening of secondary school pupils' attitudes towards religion reported over the twelve year period from 1974 to 1986 may now be gradually softening. Such a bold conclusion, however, needs two caveats.

First, a single point of change on a continuing graph is insufficient evidence on which to identify a trend. The study now requires further replication in 1994 in order to test whether the improvement in attitude recorded in 1990, over the situation in 1986, signals a new trend or reflects a temporary aberration.

Second, the fact that the sample draws pupils from only two schools may mean that the observed changes are specific to factors associated with those schools rather than representative of more general national trends. If the churches are really interested in knowing about changes in young people's attitudes towards Christianity, this kind of research needs to be realistically established over a wider sample of schools.

Third, a single short measure of attitude towards Christianity is unable to reflect adequately the wider nuances involved in the young person's response to the religious dimension more generally. Future research needs to take these wider issues more fully into account.

Meanwhile, however, the present study remains the most adequate index currently available to report on changing attitudes towards Christianity among secondary school pupils from the early 1970s into the 1990s.

Alongside this simple study concerned with monitoring teenage attitudes towards Christianity, I have also wanted to develop more sophisticated studies. These studies help us to have a better understanding of why some teenagers are more likely to drift from the churches than others. Such understanding should help the churches to plan their mission and to allocate their resources.

Some of these studies have concentrated more on the features of the local churches. As a result of such research we can better assess the value of resourcing provisions like pre-school activities,[5] church schools[6] and specialist children's ministries including Sunday Schools.[7] We can better assess the impact of a resident minister[8] and the age of that minister[9] on work among different age groups.

Other studies have concentrated more on the personal features of the young people themselves. As a result of such research we can better assess the usefulness of church primary schools,[10] and Anglican[11] and Catholic secondary schools,[12] the comparative influence of fathers and mothers on the religious development of sons and daughters,[13] the significance of denominational membership,[14] and the experience of attending Sunday School.[15] We can better assess the relative impact of personality,[16] mental health,[17] social class,[18] and scientific understanding[19] on adolescents' religious development.

These specialist studies of teenage religion conducted within the UK can be set in the much richer and wider context of the international body of research on the psychology of religious development, helpfully organized in Kenneth Hyde's recent book,[20] and the ever growing secular research on aspects of adolescence.

Properly seen, such research is a crucial resource for the church's ministries of pastoral care and mission. Properly understood, practical theology needs to keep one ear clearly tuned to the voice of God and the other ear clearly tuned to the voice of God's people. The crucial value of empirical research is precisely that it helps the voice of God's people to be heard.

Peter Brierley has a well established history of commitment to helping the churches derive maximum benefit from empirical research.[21] In the present study he challenges the churches to face the truth about their ministry among teenagers, about reaching and keeping this crucial age group. He sets out the facts from a number of researchers and describes the new findings of his own research project commissioned for this book. He sets these facts and findings alongside a vision of God's purpose for the churches and highlights the potential for growth and change.

While the perspective offered by empirical research is but one of the perspectives essential for the church's future, it is a perspective which the churches cannot and should not afford to ignore. Not only is the church's future at stake, young lives are at stake as well.

*Revd Dr Leslie Francis*
D J James Professor of Pastoral Theology
and Mansel Jones Fellow
Trinity College, Carmarthen

# 1

# *Teenagers' Social Environment*

A particular Spring Harvest meeting in April 1991 on youth work was well attended. It was being led by Maggie Everett, the Training Officer of Youth for Christ. Just before it began, however, there was an 'invasion': teenagers came in from every door and entrance and doubled the audience. This was going to be a training session with a difference! They chanted and sang, and made their presence felt. At Maggie's indication, they suddenly became silent, and then quietly filed out. Maggie addressed her audience: 'That was three hundred teenagers. What a difference their absence makes. That is the number of teenagers the English church is losing every single week.'

Three hundred *a week*! Could that be true? Yes, the English Church Census,[1] published the month before, had revealed this startling statistic: the 1980s had ended with 155,000 fewer teenagers attending the churches across the country than attended in 1979. That represents a net fall-out of 300 teenagers every week (although some would have grown out of the teenage sector, with non-replacement at younger ages). This single and simple fact made a deep impression. John Wesley once said, 'If religion is not extended to the children, what will be the outcome?' If religion is not extended to the teenagers, what will be the outcome? Nothing that churches would want or welcome. How then can they be brought back? This book, and the research behind it, arises out of the concern felt by many youth organizations to think through such an important issue.

To start, however, we need to put teenagers in Britain today into context and having done that, turn to the issues of church involvement.

### Who is a Teenager?

'Teenager' literally means those aged 13 to 19 inclusive, but this definition is almost too simple. Other phrases are now used to subdivide this group, and the ages do not start at age 13. Those aged 10 to 12 are sometimes called the 'aspirant teens', the young people who look forward to becoming teenagers, and who read books meant for teenagers (which teenagers largely do not read). Those aged 13 or 14 are sometimes dubbed the 'glad-to-be-teens' with those aged 15–19 designated the 'genuine teens'. The English Church Census specially analysed the 15–19 group, and the figures quoted above relate to this age range only.

Secondary education starts at 11 years of age and finishes at either 16 or 18. Teenagers are sometimes equated with such pupils. Further education usually finishes at about 21, and young people often leave home in their early twenties. But the 16–21 age range is not uniform. Some are studying and living with their parents (and have some money, but not much time), others are unemployed but living at home (with not much money, and plenty of time), while others are working (with plenty of money and some time especially at weekends).[2]

Even this group is too wide. For example, it is the 16–19 year olds who especially listen to music, or watch hired videos. It is those aged 16 and 17 who frequently go to the cinema.

Great changes happen during the teenage years, and teenagers can change quickly, as every parent knows. 'At age 12, a son or daughter is still considered a child. Four years later on, that son or daughter has become a young man or young woman with an adult body, reproductive ability, and a desire for independence. These four years are probably the most difficult years of a person's life,' wrote one psychologist.[3]

Change is also seen through teenage social life, much of which is spent in a pub: 44% of working teens spend at least four hours in a pub or club every Saturday. Helping this process is the rapid increase in income which many teenagers experience. Weekly income from all sources averaged £16 at 15, £35 at 16, £56 at 17, and £77 at 18[4], at 1993 prices. Teenage crime has increased in the last twenty years, and there is today widespread experimentation with sexual intercourse.

There is another whole range of terminology used for present-day teenagers, given here for reference only. It is not used in this book. It has come to us from the United States. There they talk of the 'baby boomers' and the 'baby busters', though the adjective 'baby' tends to get dropped after a while. 'Boomers' are the parents of the 'busters', and 'builders' the parents of the 'boomers'.[5] The 'baby boom generation has changed and will continue to change our society',[6] and many have written about these changes and their impact on the church and society.[7] The 'busters' have also had extensive evaluation. According to George Barna, the author of key volumes in this area, 'boomers' were born between 1946 and 1964, so would be aged 30–48 in 1994. 'Busters' were born between 1965 and 1983, so would be aged 11 to 29 in 1994. These groups follow the 'baby-boom' (whence the name originated) in America in the 1950s, when exceptional numbers of babies were born. In Britain, the baby-boom occurred somewhat later, in the late 1950s and early 1960s, so that we are up to ten years behind the Americans in this respect. Their 'buster' generation fits with our teenage group, however defined, and we shall need to look at some of the American findings. For the purposes of this study, teenagers are defined as 12 to 18 years of age, broadly secondary school age, but where relevant we look at earlier and later years as well.

*How many teenagers are there?*

Table 1: UK 15–19 year olds 1981–2006[8]

| Year | Number | Percentage of population | Percentage males |
|---|---|---|---|
| | | % | % |
| 1981 | 4,735,000 | 8.4 | 51.2 |
| 1986 | 4,479,000 | 7.9 | 51.3 |
| 1991 | 3,723,000 | 6.5 | 51.4 |
| 1996* | 3,517,000 | 6.0 | 51.4 |
| 2001* | 3,703,000 | 6.3 | 51.4 |
| 2006* | 3,914,000 | 6.6 | 51.6 |

* estimate

In the baby-boom period in Britain (late 1950s and early 1960s) extra large numbers of children were born. With the average age of having a first baby now 27 years of age, the baby-boom children themselves will mostly have their children in the late 1980s and the 1990s. The number of teenagers in the population has consequently been falling during the 1980s and the 1990s, as Table 1 shows. The number begins to increase again in the early years of the twenty-first century as the children born in the late 1980s reach the 15 to 19 age-group. The proportion of male teenagers has also slightly increased since 1981 and is projected to continue doing so.

There is very little difference in the proportion of teenagers across England, with slightly more in the West Midlands, and slightly fewer in the South West. In Wales and Scotland the proportion of 15–19 year olds in 1991 was respectively 6.5% and 6.7% (against 6.4% for England), but it was very different in Northern Ireland, where the percentage was 7.8%.

**Teenagers at home and work**

*Home environment*

Teenagers will grow up in a home with increasingly fewer children in it. In 1971 the average number of children per British woman was 2.4, but in 1991 this had fallen to 1.8, a number similar to that in France, but, apart from the Irish Republic, higher than anywhere else in the European Community[9].

Twelve to 18 year olds in 1992, the year the study was undertaken, were born between 1974 and 1980. In these years illegitimate births increased from 9% to 12%, which although well below the 1992 figure of 30%, was still substantial. Roughly one teenager in ten in Britain in 1992 was born outside wedlock.

In the 12 years since 1980 there were 1.8 million divorces. One mother hesitatingly told her twins that she and their father were separating. 'Thank goodness,' was the astonishing response of the 12 year olds, 'now we will be like all the other children in our class!' In a fascinating analysis the Government statistician John Haskey looked at the children in the families of couples who divorced in 1988/89, and worked out the likelihood that a child of 11 had a 19% chance of experiencing a divorce, rising to 24% for a 15 year old.[10]

One in six households with dependent children today are single-parent families, with the majority being single mothers. 'That divorce is associated with more adverse outcomes for children than the death of a parent and that the remarriage of a parent appears in some circumstances to add to the children's difficulties, are findings supported by a very large body of research of many different kinds'.[11]

Teenagers do not only experience the effects of divorce from their parents, they also marry and sometimes divorce themselves before they are 20. Fortunately such numbers are small (in the hundreds) though they are rising. Generally young people are tying the knot later, partly for employment/career reasons, partly economic reasons, and partly because of housing availability. Cohabitation before marriage is widespread, especially among those in their early twenties. This also affects those in their teens. In 1987 one in four young people under 20 was living with a partner, some 900,000 couples altogether, with 400,000 dependent children. So many children? Yes, because so many of these couples have a stable relationship but decide not to marry even when they have children.[12] The proportion of illegitimate children registered under two names in 1990 was 73%.[13]

It may be asked in these circumstances, what constitutes a family and what a household. This cannot be discussed in detail here, but 'the core unifying notion behind family relationships is the idea of obligation; the acceptance of social rules defining obligations which different family members owe to each other.'[14] The smaller number of households with children reflects the results of a survey undertaken by the National Council of Women which showed that having children was only third in their list of priorities, but nearly 75% agreed that 'having a stable relationship was important.'[15] As well as life style, partner relations, and personal preferences, the societal culture of power structure is felt by some to be an important determinant at individual level on having a family.[16]

## Teenage conceptions

The total number of teenage conceptions (inside and outside of marriage) did not vary greatly during the 1980s in total. However, the declining number of teenagers during the period means this was an increase in conception rate. The percentage of abortions among those aged 17 or over also increased as shown in the table opposite.[17]

The columns headed 'Conception rate per 1,000 females' are simply the number of conceptions in the first columns divided by the number of teenagers living at the given age and multiplied by 1,000. Thus of all the 19 year olds in 1990, 100

Table 2: Teenage conceptions in England and Wales 1980 and 1990

| Age | Number | | Percentage leading to legal abortion | | Conception rates per 1,000 females[18] | |
|---|---|---|---|---|---|---|
| | 1980 | 1990 | 1980 | 1990 | 1980 | 1990 |
| | | | % | % | | |
| Under 14 | 352 | 356 | 65 | 58 | 1 | 1 |
| 14 | 1,714 | 1,870 | 61 | 56 | 4 | 7 |
| 15 | 6,513 | 6,408 | 52 | 48 | 16 | 22 |
| 16 | 15,210 | 14,311 | 44 | 42 | 37 | 46 |
| 17 | 23,894 | 23,036 | 34 | 37 | 60 | 70 |
| 18 | 32,093 | 31,482 | 27 | 34 | 81 | 89 |
| 19 | 37,475 | 37,592 | 22 | 31 | 96 | 100 |
| Total under 20 | 117,251 | 115,058 | 31 | 36 | 68 | 69 |

out of 1,000 (or 10%) conceived. This was 37,592 conceptions, and there were about 375,000 19 year olds living in England and Wales in 1990.

It should be noted that about one in eight conceptions to all women in England and Wales in 1990 were to women under the age of 20. Teenage pregnancies are a significant proportion of the total.

'Childbearing teenagers, particularly in the younger age-groups, suffer more than mothers in their early twenties from a number of medical conditions . . . and are therefore more at risk of giving birth to vulnerable and 'small-for-dates' babies for every period of gestation.'[19] In 1980, for example, the perinatal mortality rate per 1,000 births was 19 for mothers aged under 16, 17 for mothers aged 16 to 19, and 13 for those in their early twenties. 'The rate of depressive disorders increases sharply during adolescence, which may make pregnancy at this time additionally problematic . . . parents of battered babies tend to be very young.'[20]

In a major book on *The British Population*,[21] published in 1992, the authors, David Coleman and John Salt comment on teenage fertility. It 'brings together many of the problems of poor knowledge and planning, the harmful consequences of unwanted fertility, and its transmission across generations. Teenage mothers are least able to cope with motherhood, being often themselves emotionally immature and sometimes physically immature. Often they possess no resources or accommodation of their own. They are twice as likely to live in council housing, twice as likely to be supported by someone in class V (if at all) than in any other class. Their pregnancies are likely to be troublesome and repetitive. In a Newcastle study, more than 70% of first illegitimate pregnancies were followed by another.

'The earlier the pregnancy, the worse the circumstances. Girls who become pregnant by their 16th birthday are likely to have parents who are divorced, separated, alcoholic, or in gaol, or to have been themselves in care or in a special school.

In one survey, 83% of the younger girls never used contraception or used it sporadically. Only 51% of the girls over 16 had attempted to avoid pregnancy; others thought that they could not become pregnant because they were too young or had sex too infrequently. Parents of teenage mothers usually married young themselves, had primary education only, were mostly in manual occupations, and came from large families. The teenage mothers like their parents had little ambition except further childbearing. Teenagers who conceived pre-maritally were five times as likely as the average to have been conceived pre-maritally themselves. More than half teenage marriages are likely to end in divorce. Teenage marriage and pregnancy have comprehensively gloomy outcomes.'

## *Employment, education and finance*

It has already been noted that income rises rapidly during the teenage years. A young person with a job will earn roughly three times what a student gets (£100 a week versus £35 in 1993). The cumulative direct spending power in 1993 of those aged 15 to 24 was £36,000 million. Of those working in 1988, 79% had a bank account, 55% a building society account and 31% a credit card, though despite this there was a fairly wide mistrust of banks.[22] What do young people spend their money on, apart from rent and fares? The top items were:

Alcoholic drinks in pubs
Clothes
Eating out
Soft drinks and 'other things' in pubs
Take-away food
Records and tapes
Cigarettes
Makeup and cosmetics
Watching or playing sport
Magazines[23]

Employment, however, is not always easy to come by. In 1975 60% of 16 and 17 year olds were employed, compared to 22% in 1988. In 1990, 53% of 16 year olds stayed on at school, and a further 22% attended youth training schemes. By the age of 18, however, many more were working: 70% of this age-group had a job in 1988, though the proportion unemployed was four times what it had been in 1975. The spectre of unemployment is high: 75% of 13 year olds in a 1992 survey[24] realised it would be difficult getting the job they wanted. Recession has hit the employment of teenagers hard, if not harder, than others. In one group of 17 year olds, only 20% had found a job.[25] The top three priorities for a 17 year old were a car, more money, and a job.

It could be that the difficulty of getting a job is one reason for the increase in the number of students. There were just under a million students in England in 1990, a number which had increased by a third over the previous ten years, and likely to continue to grow.[26] At a large comprehensive school in south-east London in November 1992, a small group of girls was asked, as part of that morning's assembly, what they wanted to do in the future. Five 16 year olds spoke. All wanted to carry on studying, either at school or college. They saw themselves at 21 as either still studying or with a 'meaningful' job. By the time they were 26 however, four expected to be married, maybe with one or two children. Three said they wanted to be 'happy', one wanted 'lots of money', and one wanted to secure her career before she got married.[27] The emphasis on study is unmistakable.

Part of the need to work is the desire to have money for legitimate wants. One of the main fears of 17–19 year olds is getting into debt: 'nine out of ten of them are terrified of going into the red.'[28] Perhaps this explains not just their desire to get a job, but to keep it as well, if they can. When George Barna asked American 'busters' how they spent their time in 1992 compared to a year previously, 53% said they were devoting more time to work.[29]

One special danger for female teenagers requiring money, but not being able to find employment, is that they will turn to prostitution. This is not just a British problem. In Montreal, Canada, there are 7,000 prostitutes, and in a study of prostitutes in Calgary, Canada, it was found that the *average age was under 16.*[30] It is all too easy in such circumstances for some to feel the Asian saying applies to them: 'A girl should be like water: unresisting, it takes the shape of the container it is poured into, but has no shape of its own.'[31] Young people (males as well as females) often do not feel valued by society—nor by the Church. Some churches spend more on flowers than they do on young people! As a consequence they can feel completely isolated.

The above comments on money fly in the face, however, of a European study. 'According to the 'Eurokids' report published by Alto, the panEuropean advertising group along with Eurodata, the EC's statistical office, materialism, money, greed and yuppies are out of favour. Tarot reading, rainforests, crystals, shamanic arts, and vegetarianism are in.'[32] How far this may be true in England is examined later; what the quotation suggests is that the contrast between the practical, financial world and the theoretical, implicitly religious world may be sharper than at least many older people think.

### Smoking and drugs

George Barna asked over a thousand Americans how important certain items were for them, with the results in Table 3.[33]

This is an interesting list, both in its order and the differences between young and old. There were three items where both groups scored about the same: their time, living comfortably, and money. The younger people were much more concerned about their career than older people, and put the importance of their career well above living comfortably and money (and their religion!). For older people, their friends, the Bible, their religion, their free time and their community were much more valued.

*Table 3: 1992 US priorities (percentage rating 'very important')*

| Importance of | Aged 18–26 | Aged 27 or over | Difference |
|---|---|---|---|
| | % | % | % |
| Family | 93 | 97 | −4 |
| Health | 84 | 92 | −8 |
| Time | 78 | 78 | 0 |
| Career | 67 | 51 | +16 |
| Friends | 64 | 78 | −14 |
| Living comfortably | 61 | 60 | +1 |
| Bible | 56 | 70 | −14 |
| Religion | 54 | 73 | −19 |
| Free time | 52 | 66 | −14 |
| Money | 40 | 39 | +1 |
| Community | 28 | 56 | −28 |
| Government and politics | 25 | 35 | −10 |

Health was regarded as the second most important item, coming only after family. Older people prized it even more. This shows the value young people, which included some teenagers, put on their physical well-being. Similar studies have not been carried out in the UK so far as I know, but it is likely that the health item would be seen to be important for British teenagers also.

Perhaps in confirmation, the proportion of younger teens who regularly smoke is small. In 1990 only 9% of boys aged 11–15 said they regularly smoked, and a further 6% said they occasionally did so. These percentages have not varied significantly since 1980. 11% of girls said they were regular smokers, and 6% occasionals, again figures which have not varied greatly. These proportions still represent one boy in seven and one girl in six who is smoking.[34]

The proportion of children who have tried drugs is small. 4% of 9–15 year olds said they had tried cannabis, and 7% one drug or another. 6% said they had been offered cannabis, and 15% some kind of drug. These may seem small percentages but they mean, if true, that something like 360,000 children between 9 and 15 have tried drugs. That there were only 1,400 drug addicts under 21 notified to the Home Office suggests that a huge number might try drugs, but do not take them regularly, or at least do not become notifiable addicts.

In 1989 there were about 30 people using drugs illegally per 10,000 aged 17–20, and about 3 per 10,000 aged 10–16.[35] We must pray that this situation does not change. In New York, it has. 'Even nine and ten year old kids in New York City are pushing drugs. Police picked up an eight year old boy in fact, up in Harlem with a little paper sack with 400 vials of crack he was selling. Eight years old! . . . Right in my face, young teens scoff and tell me, 'Just say no to all my gold chains and this £5,000 wristwatch? Say no to these designer clothes and go back to nothing? To food stamps and Salvation Army used clothes?' . . . My dad's an alcoholic, my mom's on drugs and doesn't care, I lived with my grandma and didn't have any money, dropped out school. And if I'm going to die with a bullet in my head, I'm going out in style. I'll have some money in my pocket, I'll be driving a nice car and if I go to hell, I'm going to hell in a Porsche.'[36]

## Teenagers at risk

### Teenagers and crime

What is crime? The language of what is wrong is being changed. 'In the wake of relativism, new definitions have been adopted to account for the changes in ethical thinking. Youth magazines, educators and the media generally have taken on board these new inoffensive definitions.

- Abortion is no longer murder—it is simply a woman exercising her right of privacy of her own body, or in medical terms, 'retrospective fertility control'.
- Homosexuality is merely an optional sexual preference.

- Pornography is an expression of free speech that doesn't affect anyone else.
- Adultery is 'living together'.
- Illegitimate babies are 'love children'.
- Euthanasia is 'mercy killing'.'[37]

The number of children over 10 and under 17 found guilty of or cautioned for indictable offences committed was 83,000 in 1972, 90,000 in 1982, and had reached 111,000 by 1990. In 1990 there were 125,000 such offences by young adults between 17 and 20. Of these 80% and 85% respectively were male in 1990. 'The peak age for recorded offences is from 18 for males and 15 for females.'[38] Driving offences by those under 18 trebled between 1972 and 1992.

In the United States, some families are trying to prevent crime a different way. 'Increasingly, parents are locking up their unruly kids in the psychiatric wards of private hospitals for engaging in what many therapists call normal adolescent behaviour. Busy parents who are unable or unwilling to deal with rebellious teenagers, and the profit margins of psychiatric businesses are blamed for this trend. Inpatient psychiatric care is reimbursed by insurance companies at 80–100%, compared to 50% for outpatient services.'[39] Maybe this would keep the crime rate down too!

Delinquency amongst young males has always been fairly common, but with a more robust view of the need for punishment has been better contained. The authority of the police and schools, and even parents, is gradually becoming more restricted, allowing young men to get involved more easily. A child under 10 in English law is deemed 'not to know the difference between good and evil,' and cannot therefore be taken to court. Those under 15 can no longer be detained in custody unless found guilty of murder.

Crime is increasing, though the underlying crime rate (crimes per head of population) has not greatly altered. The crime rate could increase. If we choose to redefine our terms, however, it could decrease simply because what had been a crime is so no longer—a very dangerous game to play. Keeping an eye on crime numbers therefore is of some importance. It must be recognized, however, that if all the indictable offences were committed by separate individuals (that is, no-one committed more than one) in 1990 2.1% of the 10–17 year old population and 3.9% of 17–20 year olds were involved in crime.

## Suicide

As Olaf Fogwill, the Public Relations Manager of Crusaders, the young people's organisation, was walking through a St. Albans park one day, he came across a bench with these words of graffiti inscribed:

'Dave, Lucy, Ed and Nat spend enough time getting wrecked on this bench. Procrastination is our thief of time. We are the children of the wasted years—unique, unrivalled, lost in a dream of what has gone before—WE WILL NEVER CONFORM'[40]

In 1991 16% of the 3,000 aged 15–24 who died in England and Wales did so by committing suicide, a significant percentage, though not as high as the 22% of deaths of those aged 25–34. These two percentages were by far the largest proportions for suicide out of all ages. One third of suicides in 1991 were by those aged 15–34.[41] Another study showed that by far the most suicides took place amongst those who became separated from their spouse, with divorced people being the next category but much smaller—only one-sixth the number of those separated. Going to prison is a traumatic experience for anyone, but especially for young people. In 1991 over 1,200 people under 21 mutilated themselves or attempted suicide while in prison.[42]

## Young people in transition

It is obvious that the teenage years are years of transition, tension and turmoil for most. They have to cope with so many pressures, problems and persuasions. New activities, authorities and advertisements play on their emotions. Family, friends and feelings all compete for attention. How does the church cope? Generally, not very well. That is why 300 teenagers are drifting away each week. How should the church cope? By at least recognizing two things: individual teenagers vary greatly across these vital years, and it must not patronize an 18 year old by offering a form of faith relevant to an 8 year old. It must also recognize that teenagers of the same age-group vary enormously, some being much more mature, modern and moralistic than others.

Carrick James Market Research surveyed 731 16–24 year olds in December 1989–January 1990 using face-to-face interviews and questionnaires, which involved completing 40 attitude statements. They used these to classify young people into seven types.[43] This classification is useful in showing the different groups into which young people fall, and important for the church in trying to assess how to reach these varying types. These types are described below, with the names in brackets being the titles Carrick James assigned to each group.

### *Hedonists* (Life's a party)

These comprise 18% of young people. They seek enjoyment, drink lager, support the poll tax. They have little ambition, 40% smoke, and feel little social responsibility. They tend to vote Conservative, and are fashion conscious—they like to feel good and look good. They tend to be racist (50% think 'there are too many blacks in Britain') and anti-gay (76% say homosexuals 'disgust' them), but have little moral concern. They tend to live in London and the south-east. Of all groups, they have the highest disposable income, but still think you should borrow now and pay later. 58% are men, and 49% aged between 18 and 20. They go to football matches.

Figure 1: The Hedonist

Figure 2: The Moralist

## *Moralists* (New moralists)

This category covers 13% of young people. They are austere, cautious and clean-living. They are anti-smoking, and hard working. Many have an ABC1 social background (professional, managerial, middle-class). 25% are Green voters. They emphasize keep fit, and vegetarianism. They are anti-drinking (alcohol is a dangerous drug), and egalitarian. 44% are aged 18–20. They are Body Shop regulars. Most want eventually to be self-employed. They do not live for their holidays, believing strongly in the work ethic. They certainly endorse sexual caution, and 87% do not think there is too much fuss about the dangers of smoking.

Figure 3: The Moderate

*Moderates* (Young moderates)

These make up 8% of young people. They have low income (second lowest take home pay), but 42% smoke, and they tend to buy their clothes from catalogues as they hate shopping. They are not heavy drinkers, preferring cola and hot chocolate. They are predominantly Labour voters, for whom pensions are important. They are highly family orientated.

*Cautious* (Safety seekers)

These constitute 16% of young people. They tend to take middle-of-the- road, unexceptional, views. They are not sporty, and are nervous of flying and using the Channel Tunnel. They

Figure 4: The Cautious

are not work orientated and 79% of them do not smoke though they do not hold strong views against smoking. They are mildly Green, wanting to 'do their bit' for the environment, but are certainly not in the vanguard of Green politics. 38% vote Labour. They are not heavy drinkers and think alcohol is a dangerous drug.

*Idealists* (Outsiders)

This category comprises 16% of young people. These are self-sufficient, believing in sexual and racial equality. They are of working class origins, and often on a low income (the lowest

Figure 5: The Idealist

of all). They are alienated by most politicians, but very keen on Green. They have a low education level, and 50% smoke. They tend to get their clothes from market stalls. They are unconcerned about having a healthy diet. They mistrust banks, politicians and the police. They tend to blame society or authority whenever they are given the chance. 42% just live for their holiday.

## *Authoritarians*

These make up 13% of young people. Seven in every ten authoritarians are women, and are anti-smoking (especially in public places or at work). They are very anti-gay and believe it is the woman's responsibility to organize contraception. They tend to drink gin and tonic. They support the police and the

G &T

FASHION
MAGS

Figure 6: The Authoritarian

SDP. They are in favour of work and marriage. They are happy to have a mortgage and dress fashionably. They are fairly racist. Generally they have a relatively high level of education and disposable income. They support the poll tax, and the scheme for identifying under-age pub-goers through identity cards. They are predominantly based in London and the South.

*Conventionalist* (Greying youth)

These cover 16% of young people. They tend to have old-fashioned, traditional and middle-aged views. They are cash orientated. They believe hard work is the route to success and are very keen on settling down to married life (14% are

Figure 7: The Conventionalist

engaged). 47% vote Labour. They are not entrepreneurial. They are not Green, nor sporty. On the whole, they are relatively highly educated. They worry about pensions and their personal safety. They strongly support the police. 27% smoke and 92% claim to eat what they like—as a group they believe keeping fit is unimportant.

This is an interesting analysis. Into which categories would you put your children, your young people, your youthful friends? Are any categories missing? In what ways would you try to reach each group with the Gospel message? If Jesus was telling these groups a story, which parable would he use? Which miracle might especially appeal to those in each of these different groups?

## Moloch lives today

The above analysis takes no account of spiritual factors. This next section compensates by looking at some of the hidden spiritual elements in the world today, and the malign influence of evil. It is based heavily on a disturbing book by a New Zealand biologist, Winkie Pratney, who, since his conversion in his teenage years, thirty years ago, has been an evangelist to teenagers. He has written a number of books, but *Devil take the youngest*[44] explores the world of Moloch.

Moloch is a god mentioned in the Bible as early as Leviticus.[45] He was a 'deity of unnatural cruelty to whom human sacrifice was made'.[46] He was the opposite of Baal, the Canaanite god the Lord ordered the Israelites to destroy, who was seen as the giver of life (hence the many fertility rites), whereas Moloch was seen as the destroyer of life. Men sought to appease Moloch by offering even their own children to him. Most of the Biblical references to Moloch relate to this aspect of his worship, making one's children 'pass through the fire'.[47] A backslidden Solomon allowed Moloch worship in Jerusalem for his pagan wives and concubines.[48] Moloch captured the worship of the Ammonites, the Moabites, and the Assyrians in earlier Old Testament times, and through them later the Syro-Phoenician empire and Carthage.

'Why did God tell Joshua to take the land of Canaan and to *utterly destroy* its inhabitants as mortal enemies? When we understand the national devotion of Israel's enemies to Moloch and Baal, the awful annual slaughter of pagan children as an act of worship, we can understand something of the great anger of the Living God.'[49]

'Why on earth would an advanced people sacrifice their children? Every first-born male was consecrated to him as a human sacrifice or to enter his priesthood. This was Satan's own parallel to Jehovah God's love-covenant with His people, that every first-born son in a Hebrew household would be devoted to the Lord. Israel had seen these practices in the nations around them. No wonder they were warned so strongly, and punished so severely when they adopted such strange devotions.

'This dark deity that ruled the pagan world by fear was a frightening metal Minotaur, a half-man, half-beast like the robot Gort from 'The Day the Earth Stood Still'. Moloch was represented as a human figure with a bull's head, with permanently outstretched arms to receive babies and children being sacrificed.

'If you, as a first-born child, were taken to church on that special night it was better that you were too small to know the order of the service. It was better that you did not understand the real purpose of the intensely loud music and hymns sung frantically around you. Better that you did not see the central focus of the meeting. You would not cry long during the awful music or the screaming that passed for singing. You would be too small to care how long the night's sermon was. For when the 'invitation' was given, ready or not, you were going to the front. And after that, nothing mattered.

'The huge brazen figure was hollow. Beneath its reaching arms of death was strategically placed a deadly hollow lap glowing red in the darkness by a fire kindled inside it. The newborn babies, or small children made suddenly and terrifyingly aware that they were to be made part of the nightmarish celebration, were laid in its arms to roll off into the fiery lap below. And all the while, their parents sang hymns and prayed.

'This horrible devotion took place regularly once a year on a fixed day as an atonement for sins committed, before some great enterprise or after some great misfortune . . . Nor did the act involve just one or two children a year. After one Carthaginian military defeat, they ascribed the loss to Moloch's anger over being offered boys brought up and fed for the purpose. Before, he had been given boys from the noblest families. Two hundred boys were offered up at once together, three hundred others voluntarily giving themselves up afterwards as freewill offerings for the good of their fatherland.

'. . . We can only realise the combination (of worship and sacrifice) by imagining a group of high-tech Silicon Valley executives going to church every morning at 11 o'clock to see a baby roasted alive.'[50]

Why these horrific quotations in a book on lost teenagers? Simply because Winkie Pratney goes on in his book to suggest that the Moloch principle is still very much here in the twentieth century in terms of what we are doing with today's children and young people. The 'War on the Child'[51] has come to our world. The following show not just what happens to children but in attitude to all young people, including teenagers.

*War on the Womb: Abortion.*   It is not known how many abortions there are world-wide each year, but the total might well be over 10 million, including Britain's 200,000. Who says we are not offering our children to Moloch?

*War in the Home: Divorce.*   Probably few children can handle a divorce and emerge unscathed by it. A 10 year old girl being treated for depression wrote this poem:[52]

Divorce shakes you off the ground
　Divorce whirls you all around
Divorce makes you all confused
　Divorce forces you to choose
Divorce makes you feel all sad
　Divorce pushes you to be mad
Divorce makes you wonder who cares

Divorce leaves you thoroughly scared
　Divorce makes a silent home
Divorce leaves you all alone

Divorce is supposed to be an answer
　Divorce, in fact, is emotional cancer

*War in the Home: Child slavery.* Concern was expressed in January 1993 about the amount of child slave labour in North India, partly caused by parental debt. Thousands of children are enmeshed in this process, and not only in India. They have no rights, and are, in effect, sold to Moloch.

*War in the Home: Child abuse and incest.* This is increasingly common in all parts of the world, including Britain, or, at least, is increasingly reported. Over 45,000 children were on the Child Protection Register in 1991, 30% of whom were 10 years of age or older.[53] Neglect and physical abuse account for nearly half of known abuse incidents but sexual abuse accounts for one case in every seven.

*War in the Home: Throwaways and runaways.* With more and more families where both parents are working, more and more children come home by themselves and to themselves. Not every teenager can handle such loneliness, and some invite their friends around, which can include those of the opposite sex. Some children find their home situation so unbearable that eventually they just run away: in 1983 1,074 boys aged 14–17 in Britain and 1,346 girls.[54] There were perhaps more homeless children in the Victorian era than today but the reasons then were different. Today young people are maturing earlier but because they are dependent on their parents for longer (because of unemployment or further education) find the tensions unbearable.

*War on the Heart: Kidnapping.* Children are not settled peaceably or agreeably in every divorce. There have been many instances of one partner kidnapping the child back. The number is estimated at 400,000 such children a year in the United States (figures for the UK are not available). The children do not die, but they 'are sacrificed on the altar of money, knowledge or power. Moloch lives, and love dies.'[5]u25

*War on the Heart: Child pornography.* The recent book by Madonna, simply called *Sex* sold hundreds of thousands of copies within a few months of publication. It was ostensibly aimed at youth, and derided as just 'pornography' by many. This might be pornography for youth, but there is today a great deal of pornography of youth. Paedophile rings are known to the police, and regularly uncovered. Here again is a mechanism whereby a child's natural rights (in this case to personal privacy) are stolen from him. Moloch rules.

*War on the Mind: Media exploitation of children.* The power of television is well known to commercial businesses wanting to sell their products to the child and youth world. Huge sums are paid for advertising at key times, especially just before Christmas! The number of hours that young people spend before a television set also means that its culture frequently becomes their culture too. But the TV world is not necessarily reality. Where the body might resist exploitation, here is a way to manipulate the minds of youth. This is not to suggest that TV has no positive benefits: it clearly has. TV gives a wider world view, and with more information, thinking young people ask more questions.

*War on the Mind: Hidden agendas.*   This is the term Winkie Pratney uses to describe some of the 'hidden' things children learn at school, such as vandalism, absenteeism, extortion, drug taking or pushing, drinking, gang warfare, assault, and even rape.

*War on the Mind: Technical exploitation.*   The irresistible attractions of games like Super Nintendo with an incredible 33,000 colours and fast moving 3–D graphics mesmerize children. The Nintendo Club had 660,000 members in April 1992, and new adventures are added regularly. Other manufacturers like Sega have their own games. Young people can get totally hooked on such programmes, another example perhaps of how their minds can get caught.[56]

*War in the Streets: Teenage prostitution.*   There is much child and teenage prostitution in some parts of the Third World, perhaps especially Thailand, but, as has been noted above, increasingly in the cities of the Western world. In Britain, it has not yet perhaps reached the level seen in Queen Victoria's time.

*War in the Streets: Violence.*   Gang violence has increased in many cities, and needless gratuitous violence, especially on the defenceless, sickens our eyes. Newspaper photographs are horrific. The murder of 2 year old James Bulger early in 1993 in Merseyside by two 10 year old boys brought scenes of outrage.

*War to the Death: Child and teenage suicide.*   This has already been mentioned above.

What all these add up to is simply that in many ways we are losing the minds, hearts, emotions, wills, bodies of our teenagers, either as teenagers or as younger children. Moloch desires to have children for sacrifice. Despite all the changes in the past two millennia, his spirit is still with us. We need to react similarly to Bramwell Booth, the son of William Booth. Ascertaining for himself that it was true that there was a huge traffic in street-girls in London, he wrote: 'I resolved— and recorded the resolve on paper—that no matter what the consequences might be, I would do all I could to stop these abominations, to rouse public opinion, to agitate for the improvement of the law to bring to justice the adulterers and murders of innocence, and to make a way of escape for the victims!'[57]

It is equally true that all this needs to be put into proportion. Awful things are happening to many young people, and the extent of such evil is undoubtedly increasing. But there are also millions of young people who grow up in traditional two-parent families and manage to avoid all of the evils depicted above.

### Involved teenagers

The table on the next pages gives details of membership across the UK of a number of youth organizations.[58] Generally speaking numbers increased across the 1950s, 1960s and 1970s, but began to drop off in the 1980s. If the predictions turn out to be correct, they are set to recover during the 1990s, but only back to the 1981 level by the year 2001. The change from one year to the next is better than the population change (measured here on all those under 20). Males are always slightly in the majority, but this decreased in the 1960s and 1970s and increased in the 1980s, suggesting that part of the decline in the 1980s is due to females leaving rather more than males.

The numbers of young people represented among these different youth organizations is considerable. The ages for membership vary between organizations, but the total might reasonably be compared with the number of young people aged, say, 5–20. On that basis, the 1991 total membership is 20% of the population. One young person in five belongs to

Table 4: Membership of selected organisations for young people in UK 1951–2001 (thousands)

| | 1951 | 1961 | 1966 | 1971 | 1976 | 1981 | 1986 | 1991 | 1996* | 2001* |
|---|---|---|---|---|---|---|---|---|---|---|
| Cub Scouts[1] | 192 | 245 | 246 | 265 | 296 | 309 | 332 | 349 | 369 | 388 |
| Brownie Guides[2] | 184 | 284 | 329 | 376 | 410 | 427 | 384 | 385 | 426 | 482 |
| Scouts[3] | 237 | 272 | 242 | 215 | 225 | 234 | 213 | 192 | 186 | 187 |
| Girl Guides[4] | 221 | 266 | 244 | 316 | 344 | 348 | 282 | 225 | 243 | 288 |
| Sea Cadet Corps | 19 | 18 | 18 | 18 | 21 | 19 | 17 | 16 | 17 | 17 |
| Army Cadet Corps | 64 | 44 | 38 | 39 | 42 | 46 | 43 | 39 | 35 | 34 |
| Air Training Corps | 38 | 30 | 26 | 33 | 34 | 35 | 35 | 34 | 34 | 34 |
| Combined Cadet Forces | 58 | 76 | 49 | 45 | 43 | 44 | 43 | 40 | 35 | 31 |
| Boys' Brigade[5,8] | 142 | 159 | 143 | 140 | 137 | 154 | 120 | 103 | 117 | 122 |
| Girls' Brigade | 138* | 119* | 98 | 103 | 99 | 103 | 92 | 86 | 90 | 94 |
| Methodist Association of Youth Clubs | 101 | 110 | 121 | 115 | 131 | 127 | 78* | 40 | 49 | 66 |
| National Association of Boys' Clubs | 146* | 156 | 158 | 164 | 169 | 186 | 172 | 155 | 158 | 169 |
| National Federation of Young Farmers Clubs[6] | | | | | | | | | | |
| – Males | 24* | 32 | 24* | 24 | 24* | 28 | 24 | 18 | 22 | 21 |
| – Females | 18* | 18 | 18* | 16 | 18* | 23 | 20 | 15 | 19 | 19 |
| Young Mens' Christian Association[7] | | | | | | | | | | |
| – Registered males | 29* | 33 | 34 | 35 | 31 | 36 | 39* | 43 | 42 | 43 |
| – Registered females | 0* | 5 | 8 | 13 | 16 | 19 | 26* | 32 | 34 | 39 |

*Table 4 (cont)*

| | 1951 | 1961 | 1966 | 1971 | 1976 | 1981 | 1986 | 1991 | 1996* | 2001* |
|---|---|---|---|---|---|---|---|---|---|---|
| **Duke of Edinburgh's Award:** | | | | | | | | | | |
| Participants | — | 80 | 102* | 122 | 140* | 170 | 165 | 200 | 216 | 235 |
| Award gained:[12] | | | | | | | | | | |
| Bronze | — | 9 | 16 | 18 | 21 | 23 | 20 | 35 | 34 | 38 |
| Silver | — | 4 | 7 | 7 | 8 | 10 | 9 | 13 | 14 | 15 |
| Gold | — | 1 | 3 | 3 | 3 | 5 | 5 | 6 | 7 | 7 |
| Crusaders – boys | 18* | 18[9] | 19 | 18 | 15 | 10 | 8 | 9 | 10 | 1 |
| – girls | 3* | 4[9] | 7 | 10 | 10 | 8 | 7 | 8 | 12 | 16 |
| **Youth Clubs UK[10]** | | | | | | | | | | |
| – boys | 58 | 94 | 133 | 179 | 276 | 430[11] | 328[13] | 310 | 423 | 466 |
| – girls | 78 | 86 | 106 | 140 | 243 | 341[11] | 239[13] | 290 | 343 | 375 |
| Total | 1,768 | 2,130 | 2,137 | 2,386 | 2,699 | 3,097 | 2,667 | 2,589 | 2,880 | 3,138 |
| Males[14] | 1,004 | 1,192 | 1,175 | 1,232 | 1,366 | 1,618 | 1,443 | 1,379 | 1,509 | 1,622 |
| Females[14] | 764 | 938 | 962 | 1,154 | 1,333 | 1,479 | 1,224 | 1,210 | 1,371 | 1,516 |
| % Male | 57% | 56% | 55% | 52% | 51% | 52% | 54% | 53% | 52% | 52% |
| Proportion change of total (1971 = 100) | 74 | 89 | 90 | 100 | 113 | 130 | 112 | 109 | 121 | 132 |
| Population change for under 20 (1971 = 100) | 83 | 93 | 99 | 100 | 99 | 94 | 88 | 85 | 87 | 90 |

* Estimates

1 Includes Beaver Scouts (6–8)
2 Includes Rainbow Guides (4–7)
3 Includes Venture Scouts (15–20) since 1971, Senior Scouts (15–18) and Rover Scouts (18–24) previously
4 Includes Ranger Guides (14–18) and young leaders (15–18)
5 British Isles
6 England, Wales and the Channel Islands, aged 10–25 up to 1971 and 10–26 from 1981
7 Under 25s
8 Includes those aged 6 or over since 1978
9 1956 figure
10 Previously National Association of Youth Clubs
11 Since 1981 includes membership of clubs affiliated to four local associations
12 Not included in total
13 1985 figure
14 Estimated where not given by assuming pro-rata to where given

a club or scheme or group of some kind. That means four-fifths don't.

What kind of church programme is needed to accommodate youngsters who don't want to join anything? What kind is required for those who do? David Winter, the well-known author and broadcaster, has close links with Oxford Youth Works, and draws a helpful distinction between three groups of young people:[59] those who belong to formal clubs (like many of those listed), those who belong to informal clubs (like those put on by many churches), and those who do not belong at all.

How many are there in the second group? On the basis of the number of young people attending church in England in 1989 and adding the excess of church members over churchgoers (as not every youngster going to a church club goes to church), 18% of those aged 5–20 could be involved in church groups. Of course there may well be overlap between church groups and non-church groups. In any case, some of the groups listed in the table are specifically church groups, amounting to about 10% of membership in 1991. This suggests that perhaps:

  10% of young people belong to a 'formal' club *and* a church
    club
  10% belong *only* to a 'formal' club
  8% belong *only* to a church club
  72% of young people don't belong to any type of club

If these figures are even only roughly right, there's a considerable number of young people whose philosophy is either against joining clubs and activities or at least have not come across a club that appeals to them, or might be too busy studying, etc.

Table 4 shows that membership of these organizations dropped from 3,097,000 to 2,589,000 between 1981 and 1991, or a decline of 16% across the whole UK. In England, it represents a decline of 1,000 youngsters *every week*—300 teenagers and 700 children. The churches in the same decade also lost 300 teenagers every week and 400 children.

This puts the decline in teenage church attendance in perspective. Yes, the combined churches did lose teenagers. But the combined youth organizations also lost them *at the same rate*! The churches, however, lost fewer younger children —showing the continuing attractiveness of children to church activities.

Here then is a clue which is important. The teenagers who are leaving the churches are not necessarily abandoning Christianity but are rejecting 'belonging' or 'involvement' or whatever relates them to the adult world into a world of their own. 75% of those interviewed in the *Finding Faith Today* study[60] once belonged to some kind of church club.

Could this be the reason why a number of churches experimenting with 'youth congregations' or 'youth churches' have in the main found them successful? St Thomas Crookes, Sheffield, has been one of these and spectacularly successful— the Nine O'Clock Service (9.00pm!) has grown so large that the church is no longer big enough, and the church seats 600! Other churches have seen the same, and the largest and most successful church in Helsinki, Finland (the Lutheran Thomas Mass Church), which, despite having Lutheran ministers is independent of any one denomination, is largely a youth-only church.

Of the six experienced youth workers interviewed at length for this study, four were in favour of 'youth churches', one was against, and one was uncertain. Of the four in favour, three were cautious for the same reason as the person who was negative—the purpose of the church is to build a complete community, and that community needs to involve young people, not have them as a separate unit. But if the choice is between young people doing their own thing alone, or not coming to church at all, the majority were clearly in favour of them coming on their own terms.

The figures above are very tentative, but if the projections to 2001 are correct, during the 1990s teenagers will begin to return to 'formal' clubs, with the proportion in church clubs rather less than before. In other words, youth may return to a degree of formality; how we treat them in the meantime is therefore particularly important. The father did not criticise the way his prodigal son had spent his money when he returned, but welcomed him with love. The churches will need to do the same. Are they ready?

### Summary

- Teenagers vary greatly across the teenage years in maturity, interest, values and experiences.
- There were 3.7 million young people aged 15–19 in the UK in 1991, 6.5% of the entire population.
- 7% of women will conceive before the age of 20, and 2.5% will have an abortion.
- Personal income rises rapidly between 15 and 20, and is spent on alcohol, clothes and eating out (in that order).
- Getting a job and getting qualifications are key priorities for the average teenager.
- One teenager in six smokes, and one in 14 has tried drugs.
- Crime amongst teenagers is increasing, especially by men.
- 12% of the 3,900 suicides in England and Wales in 1991 were by those aged 15–24.
- Seven types of young people were identified in one study—the Hedonists (18%), Cautious (16%), Idealists (16%), Conventionalists (16%), Moralists (13%), Authoritarians (13%) and Moderates (8%).
- The ancient Moloch god is still demanding youthful sacrifice.
- Youth organizations were attended by 2.6 million aged 5–20 in 1991, 20% of that population.
- In the 1980s these youth organizations lost 300 teenagers a week—the same as the churches—but could gain them in the 1990s.

# 2

# *Teenagers and Their Leisure*

'Young people want . . .
Something to do
Somewhere to go
Someone to confide in'

said the BBC commentator on a radio programme early
in 1992.[1] The actual programme is forgotten but the categories are useful. The 'Reaching and Keeping Teenagers'
Research Project (RAKT Project) explored leisure activities
with 900 churchgoing teenagers and 1,500 school-age teenagers, and the results will be broken down into these three
areas. (The detailed methodology of the study is given in
Appendix 2.)

## Something to do

Seven activities under this broad heading were suggested, with
the results in Table 5.

Apart from the hobbies/interests, the order is the same
for both groups with the top three well ahead of the others.
These same three also emerged as the key areas in a Gallup
survey of 14–16 year olds in 1991.[2] They also asked them
how long they spent doing each of them, with the results in
Table 6.

*Table 5: Teenage activities 1992*

|  | Church groups | School groups |
|---|---|---|
|  | % | % |
| Watching television | 91 | 92 |
| Listening to music | 86 | 86 |
| Doing homework | 84 | 80 |
| Other hobbies/interests | 62 | 55 |
| Watching videos | 59 | 70 |
| Playing sport | 53 | 62 |
| Playing home computer/ electronic games | 40 | 54 |

*Table 6: Average daily time spent on leisure activities by 14–16 year olds 1991*

| | |
|---|---|
| Watching television | 3 hours 40 mins |
| Listening to music while doing something else | 2 hours 30 mins |
| Listening to music while doing nothing else | 1 hour 30 mins |
| Doing homework | 1 hour 25 mins |
| Reading a book for pleasure | 45 mins |

I'm not sure every teenager would regard homework as leisure! Doubtless that was one of the things done while also listening to music! The time spent listening to music and watching TV totals 7 hours 40 minutes, almost one-third of a day. What a tremendous influence such music and pictures have! Another major study through 150 church youth groups, also in 1991, confirmed the same dominance,[3] and a study of 5,400 secondary school pupils in Dundee gave similar average watching times.[4]

*Watching television*

The RAKT Project found no significant variations to this dominance of television viewing by gender, age, strength of

Christian commitment, denomination, churchmanship, geographical location, environment (rural, suburbs, council estate or city centre), marital status of parents (asked in school sample only) or religion (Christian, Muslim, another or no religion—again asked in school sample only). In other words, TV is a dominant activity for virtually every teenager in the country regardless. (There was a suggestion in the school study that strongly committed Christian teenagers watched it slightly less—85% against 92%). Showing how much times have changed over the last thirty years, a 1963 study revealed only 24% of boys and girls watching television, though this was still their most popular activity.[5] In the 1990s however, many teenagers have their TV set in their bedrooms, increasing personal watching time and removing parental control over what is watched.

Such prolonged exposure to television has important consequences. It 'has produced dysfunctionalism more than anyone is willing to admit'[6] says the author of an encyclopaedia on the Sunday School. In the first place, television presents news items in bite-size chunks; watchers experience a breadth of information and not always depth; much detail but not always evaluation. This can lead to quick impression-making. Secondly, the popular TV soaps never end and their situation and culture become a part of life. Watchers get caught on a series of non-issues, and it is easy to transfer that to real life. The African famine is an issue today, the Iran War one tomorrow, the fall of the Berlin Wall something from yesterday. Life rolls by without the opportunity of indepth focusing on anything. Thirdly, teenagers get their views on God not from the church but from the TV and music they watch and listen. They have as a consequence 'a watered down view of God, the church and ministers'.[7] They therefore tend to be pluralistic, and supernatural (plenty of demons in TV movies). They 'have seen the realism of *The Exorcist* and the surrealism of *Ghostbusters*.'[8]

Some months ago I had the privilege of speaking with a

senior member of the Exclusive Brethren. 'We don't have television sets in our houses,' he remarked at one stage, 'I would be afraid that my family and I would become addicted.' Maybe he was right. One group of 15 families volunteered to go without television for a month and kept a diary to see what difference it made. The first few days were weird (withdrawal symptoms?) but then they wondered what to do with the 'oceans of time' that appeared.[9] One writer asked anxiously, 'What are we doing to our young people? How can I compete with the lies they're getting for hours on end every day on TV?'[10]

## Listening to music

This is the second most popular teenage activity, occupying up to four hours a day, according to Gallup. It is slightly more popular with females than males (91 against 81%), and with 17 and 18 year olds than with those aged 11 or 12 (95 against 75%). It is a massive increase since 1963 when the percentage was 8%, but that was via records or the radio! Today, Walkman rules, OK? And so do the stereo systems many teenagers have in their rooms.

What kind of music do they listen to? In the church youth group study 98% of teenagers listened to soul/rock music with artistes like Phil Collins, Whitney Houston 'one of their favourites'.[12] Gloria Estefan, U2, Eurythmics and Michael Jackson were 'enjoyed sometimes'. On an enjoyment score varying from −2 to +2, such music rated an average score of +0.7.

The same study showed that 95% of church youth also listen to reggae/rap/pop music (MC Hammer and UB40 positively acclaimed), and 98% to overtly sexual music, such as comes from Madonna, Simply Red, George Michael, or Tina Turner. On the whole though such music was endured, not enjoyed. Heavy metal music was listened to by 85%, with Guns N Roses the most popular, but still not positively appreciated. Whitesnake and KISS were less well known, but disliked by those who knew them.

In contrast, less than half these church teenagers listened to Christian music and only a third Christian heavy music (Petra and Stryper).

What is the impact of such music? It has to be heard repeatedly to be understood (30 or 40 times I was told by one rock singer), by which time the lyric will be well implanted in a person's memory. Some (many?) of the words in these songs have a New Age spirituality, or anti-Christian sentiments, and these can form the backcloth to a person's attitude to Christianity.

Secondly, such music is frequently listened to on a personal stereo. This individual listening is symptomatic of a key characteristic of teenagers today—they live in a world of their own isolation. Compare how the generations have danced. Teenagers' grandparents danced hugging and squeezing each other on the dance floor. Teenagers' parents twisted, and worked in perfect grace and harmony but seldom touched. Teenagers today dance alone. No-one else is on the stage with Madonna—they dance with themselves. They are the isolated generation.

This liking of certain music, and dislike of other music was turned to good use by a San Francisco teacher who enhanced detentions by giving 'Frankies' instead. Pupils who get one don't just have to stay in school for an extra half hour or so; they have to stay behind and listen to tapes of Frank Sinatra's greatest hits. The kids just loathe it. 'It drives them crazy,' said the sadistic if inspired pedagogue responsible for thinking up the scheme. 'They find Frank Sinatra real excruciating!'[14]

## Doing Homework

Five teenagers in six do this in their spare time, rather more by girls than boys (85 against 79%), rather more in rural areas than on council estates (93 against 80% in the church group), and in the south of England than in London (90 against 76% in the church group).

The church and school groups differed in that younger people did more homework than older teens in the church group (89% of 14 year olds against 63% of 18 year olds), but the reverse was true in the school group (85% of 11–13 year olds against 96% of 18 year olds). Exam pressure will undoubtedly play a part.

## Other hobbies/interests

These were more popular with church teens than school teens (62 against 53%), and with younger teens than old (63% of 11 year olds against 46% of 16 year olds). We did not ask what those hobbies might be, so cannot list them.

## Watching videos

This was more popular with school teens than church teens (70 against 59%), and with males than females (74 against 66% in school groups). In the church groups those from Independent and Methodist churches were the most avid watchers (71 against 53% for Anglicans).

The church youth group study showed that teenagers tended to watch videos with a rating older than their age. Thus 39% of 13 year olds watched 15 rated videos, and another 39% 18 rated. 67% of 16 and 17 year olds watched 18 rated videos.[15]

## Playing sport

This is an activity which engaged half the church group and five-eighths of the school groups. In both cases the males played much more than the females (75 against 42%). In the church group however older teens played more than younger ones (71% of 19 year olds against 57% of 11 year olds) but the reverse was the case in the school groups (58% of 18 year olds against 72% of 11 and 12 year olds).

## Playing electronic games

This was more popular with school teens (54 against 40%) than church teens, and definitely much more a male occupation! 64% of boys played with home computer games against half that percentage, 31%, of girls. This was also something which declined with age: 62% of those aged 11 and 12 played such games, against only 20% of 17 year olds. It was also a feature of London and city centre life more than suburban life (54 against 40%).

Computer games are likely to be a continuing feature of young teenage life. Sega Megadrive alone had over 40 different games available in 1992.[16]

## Reading

The RAKT Study didn't ask directly about this. Gallup reported that 14–16 year olds spent an average of 45 minutes a day reading for leisure. An American study showed 23% of those aged between 18 and 26 had read a Christian book in the past month.[17] A survey of Christian reading habits in a large Southampton congregation in 1987[18] showed:

- Those who read Christian books are likely to read secular books as well
- Teenagers (16–18) on average read less than two Christian books a year, and less than three secular books
- The most avid readers were aged 30–44 or 65 and over
- A third of their teenagers read no books at all
- Half the teenagers bought books from a Christian bookshop and two-thirds borrowed them

Another Gallup study found that one young person in 14 aged 15 or 16 never read a daily newspaper in 1985 and twice as many never read a Sunday newspaper.[19]

There is however a vast array of teenage magazines and they would not be published if they were not being read. A summary of those is given in Table 7.[20]

John Buckeridge, the Editor of *Youthwork* magazine, who initially drew up this list, comments on two magazines specially. 'Despite its name *Just Seventeen*, the best-selling magazine for teenage girls is mainly read by 11 to 15 year olds. The content features a mix of fashion and beauty tips, interviews with pop and TV celebrities, gossip, horoscopes and trivia, plus an

Table 7: Teenage magazines available in March 1992

| Title | Price | Readership | Frequency | Age range | Content |
|---|---|---|---|---|---|
| Viz | £1 | 1,065,000 | Bimonthly | Legally 18+, in fact 13+ boys | Includes pornographic and bestial 'jokes' |
| Smash Hits | 60p | 420,000 | Fortnightly | Teenage | Pop music magazine |
| Big! | 65p | 257,000 | Fortnightly | Young teens | TV, pop and film stars |
| Looks | £1.10 | 299,000 | Monthly | 15–19 girls | Fashion and beauty |
| Just Seventeen | 60p | 225,000 | Weekly | 11–15 girls | Fashion, horoscopes and advice column |
| 19 | £1 | 185,000 | Monthly | Older teens | Fashion and image |
| Fast Forward | 45p | 166,000 | Weekly | 8–13 | Pop and soaps |
| Shoot | 55p | 156,000 | Weekly | 8–14 | Football |
| Mizz | 60p | 140,000 | Fortnightly | 11–15 girls | Horoscopes and straight talking on sex |
| Sky | £1.30 | 140,000 | Monthly | 16–20 | Youth culture, trends and entertainment |
| Number One | 65p | 137,000 | Weekly | 14–18 girls | Pop music and its stars |
| Look in | 45p | 128,000 | Weekly | 8–13 | Chart songs, lyrics |
| 2000 AD | 50p | 96,000 | Weekly | Teenage | Graphic gore and violent sex |

authoritative three-page advice column for girls and boys. Although some of the advice is sound, absolutes on what is right or wrong are fuzzy at best. About 20% of the content deals with sex and sexuality: losing your virginity, your first date, tips on looking desirable etc.' From personal observation I support these comments.

John Buckeridge continues, 'Legally *Viz* should only be sold to the over 18s. This has not stopped it becoming the most popular read for teenage boys. In almost every school playground in the country *Viz* is compulsory reading. Selling 1 million copies of every bi-monthly issue its contents include pornographic, bestial, blasphemous, sexist, violent and sometimes racist 'jokes'. *Viz* and its many imitators joke about anything—vicars who are invariably portrayed as sexual perverts are a favourite target.'

The incredible total average readership of these 13 magazines is 1.57 million readers, enough for one in every 6 people aged 8–19 in the whole country, *per week*. If a person reads only every fourth issue, that is equivalent to two-thirds of our young people reading one of these magazines once a month, every month on average. Again the cumulative influence by such output is enormous. Where are the church counterparts? How does the church try and put across alternative cultures and ethics in as popular a fashion?

## Somewhere to go

Where do young people go? They go to different places, and whereas what they do does not vary greatly between churchgoers and non-churchgoers, where they go does, as Table 8 indicates.

The differences between these two groups are especially marked for church activities (as might be expected), youth clubs (many of which will be church youth clubs) and games arcades.

The order is also interesting. The order in the table reflects

*Table 8: Location of activities 1992*

| Activity | Church groups | School groups |
|---|---|---|
| | % | % |
| Churches | 53 | 12 |
| Cinemas | 46 | 51 |
| Youth clubs | 44 | 24 |
| Discos/nightclubs | 24 | 36 |
| Pubs | 19 | 22 |
| Games arcades | 12 | 27 |

church groups' preferences. The school groups order is cinemas, discos/nightclubs, games arcades, youth clubs, pubs, and church activities.

## *Church activities*

Many churches have mid-week church activities or other activities apart from the Sunday services. Sunday services are considered in the next chapter, but other church activities varied greatly. Teenage attendance at these activities varied, and the lowest and the highest percentages in various categories are given in Table 9.

Thus, of church teenagers, only 23% from Roman Catholic churches are involved in church activities outside of Sunday, but 70% are from New (or House) Churches and so on. What this suggests, as might otherwise be expected, is that it is the 'keenites' who get involved in church activities especially among groups with a high sense of mission.

Although the school group involvement with church activities is 12% on average, half of this is made up from the 10% in the schools who classified themselves as 'strongly' committed, and the other half from the other 90%.

There is an important distinction here. Most of the strongly committed might be expected to get involved in church activities but in both the church and school groups only about

Table 9: *Variations on church activities by church groups*

| Factor | Lowest | Highest |
|---|---|---|
| Denomination | Roman Catholic (23%) | New/House Churches (70%) |
| | | Baptists (69%) |
| | | Methodists (66%) |
| Churchmanship | Non-evangelical (42%) | Evangelical (63%) |
| Environment | City centre (46%) | Rural (63%) |
| Geographical area | London (46%) | North England (57%) |
| By church commitment | Never a Christian (32%) | Strongly committed (66%) |

half do so in fact. In other words, half who describe themselves as strongly committed Christians do not get involved in any church activity outside Sunday church attendance. How then do they express their strong commitment?

As might be expected, those who are not strongly committed do not get involved in church activities in the main, though 1 in every 11 (9%) does. Could this be a cutting edge of opportunity? How can one help the not very committed to get more involved?

*Cinema*

Half the teenagers surveyed went to the cinema at least occasionally, a massive increase from the 8% in 1963.[21] In the school sample Christians went more than non-Christians (53 against 44%). In the church sample females went more than males (51 against 41%), and those living in the suburbs more than the rural areas (52 against 38%).

The main differences were by age, however, as is seen below:

*Table 10: Church group cinema-goers by age*

| Age | % |
|---------|-----|
| 11,12 | 29 |
| 13 | 37 |
| 14 | 47 |
| 15 | 52 |
| 16 | 52 |
| 17 | 60 |
| 18,19 | 55 |
| Overall | 46 |

Note that the percentage peaks at age 17, something found in other studies also.

## Youth club

Four out of nine teenagers in the church groups went to a youth club, in many cases the church youth club, with many more evangelical churches than non-evangelical churches involved (54 against 32%).

In the schools group, 26% of Christian teenagers went to a youth club, and 26% of Muslim teenagers also, but only 16% of other non-Christians. Attendance was highest among the younger teens (30% of 13 and 14 year olds against 8% of 17 year olds).

## Discos/nightclubs

About a quarter of church teenagers went to discos, and over a third of school teens. Girls went more than boys, though not by a wide margin. Older teens went more than younger teens—in the church groups 43% of 17 years olds against 11% of 13 year olds, and in the school group 70% of 18 year olds against 27% of 11 and 12 year olds. In the church group, 36% of Roman Catholics and 33% of those at New/House Churches attended, against 20% of Anglicans and 18% of Baptists.

In the school groups 36% of Christians and 40% of non-Christians went, but only 15% of those in other religions. 18% in church groups and 22% in school groups who were strongly committed Christians went, but of those who were 'no longer a Christian', 82% in church groups and 52% in school groups attended a disco or nightclub. Here then is an activity which those who break away from Christianity see as particularly open to them. The more dedicated are much more conservative.

## Pubs

The same was true of the public house. About a fifth of both groups went, but this percentage varied. Of those in the church groups only 18% who were strongly committed went, and just 8% of these in schools. But 55% went in the church group who were no longer a Christian and 34% in the school group.

As with the discos, it was the Roman Catholics (27%) and

New/House Churches (33%) who had the highest proportions attending. This is fascinating as it is precisely these two groups, out of all the denominations, which have continued to attract teenagers into their churches, whereas every other denomination has lost them.

Could it be that their 'Christianity' allows involvement in the world, as it were, whereas other denominations tend to repress it, with the result that if people break away they immediately find an alternative place to 'belong' in the local pub, influenced, perhaps, by the pull of their peer group.

*Games arcades*

This is another place which those no longer a Christian frequent much more than the strongly committed (42 against 23% in the school group). It is massively a male domain (21 against 4% females in church groups and 45 against 9% females in school groups). It is a central London rather than a suburban activity (19 against 7% in church groups and 33 against 23% in school groups). It is an activity for younger teens (35% of 11 and 12 year olds against 8% of 18 year olds in school groups).

What are the implications of all these figures? Teenagers want somewhere to go, and where they go depends to some extent on their Christian traditions. Christians (of all kinds) tend to go to church activities and youth clubs, and to the cinema. Roman Catholics and New/House Church Christians, but not others, are more likely to go to discos and pubs.

Non-Christians and those who have renounced their faith were likely to go to discos, the cinema, pubs and play arcade games. A different style is emerging. One can almost discern two separate groups here: the Christian and the non-Christian, one meeting with others in a 'safe' environment (I am deliberately being patronizing) and the others meeting where the world meets. Is this a fair interpretation of the situation? One group is in clubs, the other group meets in pubs and discos. The culture, language, ethos and experience of the two groups are enormously different. But if the church is to reach teenagers somehow this bridge must be crossed, and it appears that perhaps the Catholics and New/House Churches (two very different groups) have made some progress in this area.

Why should this be? The question was explored with some of those interviewed, one of whom was a Roman Catholic Youth Officer. Patrick Harrison pointed to three things: (a) the commitment expected by Roman Catholics to the church, (b) the fact that a person was a 'Catholic', and so tended not to drift to other denominations, and (c) the resources given to youth work generally by the Catholics with the implicit expectations this had on the adult members.

The New/House Churches, others indicated, would in some ways agree with these emphases. (a) A high commitment was expected, not so much to the church, but to the process of church planting in which so many were engaged. (b) Without doubt, House Churches have a very special ethos, and in particular, because they are largely young churches, have few traditions to hinder them, allowing them to change to meet situations as required. (c) House Churches likewise pay attention to their young people, and expect them to be part of the whole framework of the church and not a special department.

Commitment, ethos and resources help keep teens in church. What about your church? There is one other element which unites Roman Catholics and New/House Churches in this particular sphere, which Steve Chalke, Director of Oasis Trust, helpfully noticed. They both use pictures and symbolism a great deal (although in very different ways).

### Someone to confide in

In the questionnaire only two areas of teenage spare-time activity had to do with companionship: friends in general and boy/girl friends in particular. (The RAKT Study did not explore family relationships—other studies have done this and their results are given later.) The next table shows how many

*Table 11: Activities of companionship 1992*

| Companions | Church | School |
|---|---|---|
| | % | % |
| Hang around with friends | 70 | 78 |
| Spend time with boy/girl friend | 25 | 33 |

*Table 12: Time spent with different companions, by age*

| Age | Friends | Boy/girl friend | Total (=100%) |
|---|---|---|---|
| | % | % | |
| 11,12 | 74 | 23 | 416 |
| 13 | 71 | 21 | 418 |
| 14 | 78 | 26 | 265 |
| 15 | 76 | 33 | 333 |
| 16 | 75 | 35 | 223 |
| 17 | 72 | 40 | 175 |
| 18,19 | 72 | 49 | 123 |
| Overall | 74 | 29 | 1,953 |

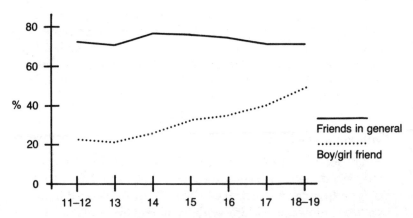

Figure 8: Time spent with different companions

indicated they spent time with different companions. The question was 'What do you do in your spare time?' with 15 suggestions being given, of which these were two. The percentages do not total 100% since multiple answers were allowed for the whole question.

Inevitably time spent with friends and time with a boy/girl friend varied with age, as shown in Table 12 which combines both school and church groups.

## With friends

Apart from watching TV, listening to music and doing their homework, hanging around with their friends is the fourth most important activity for teenagers. Their peer group is very significant for them.

For church groups this was more important for females than males (74 against 65%), and for 14–16 year olds than 13 year olds (76 against 61%). It happened more on council estates than in rural areas (76 against 62%).

For school groups, those following non-Christian religions were more reserved than Christians (62 against 78%). It was more important for those who were not sure if they were a Christian than for the strongly committed (83 against 67%).

Time spent with a boy or girlfriend tends to increase with age (though it dips slightly at age 13). However, this makes little difference to spending time with friends in general (though this also dips at age 13 slightly). In other words, as teenagers get older, they make increasing time for one special friend without relinquishing their wider circle of friends.

## With boy/girl friend

This was another area where those who have left the faith outdo those who have not: 65% of the former reckoned on spending time with their boy/girl friend against only 20% of strongly committed Christians. Having forsaken their divine friend they turned to a human replacement.

It was also an area where the marital status of parents was important. In the school group, 31% of those whose parents were married spent time with their boy/girl friend, but 41% did so whose parents were divorced—the loss of a parental figure being made up by one of their own age (presumably).

Both situations reflect the inherent loneliness many teenagers feel. This is one element to which we shall return in the next chapter. It is also one part of the 'isolated' feeling which has been mentioned already.

Does it stop there? No it doesn't. The present teenagers are not only an isolated generation, but a unisex generation also, the first generation to grow up being so. As Elma Towns, the American youth specialist has put it: 'Unisex is a movement towards the centre. Both boys and girls wear jeans, T-shirts and have the same length hair. Outward adornings are not the issue. There seems to be no mystery in the boy-girl relationship. Buster children have grown up with sex education. They have seen nude pictures, can identify the plumbing fixtures, know what they are expected to do in copulation and can explain it with proper identification of the organs. But they don't know the mystery of the sexual relationship. Even in marriage, there is often a contracted agreement. They have not experienced what Jesus described, "The two shall be one flesh".'[12]

## Teenage sexual activity

The first issue of *Youthwork*, then included as part of *Alpha* magazine, highlighted the following disturbing facts about teenagers:[23]

- 51% of parents disagree with the view that 'parents should tell their children sex before marriage is wrong'[24]
- 41% of teenagers say they lost their virginity before their 16th birthday[25]
- 14% of church-going young people say they lost their virginity by the age of 16[26]

- 34% of 12–15 year olds agree with the statement: 'AIDS is only a problem if I get it'[27]
- In the United States, although the incidence of AIDS among teenagers is still low, it is doubling every 14 months[28]
- By the age of 18 the average person will have watched on television 9,000 actual or suggested acts of sexual intercourse
- In England and Wales more than 8,500 girls under the age of 16 become pregnant each year[29]

The results of two surveys into sexual activity by 15–19 year olds are given in Table 13 on page 76.

Figures for the two years are not strictly comparable: the 1963 study[30] was based on the general population and the 1991 figures are based on church youth groups of which 84% claimed to be Christian.[31] The 1991 study omits responses for 13,14 and 20 year olds for ease of comparison. The categories used are for the 1963 study, and have been equated in the first category to holding hands in the 1991 study. The second category in 1991 was defined as 'embraced and kissed/heavy 'french' kissing'. The third category was defined as 'fondling breasts/genitals'. The fourth category combines the 1963 categories of intercourse with one partner and intercourse with more than one partner.

Nevertheless the comparison has a number of points of interest.

- Far fewer 15 and 16 year olds had little or no contact with the opposite sex in 1963 than 1991
- Only experiencing a limited amount of sexual activity is much less common across all ages in 1991 than it was 28 years earlier
- Experience of intimacies short of intercourse is much more widely prevalent in 1991, except at age 19.
- Actual experience of intercourse is higher across all ages, doubling at ages 15 and 16, but increases much less at ages 17 and 18, with a large increase at age 19.

*Table 13: Sexual intimacies of teenagers 1963 and 1991*

| Level of intimacy | 1963 | | | | | |
| --- | --- | --- | --- | --- | --- | --- |
| | 15 | 16 | 17 | 18 | 19 | Total |
| | % | % | % | % | % | % |
| Little or no contact with opposite sex | 25 | 17 | 7 | 6 | 5 | 12 |
| Limited experience of sexual activities | 52 | 47 | 42 | 32 | 29 | 42 |
| Intimacies short of intercourse only | 18 | 29 | 33 | 40 | 36 | 32 |
| Sexual intercourse | 5 | 7 | 18 | 22 | 30 | 16 |
| Total number (= 100%) | 275 | 487 | 454 | 486 | 189 | 1,873 |

| Level of intimacy | 1991 | | | | | |
| --- | --- | --- | --- | --- | --- | --- |
| | 15 | 16 | 17 | 18 | 19 | Total |
| | % | % | % | % | % | % |
| Little or no contact with opposite sex | 9 | 7 | 5 | 4 | 6 | 6 |
| Limited experience of sexual activities | 33 | 30 | 23 | 19 | 18 | 25 |
| Intimacies short of intercourse only | 49 | 49 | 50 | 51 | 33 | 46 |
| Sexual intercourse | 9 | 14 | 22 | 26 | 43 | 23 |
| Total number (= 100%) | 309 | 293 | 236 | 190 | 101 | 1,129 |

- The 1991 figures show that half the teenagers between 15 and 19 went so far but no further but this barrier broke down at age 19.

In short this shows much greater intimacy at 15 and 16 in 1991 than in 1963, a little more at 17 and 18, but the floodgates beginning to open at age 19. If one takes into account the fact that the 1991 percentages are mostly for Christians and that equivalent non-Christian percentages would be likely to be higher (the only known point of reference is the number having had sexual intercourse at 16: 41% non-Christian against 14% Christian), then it is easy to see that the floodgates have opened. Late teenagers are likely to have been swept away on a vast tide of sexual intimacy on a scale not dreamt of in 1963.

The 1963 study showed that when men started sexual intercourse they continued, whereas women hesitated longer before allowing full intercourse. The greater availability of both contraception and abortion have probably been responsible for sweeping away even this hesitation now.

The 1963 study found that the reasons for and reactions to the first experience of sexual intercourse were:

*Table 14: First experience of intercourse 1963*

| Reasons | Men | Women |
|---|---|---|
| | % | % |
| Sexual appetite | 46 | 16 |
| Curiosity | 25 | 13 |
| Love | 10 | 42 |
| Other reasons | 19 | 29 |
| Reactions | | |
| Liked it | 48 | 30 |
| Disappointed | 14 | 7 |
| Ashamed | 10 | 25 |
| Disliked it | 7 | 7 |
| Afraid of it | 5 | 15 |
| Other reactions | 16 | 16 |

The 1963 study also found that people were likely to have sex the more alcohol they drank, the more money they had, the more they smoked, the more they learned the facts of life from their friends and the more restless people were.

The consequence initially for boys was to depress ambition, for girls greater religious antipathy, and for both an increased dislike of holidays with their parents.

The 1963 study found no significant difference in the amount or type of teenage sexual activity between Anglicans, Free Church, Roman Catholics or Jews.

Similar details are not available in more recent studies. The large Exeter University study by Dr Nicholas Ford, lecturer at their Institute of Population Studies, updated one item, however: he found romantic reasons for the sexual experience at 33% for men and 60% for women,[32] against the 10% and 42% respectively given in 1963.

Josh McDowell in his book *Teens speak out* quotes a conversation between a young man and his friend. 'It says in this book,' says the young man, 'that teenage boys think about sex 17 seconds out of every minute.' 'Really,' replied his friend, 'that's unbelievable.' 'Why?' asked the first. 'Well,' said his friend, 'What else is there to think about the rest of the time?'![33]

Such is the sexual image of the 1990s. How do the churches combat it, and such incredible statements as that of Madonna, 'I saw losing my virginity as a career move.'[34] Terry Mattingly, a communicator on culture at Denver Seminary suggests, 'keep asking those to whom we minister if the culture is delivering what it promises. Ask young people if modern sexual practices are creating happiness in the lives of those around them. Ask if premarital sex has brought feelings of acceptance and security.'[35]

Cohabitation is a further excursion which a few teenagers are trying. It is not discussed here as it is much more common with those in their early twenties, but helpful ways of handling young people, and your own children if they begin to cohabit, are given in Rev Edward Pratt's booklet *Living in Sin?*[36]

## Priorities

Companionship is important for teens as is going to the pub. But judging by the percentages who opt for particular types of activity does not give a sufficient understanding of their relative importance. Few surveys seem to ask how teenagers prioritize the many influences on them. Gallup asked 518 14–16 year olds the two or three most important things in their life and found 51% included education and examination results, 49% their home and 48% their friends.[37]

In any case, priorities change with age. A Trustee Savings Bank study found the main activity for 12 year olds was watching television, but this had slipped to second place for 16 year olds, and fourth place for 17–19 year olds. On the other hand 17–19 year olds put discos top of their list, whereas it rated third for 16 year olds and sixth for 12 year olds.[38]

There are three other aspects of life which for some teenagers take high priority. The first is lack of activity, unemployment. In Spring 1992 the percentage of teenagers in Great Britain aged 16–19 out of work was 16.4%.[39] In a brilliant analysis of over a thousand unemployed young people, the researcher Leslie Francis finds two main consequences of the lack of employment: depression and radicalism. 'The depression factor brings together notions of loneliness, anxiety, worry, isolation, self doubt, despondency and dependency. The young people who were depressed tended to say that they often felt lonely and that they feel no-one really knows them. They were the people who worry a lot about what they are doing. They become very anxious about their relationships with others and they worry a lot about their sex lives. They begin to doubt their worth as individuals.

'The radical young person wants to reject the moral values that society imposes on issues like abortion, divorce, homosexuality and the use of drugs. They rejected the demands placed on them by the law of the land . . . They have learned to distrust and dislike the police. Their interest is in enjoying the present moment, not in saving up for their future . . . They reject God and all that the church stands for.'[40]

The second activity is that of vandalism. 'In a 1987 survey of 1,100 secondary school children in England, 66% admitted to acts of vandalism, from arson to breaking windows, and 35% said they would do more. Some 34% saw little harm in vandalizing bus shelters, 40% in scrawling graffiti, and 64% in damaging plants in a garden.'[41] There could be as many as six million acts of vandalism a year (only one in ten is reported), four out of every nine by someone under 21. It costs the country £2,000 million a year.[42] In Australia, 'almost all young offenders are either from single parent or blended (two adults, not both the original parents) families. Mothers are not able to offer a male role model to their sons,' says John Smith, the evangelist to kids on motorbikes.[43] This shocking result, so offensive to lone mothers, is not necessarily true in the United Kingdom, where the detection rate of juvenile crime is low.

The third activity is that of:

## Occult involvement

There is no question but that the occult is a growing reality today. The activities of some pseudo-Christian groups, of which there are a large and growing number, are scary. Allegations are difficult to substantiate, but young people can easily be drawn into the dark world of destruction and pain, which can dramatically alter their personality, behaviour and friendships. 'Teenagers are often interested in contemporary witchcraft because of its air of mystery, its dedication to the 'natural' world, and its ability to intrigue one's imagination and creativity,' write the authors of a useful but disturbing book on teenagers and the occult, *When the Devil Dares Your Kids*.[44]

The RAKT study asked about teenage involvement with nine occult practices. One of these included 'meditation' which a number misunderstood as 'Christian meditation' rather than 'transcendental meditation', so these answers are disallowed. The other answers are given below.

Table 15: Involvement with occult practices

| Practice | School group | Church group |
|----------|--------------|--------------|
| | % | % |
| Ouija boards | 26 | 8 |
| Astrology | 18 | 10 |
| Tarot cards | 13 | 6 |
| Hypnosis | 5 | 3 |
| | | |
| Crystals | 3 | 2 |
| Reflexology | 3 | 2 |
| Channelling | 3 | 1 |
| I Ching | 2 | 1 |

In every instance teens in schools were more heavily involved than those in the church groups; in that sense the church groups were more protected. But the above numbers are alarming. If the school sample is representative then 26% of secondary school pupils on their own admission are involved with ouija boards—that's over 840,000 secondary school pupils in the United Kingdom! Many are likely to be involved in more than one category. Suppose of those who do not play with the ouija board one in ten were involved in something else. That would then make about one million pupils involved with the occult in total. 1,000,000 young people in Britain playing with fire! That's an extremely high number—about 30% of all secondary school children. What an influence it is bound to have.

Table 15 shows that there are only three main types of occultic practices (out of this list of eight) practised much by teenagers—ouija boards, astrology and tarot cards, with astrology being highest for church youth. If this sample is

*Table 16: Occult involvement by Christian commitment*

| Christian Commitment | Ouija boards | | Astrology | | Tarot cards | |
|---|---|---|---|---|---|---|
| | School | Church | School | Church | School | Church |
| Strongly committed Christian | 14 | 6 | 8 | 9 | 6 | 4 |
| Christian but not very committed | 22 | 10 | 18 | 10 | 12 | 6 |
| Unsure whether Christian | 26 | 6 | 19 | 12 | 12 | 9 |
| No longer Christian | 44 | 27 | 28 | 36 | 22 | 0 |
| Never been Christian | 34 | 8 | 18 | 4 | 19 | 8 |
| Overall | 26 | 8 | 18 | 10 | 13 | 6 |

*Table 17: Occult involvement by gender*

| Gender | Ouija boards | | Astrology | | Tarot cards | |
|---|---|---|---|---|---|---|
| | School | Church | School | Church | School | Church |
| Males | 22 | 5 | 15 | 6 | 11 | 6 |
| Females | 29 | 10 | 21 | 13 | 16 | 5 |
| Overall | 26 | 8 | 18 | 10 | 13 | 6 |

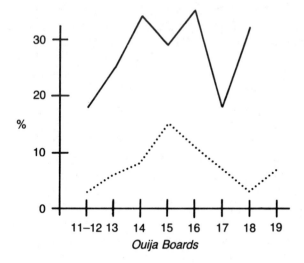

*Ouija Boards*

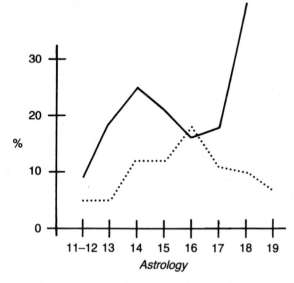

*Astrology*

Figure 9: Occult involvement by age

representative, it suggests 33,000 teenagers attending British churches in 1992, which might gross to 40,000 if all types of practice are involved. This is about 6% of the estimated 670,000 church children in England aged 11–19.

The strength of Christian commitment is an important factor in the three main practices, as may be seen in Table 16.

The strongly committed Christian is much less active in these practices than others. The not so strongly committed are involved more, but usually not as much as those not sure. Those who are 'no longer a Christian' are extremely active for the most part and have the highest participation rates, higher than for those who have never been a Christian. The experience of those 'no longer a Christian' is perhaps like those of whom Jesus spoke when He said 'When the unclean spirit has gone out of a man, . . . he says, 'I will return.' . . . then he goes and brings seven other spirits more evil than himself and they enter and dwell there; and the last state of that man becomes worse than the first.'[45] As Table 17 demonstrates, females are more likely than males to become involved with the occult, although gender differences are not as great as those related to Christian commitment.

Occultic involvement also varies with age, as shown in Figure 9, on page 83. This shows a general increase in interest in the mid-teens for ouija boards, early teens in schools for astrology, later teens in churches for astrology, and then a dying away of interest with a sudden resurgence at the highest ages. The age group changes for tarot cards are similar to those for ouija boards.

Environment, area of the country lived in, or (for churches) whether they were evangelical or not did not affect occultic involvement.

There is an interesting variation in church groups by denomination: Roman Catholics and New/House Church teens are more likely than those in other denominations to be involved with tarot cards and ouija boards, and Roman Catholics with astrology. The high New/House Church

*Table 18: Occult involvement by denomination*

| Church | Ouija boards | Astrology | Tarot cards |
|---|---|---|---|
| | Church % | Church % | Church % |
| Roman Catholics | 13 | 15 | 11 |
| New/House Churches | 16 | 7 | 9 |
| All others | 7 | 9 | 4 |
| Overall | 8 | 10 | 6 |

*Table 19: Occult involvement by parents' marital status*

| Marital Status | Ouija boards | Astrology | Tarot cards |
|---|---|---|---|
| | Church % | Church % | Church % |
| Married | 23 | 17 | 12 |
| Separated | 31 | 17 | 19 |
| Divorced | 33 | 23 | 25 |
| Unmarried | 32 | 7 | 7 |
| Widowed | 41 | 21 | 18 |
| Overall | 26 | 18 | 13 |

percentage perhaps reflects their emphasis on deliverance from the occult, thus attracting more who have been involved.

Teenagers whose parents are married are less likely to be involved in occult practices than those with divorced or separated parents or who have lost a parent by death.

These occult practices are only the fringe and the tempting start to deeper involvement. 'Of course, 'black' magic exists—Satanism, of the extremely immoral and harmful kind, is by no means dead. There is also that 'harmful' Crowley-orientated magic of heavy metal music, a form of chaos-magic, the basic idea behind it being that we are locked rigidly within conventions which must be broken for us to be able to escape, and such destruction yields power. It is through this disordering of our belief structures that we attain inspiration and enlightenment.'[46] The author, Dr David Burnett, lecturer at All Nations Christian College, in his book, *Dawning of the Pagan Moon*, suggests there could be 100,000 witches in the UK (in 1989), and quotes the Occult Census of that year to show that 67% of them became interested in occultism *before the age of 18!*[47]

We have looked at teenage leisure from the viewpoint of something to do, somewhere to go, someone to confide in and their involvement with the occult. If the church is to make headway into the leisure world of the teenager it needs to work along similar lines. The church can readily follow some of the secular activities many teenagers enjoy, but it is in the areas of somewhere to go and someone to confide in where help is needed and the alternatives less common. These are also probably the hardest areas.

One imaginative approach is that of the Ichthus Christian Fellowship which has bought the Brown Bear public house in Deptford, serving non-alcoholic drinks only, to provide a practical place for teenagers to go. Could others do the same? Some churches have given one room for teenagers to use as a lounge, with armchairs, etc., and this helps, but for those attending modern sixth forms, often with their own microwave and television and telephone, such basic amenities might need to be enhanced.

Providing companionship and help is crucial, but this takes time—what so many church people do not have. More and more churches are attempting to resolve this problem by appointing specific Youth Workers, Youth Pastors or Youth Directors. This helps, but ultimately the church needs a selection of folk willing to listen, unshockable, but caring, loving and able to give Godly wisdom to the problems presented. Could it train more singles, more couples to help in this way? The work of Scripture Union, Frontier Youth Trust, Youth for Christ, Agapé, the Boys' Brigade,

Girls' Brigade and other youth organizations brings many contacts with young people, often completely away from the church.

The church needs also to mobilize more people to pray, for otherwise the next such survey may reveal not one but two million youngsters involved with the occult.

## Sources of further information

The present generation of young people is probably the most researched group in the world. There are dozens of studies available! For those who want to go deeper here are a few additional starting places:

- The National Youth Agency, which sponsors the National Youth Bureau, has a mine of information encompassing work with young people. They have a comprehensive list of publications; they produce *The Youth Action Action Group*; they provide a *Directory of Senior Personnel in Local Authority Youth and Community Services*; they publish reports like *Taking Shape* which updates developments in Youth Service policy and provision. In particular they publish *Young People Now* the most widely read magazine amongst (secular) youth workers. Their address is 17–23 Albion Street, Leicester, LE1 6GD. Telephone: 0533 471200.
- The Department of Employment publishes an annual report on its research. The 1992 Report listed 28 projects on youth work. Details are available from their Resources and Strategy Directorate, Moorfoot, Sheffield S1 4PQ. Telephone: 0742 753275.
- Essex University keeps a data archive of the data collected in many studies. Details of these are published regularly in the ESRC Data Archive Bulletin. That for May 1992, No 50, for example listed 20 datasets on children and adolescents recently acquired. Their address is the University of Essex, Colchester, Essex CO4 3SQ. Telephone: 0206 872001/872103.

- For those interested in Christian work among young people the 1992/93 edition of the *UK Christian Handbook* (produced every two years) listed 94 different youth organizations in this country, together with address and telephone number, and a brief description of the particular kind of work they undertake. This book may be bought from the Christian Research Association, Vision Building, 4 Footscray Road, Eltham, London SE9 2TZ. Telephone: 081–294 1989.
- The only cross-denominational magazine for Christian youth workers, and a source of news, information, youth trends, features and ideas is *Youthwork*, available from 37 Elm Road, New Malden, Surrey KT3 3HB. Telephone: 081–942 9761.

### Summary

- The main teenager leisure activities are watching television (92%), listening to music (86%) and doing homework (82%).
- Other activities include watching videos (64%), hobbies (58%), playing sport (57%) and computer games (47%).
- There are sufficient youth magazines for two-thirds of youngsters to read one a month.
- Favourite places to go are the cinema (51%), discos (36%) and games arcades (27%) for school teenagers, and church activities (53%), the cinema (46%) and youth clubs (44%) for church teenagers.
- Most teenagers (74%) reckon on spending time with their friends.
- 14% of church 16 year olds have lost their virginity, 43% by the age of 19. 41% of non-church 16 year olds have done likewise.
- Perhaps one million secondary school pupils are involved with some occult practices.

# 3

# *Teenagers and the Church*

Only four people are positively identified in the Scriptures as being in their teenage years—and they all had problems! Ishmael was 13 when he was circumcised by Abraham;[1] later he was sent away with his mother Hagar to avert a clash between him and the promised line through Isaac. Joseph was 17 when he was sold into Egypt,[2] and, apart from a fleeting glimpse when he buried his father 57 years later, he never returned to his native land, although his bones were brought back.

The other two were both young kings. King Uzziah (or Azariah) was crowned when he was 16,[3] reigned for 52 years and died a leper. 'When he was strong, he grew proud,' the Chronicler tells us.[4] The penultimate King of Judah, Jehoiachin, was 18 when he became king,[5] but lasted just three months and ten days, surrendering to Nebuchadnezzar who imprisoned him in Babylon.

Others come close. Manasseh was 12 when he became king,[6] and Jesus was 12 when he went with his parents to Jerusalem.[7] Jairus's daughter was 12 when Jesus healed her.[8] It may be deduced that Jacob was 15 when his grandfather Abraham died but the text doesn't actually say so. Isaac may have been in his teens when Abraham took him up Mount Moriah but we don't know for certain. Although Mary's age is not specifically mentioned when she gave birth to Jesus, all major scholars would reckon she was a teenager, probably 14–16 at the time. The Jewish custom then was for girls to marry as young as 12 or 13, and any unmarried by 19 would be regarded as 'on the shelf'!

Of the four we know, the first was seen as a threat and removed, the second was a favourite and sold out of jealousy, the third became proud and ill, the fourth was a coward and poor—all human weaknesses affecting church teenagers, and other groups, today.

In this chapter we look at teenagers and their relationship with the church nationally, locally and through their own experience.

## Teenagers in the national Church

In 1979 13% of England's teenagers attended church. Ten years later the proportion had fallen to 9%, the dramatic fall which initiated the RAKT Study. This was a decline from 490,000 15–19 year olds to 345,000. But the drop for all teenagers (those aged 10–19) is even greater. Estimating the numbers in church for every ten-year age group in 1979 compared with 1989 figures in the same cohort reveals a decline of nearly half in numbers of teenagers attending in 1979 attending (as those in their twenties) in 1989.

*Table 20: Church attendance by ten year cohorts 1979/1989*

| Age group | 1979 | 1989 | Percentage change |
|-----------|------|------|-------------------|
| 0–9 | 940,000 | 820,000 | – |
| 10–19 | 960,000 | 760,000 | −19% |
| 20–29 | 600,000 | 490,000 | −49% |
| 30–39 | 580,000 | 560,000 | −7% |
| 40–49 | 560,000 | 550,000 | −5% |
| 50–59 | 550,000 | 540,000 | −4% |
| 60–69 | 600,000 | 580,000 | +5% |
| 70 or over | 650,000 | 630,000 | +5% |
| Total | 5,440,000 | 4,930,000 | −9% |

These figures are net changes not gross. So any who joined were offset by as many more leaving. Why did they leave? 'Church is utterly weary and has nothing of interest,' wrote one 13 year old in response to our questionnaire, 'but who will listen to me?' If we do not listen we will lose more still.

So where have the number of teenagers aged 15–19 been lost? Figures 10 and 11 show the proportion of church-goers aged 15–19 by county for 1979 and 1989 respectively. Figure 12 shows how these percentages changed. The percentages increased only in six counties—Buckinghamshire, Northamptonshire, Oxfordshire, Shropshire, Somerset (all rural counties with increasing populations) and Tyne and Wear. They were static in five—Berkshire, Dorset, Gloucestershire, Lancashire and West Sussex, and declined in the remaining 35 counties out of the 46 in England, as is illustrated in Figure 12. It shows some growth in the centre (south midlands), but decline in most other areas.

The English Church Census recorded that 7% of all church-goers in 1989 were between 15 and 19,[9] or an average of 9 teenagers per church, compared with 9% in 1979 or 13 per church. Similar studies in Wales in 1982[10] and Scotland in 1984[11] showed this proportion as 7% and 5% respectively or 5 and 11 teenagers per church on average.

Similar percentages by different categories are given in Appendix 1, where the larger Roman Catholic churches may be identified through their larger numbers of teenagers. Catholic churches attract on average over 30 teenagers per church, and Independent Churches (which includes the New/ House Churches) and larger churches with congregations over 200 are also comparatively successful in attracting teenagers.

Small churches, remoter rural churches, Low Churches, Broad Churches, URC churches and Methodist Churches all have few teenagers per church. The feeling of isolation will therefore be especially relevant here. Since teenagers like to talk with friends, and do things together, the value of larger teenage groups in a church is that they can bind together 'as

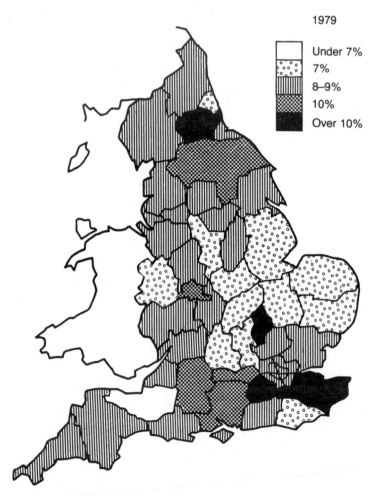

Figure 10:Proportion of churchgoers aged 15–19 by county 1979

a gang' much better. If on average it is only the Roman Catholics, New/House Churches and large churches which do this, how will all the other 80% of churches manage? It is critical to answer this question. Nick Aiken, Youth Officer for the

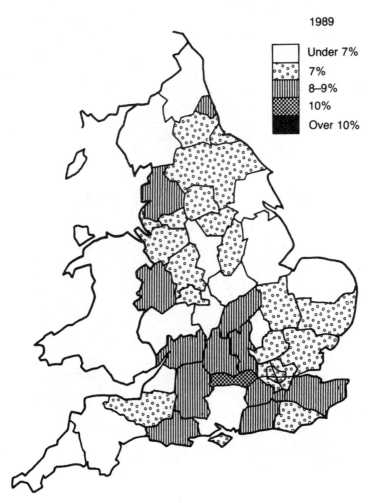

1989

Under 7%
7%
8–9%
10%
Over 10%

Figure 11:Proportion of churchgoers aged 15–19 by county 1989

Diocese of Guildford, rightly calls it a crisis, and sum-
marises it thus: '70% of all those who enter the teenage
years fall out from any meaningful relationship with the
Church by the time they hit 20.'[12] After Table 21, we

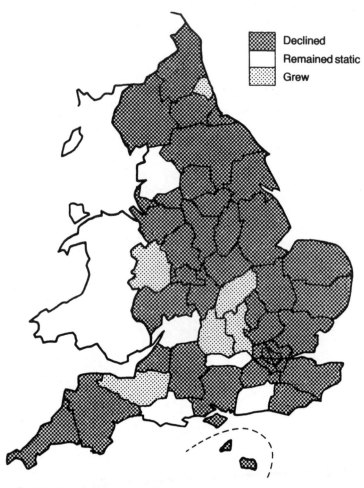

Figure 12: Percentage change in churchgoers aged 15–19
1979–1989

turn to what the teenagers themselves said in the RAKT
Study.

Table 21: Teenage churchgoers by denomination in England 1989

| Denomination | Percentage of churchgoers of all ages | Percentage aged 15–19 | Approximate number aged 15–19 | Percentage of churchgoers aged 15–19 | Sampled percentage of church youth 12–19 |
|---|---|---|---|---|---|
| | % | % | % | % | % |
| Methodist | 10 | 5 | 23,600 | 7 | 7 |
| Baptist | 6 | 7 | 17,400 | 5 | 14 |
| United Reformed | 3 | 4 | 5,500 | 2 | 9 |
| Independent | 9 | 16 | 62,800 | 18 | 9 |
| Afro-Caribbean | 2 | 9 | 8,700 | 2 | } 7 |
| Pentecostal | 3 | 9 | 10,900 | 3 | |
| Other Free | 2 | 6 | 6,200 | 2 | 2 |
| Total Free Churches | 35 | 8 | 135,100 | 39 | 48 |
| Anglican | 30 | 8 | 73,600 | 22 | 35 |
| Roman Catholic | 35 | 5 | 135,400 | 39 | 17 |
| Orthodox | 0.2 | 7 | 900 | 0.3 | 0 |
| Total all Churches | 100 | 7 | 345,000 | 100 | 100 |

## Churches attended

Which denominations did those connected with churches attend? The sample selected was deliberately deficient in Roman Catholic churches so that more of the smaller denominations could be included. Table 21 and Figure 13 give details of the overall numbers and proportions of 15–19 year old churchgoers in England.

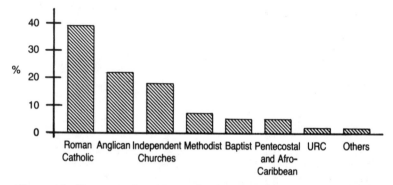

Figure 13: Teenage churchgoers by denomination in England 1989

## Teenagers in the local Church

### Frequency of attendance

The English Church Census counted teenagers present in church on one particular Sunday, but how often do they go? The results are given below, with 'several times' taken as four times a year to get the totals, and 'nearly every week' taken as 44 times a year to allow for the weeks when the youth club would be closed.

It was to be expected that church teenagers would go to church more frequently than school teenagers. Gender did not influence frequency, interestingly. Many studies have shown that girls are more likely to attend church than boys, but this study shows that once part of a church—in whatever proportions

*Table 22: Frequency of teenage church attendance 1992*

| Frequency | School groups | Church groups |
|---|---|---|
| | % | % |
| Most weeks | 15 | 84 |
| At least once a month | 6 | 8 |
| Several times a year | 8 | 4 |
| Once or twice a year | 13 | 2 |
| Hardly ever | 58 | 2 |
| | | |
| Total (=100%) | 1,069 | 861 |
| Average visits per year | 8 | 38 |

—attendance frequency is much the same. Nor did frequency vary by much throughout the country or by type of area (rural or suburban) or by whether the churches were evangelical.

Those attending church groups did vary though by age and denomination and the strength of their Christian commitment, as shown in Table 23.

*Table 23: Church groups church attendance by various categories*

| Age | Visits per year | Christian commitment | Visits per year | Denomination | Visits per year |
|---|---|---|---|---|---|
| 11–12 | 40 | Strong | 42 | New/House Church | 43 |
| 13 | 40 | | | Baptist | 41 |
| 14 | 40 | Weak | 38 | Roman | |
| 15 | 38 | | | Catholic | 40 |
| | | Unsure | 34 | Methodist | 39 |
| 16 | 36 | | | Other Free | |
| 17 | 35 | No longer | 31 | Churches | 38 |
| 18 | 38 | | | Anglican | 36 |
| 19 | 32 | Never | 26 | Independent | 34 |
| | | | | | |
| Overall | 38 | Overall | 38 | Overall | 38 |

*Table 24: School groups church attendance by various categories*

| Age | Visits per year | Christian commitment | Visits per year |
|---|---|---|---|
| 11–12 | 8 | Strong | 29 |
| 13 | 11 | | |
| 14 | 10 | Weak | 9 |
| 15 | 5 | | |
| | | Unsure | 3 |
| 16 | 6 | | |
| 17 | 5 | No longer | 3 |
| 18 | 3 | | |
| | | Never | 2 |
| Overall | 8 | Overall | 8 |

| Religion | Visits per year | Parents' marital status | Visits per year |
|---|---|---|---|
| Christian | 10 | Married | 9 |
| Muslim | 18 | | |
| Hindu | 1 | Separated | 6 |
| Sikh | 20 | | |
| Jew | 33 | Divorced | 4 |
| Buddhist | 4 | | |
| Other | 24 | Unmarried | 2 |
| None | 1 | Widowed | 7 |
| Overall | 8 | Overall | 8 |

The range of variation is quite small, suggesting commitment to the youth club as well as other church activities. The greatest variation is in Christian commitment with those who have lapsed or never been a Christian attending least often, but still at least once a fortnight.

Likewise the frequency varied for those in the school groups, as seen in Table 24. The questionnaire asked members of non-Christian religions to answer with respect to that religion, so the figures relating to the different religions need to be so interpreted. The Christian figures show a high degree of nominalism, even in the teenage years. As with the schools there was no significant variation by gender.

These figures might suggest that the age of 'fall-out' begins at 15, the year many children will start their GCSE courses. Could there be a clash of priorities? Basic commitment is clearly important, and it is interesting that the New/House Churches and Roman Catholics (with the Baptists) head the list of denominations on frequency. In the school group it is also noticeable that most other religions manage to command higher regularity of attendance than the Christians do, apart from Hindus and Buddhists. But 15 years of age might also be the time when normal church youth activities pall, and attendance frequency consequently lessens.

## *The lapsed attender*

Almost half, 49%, of the school respondents said they had attended church regularly, that is, at least once a month. How long did they attend in fact? On average 3 years. Almost three-fifths had attended for up to two years, a fifth for up to five years, and a fifth longer.

What denominations had the lapsed attended? Three-fifths (60%) had gone to an Anglican church, 13% to a Methodist and 12% to a Roman Catholic, with the remaining 15% spread over all the other denominations. Since those going to Anglican, Methodist and Roman Catholic churches account for 77% of the actual total of churchgoers of all ages (31%, 11% and 35%

respectively) this suggests that many Anglican and Methodist churches fail to keep their young people, and Roman Catholics and the Free Churches are much more successful in retaining them.

Two-thirds of the lapsed (66%) went with their family (the main reason for going), and half (47%) sat with their relations. A third (30%) went with their friends but half (51%) sat with them (rather more girls than boys). Only a small minority went by themselves (4%) or sat by themselves (2%). The family has a strong influence therefore in getting some teenagers to church, but it is likely to be their friends which keep them going.

Two-fifths of the lapsed (40%) joined the youth group, 14%, or one in seven, joined a home group/Bible study group, 6% a music group, 6% a prayer group, 1% an evangelistic group, and 15%, or one in seven, some other kind of group. Clearly it is the youth group which attracts.

How old were they when they stopped going to church? A third (34%) had stopped before they were 10 years old, half (51%) before they were 11 (and going to secondary school) and two-thirds (67%) by the age of 12, three-quarters (78%) by 13, 89% by 14, 94% by 15 and 98% by 16. These figures are graphed in Figure 14. They give a clear message.

*Table 25: Reasons for stopping going to church*

| Reason | % |
| --- | --- |
| Boring worship service | 45 |
| Few other young people | 36 |
| No activities for young people | 24 |
| Old-fashioned services | 23 |
| Serious doubts about the Christian religion | 17 |
| Congregation not welcoming | 5 |
| Others | 45 |

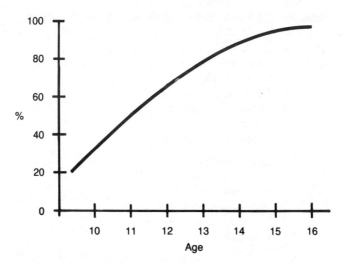

Figure 14: Percentage who had stopped going to church, by age

The experience of those who once attended church and then stopped is therefore mostly with child-like eyes and not teenage eyes. This makes Sunday School so important as this is how many will experience church. Why did they stop going to church? Table 25 gives the details.

Had they been involved in doing anything in the church (doing something at least once every six months) while they attended it? Three in seven said NO, but that means four in seven (58%), over half, had helped in some way, as indicated in Table 26.

Three-quarters of those who left the church had done so before they were 13, too young to be usefully involved in many of these activities. The list in Table 26 does not suggest those willing to help were not used. It was not the lack of (minimal) involvement that drove them away, nor the commitment of regular involvement that made them stay (none has a high percentage, and the choir is the only item requiring presumably some longer term commitment).

*Table 26: Young people's involvement in church services*

| Involvement | % |
| --- | --- |
| Take collection | 28[1] |
| Sing in choir | 17 |
| Read lesson/Bible reading | 16 |
| Serve refreshments | 14 |
| Dance/drama | 12 |
| Play in music group | 6 |
| Serve at altar | 6 |
| Welcome visitors | 6 |
| Lead prayers | 4 |
| Help with creche | 4 |
| Teach in Sunday School | 3 |
| Ring bells | 2 |
| Preach | 1 |

[1] 19% male; 37% female

One argument sometimes made is 'to keep young people you must use young people.' However desirable involvement in church service is, it does not appear to be an important factor in retaining youngsters.

So much for the responses of those at school who once belonged to a church. Their length of stay was reasonable, many had friends to sit with, over half were involved in activities in some way, but they all left, mostly before they became a genuine teenager, with boredom and loneliness given as the main reasons. Do other answers illumine these facts further?

Those who never became Christians stayed only half as long as the rest, a year and nine months on average. Lapsed Christians stayed half as long again as the rest, five years on average. But as both categories still left at much the same age as everyone else this simply suggests the first came in later, looked around 'quickly' and left, whereas the second group came much earlier and was therefore around longer. Those who are no longer Christians were predictably the main ones to have serious doubts about Christianity (68% against 11% for all others). Why did they get such doubts? What made them doubt?

At what age then did they start coming to church? Obviously at all ages, but they appeared to come in two main groups—at 7 or 8 years of age, presumably when established at junior school, and at 10 or 11 just before transferring to secondary school. This suggests that this transition period needs to be handled especially carefully by churches. One church I visited in August 1991 held a special meeting for all children about to go to secondary school (not for their parents but for the children) 'to help them act Christianly and keep their faith amidst the new challenges that faced them.' Adults forget the trauma of going to a new school; other churches could copy this example, if only because this study shows that many children leave their church within a year or two of going on to secondary school. It was also at the age of 13 and 14 that 'the boring services' response reached its peak (57% against 41% for other ages).

The ages of 11–13 are also when puberty begins and this could affect their emotions and habits. It is also that time of age when increasingly young people are less controlled by their parents, and therefore have more choice over their leisure time. If they then choose to go less, it is important parents and churches help young people to *want* to attend when they no longer *have* to attend.

These children did not just turn up once and never come again. For whatever reason (parents, friends, youth club), they gave the church a fair trial—maybe more than one church of course. On average these young people attended a church reasonably regularly for nearly four years before giving it up. The later they stopped coming the later they started coming. Four years is an average, but few gave it 10 years. We must not presume therefore, as we tend to do with adults, 'here

*Table 27: Denominational allegiance of teenagers*

| Denomination form sent to | Denomination actually attended | | | | | Total |
|---|---|---|---|---|---|---|
| | Anglican | Methodist | Independent | Other Free | Roman Catholic | |
| Anglican | 93 | – | 1 | 6 | – | 100 |
| Methodist | 2 | 95 | 3 | – | – | 100 |
| Independent | – | – | 97 | – | 3 | 100 |
| Other Free | 2 | – | 18 | 80 | – | 100 |
| Roman Catholic | 6 | 1 | 1 | – | 92 | 100 |
| Total | 103 | 96 | 120 | 86 | 95 | 500 |

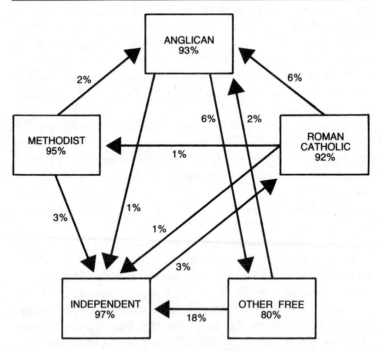

Figure 15: Switching between denominations

now, here forever.' These young people are, maybe unconsciously, evaluating their experience. After four years or so, half of them stopped coming. Do they come back? One-third did in the church youth group, but the other two-thirds left altogether.

A major study on nominality by Professor Eddie Gibbs,[13] showed that when young people leave the church, they tend to leave on average for eight years (and that's based on those that come back!)

## Changing denominational allegiance

The churches sampled, shown in the first column of Table 27, were sent questionnaires, 500 in all, for their young people to complete. We asked them the denomination of the churches they attended. Naturally the majority—three-quarters—named the one under whose auspices they were completing the form! The interest, however, is in the other quarter who gave other answers, a surprisingly high proportion, as detailed in Table 27.

On forms sent to Anglican churches, 93% of respondents indicated they attended an Anglican Church, 1% said they went to an Independent church, and 6% went to Other Free Churches. None said they went to Methodist or Roman Catholic churches. Methodists, on the other hand, scored 2% of their young people going to Anglican (a one-way road, therefore) and 3% to Independent churches (also a one-way road).

Independent churches retained the large bulk of their young people—more than any other group—but 3% said they went to Roman Catholic churches. This may seem a strange finding, but 5% of Independent churchgoers had a 'catholic' churchmanship in the English Church Census,[14] and it should not be surprising if some of that isn't reflected amongst the teenagers.

Other Free Churches lost out most, and mostly to the Independent churches, to which one person in six went. Some transfers cross the major Anglican/Roman Catholic/Free Church boundaries, but the greatest proportion are within the

Free Church group themselves with the Independents gaining and Other Free Churches losing out. The Independent Churches are a composite group: they include New/House Churches and other Independent churches such as the Christian Brethren, FIEC (Fellowship of Independent Evangelical Churches) Churches and other smaller groups. The New/House Churches retain their young people. It is the non-House Church Independent Churches which are losing large numbers of teenagers to New/House Churches, and this group also includes the 3% going to Roman Catholic churches. Roman Catholic churches lost a few of their teenagers to Methodist and Independent churches and 6% to an Anglican church.

All these swings and roundabouts are totalled in Table 27. The main 'winner' is the Independent churches and the main loser the Other Free Churches. There was a small exodus from Methodist and Catholic churches and a small gain by the Anglicans. Switching? Yes, but this is common with young people. Researcher George Barna found 'youth' the key characteristic of movers, over other age-groups, gender, marital status, environment, race, denomination and churchmanship.[15]

In addition 100 teenagers were personally interviewed with a short questionnaire, of whom 26% said they were or had been Anglican, 16% Roman Catholic, 12% Independent and 46% Other Free Churches. Interviews were concentrated on those who had left the church or were outside it, but 16 were with regular church members. Exactly half had changed their church or denomination, 3 to a New/House Church, 3 to a Methodist, 1 to a Baptist, and 1 to an Independent. Asked how they would find another church if they were going to move half said they would keep visiting until they found one where it 'felt right', two would ask their present leader before they left, two would look for active youth organizations, one would look for good singing, and three would stop going. Thus, in moving, denominational allegiance is small. Asked by George Barna if they always or usually attended the same church, or regularly attended at least two, 18–26 year olds replied 59%,

31% and 9% respectively, the 31% being the highest percentage for any age group.[16]

*Reactions to services*

What did teenagers think of church services? This is reflected in the next table, and illustrated in the following graph.

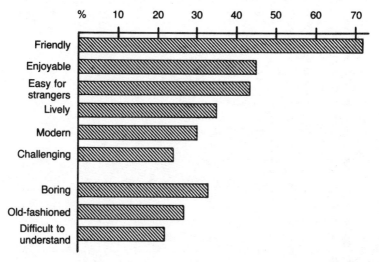

Figure 16: Teenagers' opinions of church services, by denomination

Table 28 is interesting as it represents the views of teenagers and not the church corporate. Most young people reacted positively to the church services they attended, with positive replies outnumbering the negatives by more than double on average.

New/House Churches and Baptist Churches emerge extremely positively; Methodists, Other Independents and Roman Catholic churches far less so, but still overall positive.

New/House and Baptist Church strengths are their friendly and enjoyable services. New/House Churches are especially lively, modern and challenging (the only group which scored over half for any of these descriptions, in fact scoring over half for

Table 28: Teenagers' opinions of church services, by denomination

| Opinion | Anglican % | Methodist % | Baptist % | New/ House Church % | Other Independent % | Other Free % | Roman Catholic % | Overall % |
|---|---|---|---|---|---|---|---|---|
| Friendly | 72 | 67 | 83 | 79 | 67 | 72 | 67 | 72 |
| Enjoyable | 39 | 38 | 68 | 72 | 53 | 47 | 28 | 45 |
| Easy for a stranger to join in | 45 | 31 | 63 | 44 | 30 | 43 | 40 | 44 |
| Lively | 33 | 24 | 46 | 77 | 28 | 37 | 22 | 35 |
| Modern | 30 | 21 | 36 | 65 | 23 | 28 | 25 | 30 |
| Challenging | 20 | 17 | 34 | 51 | 33 | 23 | 14 | 24 |
| Boring | 33 | 45 | 24 | 19 | 36 | 31 | 38 | 33 |
| Old-fashioned | 30 | 40 | 9 | 7 | 28 | 27 | 37 | 27 |
| Difficult to understand | 24 | 35 | 12 | 16 | 38 | 22 | 13 | 22 |
| Depressing | 6 | 10 | 7 | 5 | 12 | 10 | 10 | 8 |
| Irrelevant | 4 | 5 | 2 | 2 | 8 | 4 | 7 | 4 |
| Total number (100%) | 303 | 58 | 106 | 43 | 61 | 169 | 135 | 875 |
| Average of positives | 40 | 33 | 55 | 65 | 39 | 42 | 33 | 42 |
| Average of negatives | 19 | 27 | 11 | 10 | 24 | 19 | 21 | 19 |
| Positive ÷ negative 'score' | 2.1 | 1.2 | 5.0 | 6.5 | 1.6 | 2.2 | 1.6 | 2.2 |

them all). Baptist Churches scored highest for being easy for a stranger to join in—by comparison the New/House Churches did less well here (their weakest factor).

Reactions to Anglican and Other Free Churches were generally neither strongly positive nor negative. Methodist and Other Independent Churches were regarded as being particularly difficult to understand, with the Methodists and Roman Catholics especially thought to be old-fashioned, and the Methodists highly boring. Other Independent church services were thought challenging and enjoyable but not particularly lively or modern. The 'score' at the bottom of the Table 28 has no significance except as a comparison for the percentages given. They show how different teenagers consider Baptist and New/House Church services to be.

Females tended to feel services were easier for strangers to join in than males. Services in evangelical churches were regarded as more lively, challenging, modern and enjoyable than those in non-evangelical churches, and less old-fashioned. But these were the only differences in gender and churchmanship. No significant variations occurred for area of the country, or church environment. It is remarkable how these four factors have so little influence on the whole. The three important ones are the denomination, age of churchgoer, and commitment to Christ in most cases, but age was largely irrelevant here, too. Older teenagers (17–19) found services more challenging than younger ones (11–14), who complained that they were difficult to understand.

'Boredom' was teenagers' commonest negative opinion of church services. It was the reason most frequently given by the youngest people who have stopped attending church, Professor Eddie Gibbs found in his study on nominality.[17] Non-churchgoers in Scotland don't go because they feel services are 'boring and uninspiring'.[18] The Bishop of Motherwell, Rt Rev Joseph Devine, responded to the Scottish Church and Social Concerns Survey findings by suggesting the Church's image must change. 'We must show that services are relevant

Table 29: *Teenagers' opinions of church services, by Christian commitment*

| Opinion | Strong % | Weak % | Unsure % | No longer % | Never % | Overall % |
|---|---|---|---|---|---|---|
| Friendly | 82 | 73 | 64 | 64 | 25 | 72 |
| Enjoyable | 59 | 43 | 35 | 9 | 17 | 45 |
| Easy to join in | 51 | 44 | 38 | 46 | 21 | 44 |
| Lively | 44 | 33 | 28 | 36 | 13 | 35 |
| Modern | 40 | 29 | 23 | 9 | 8 | 30 |
| Challenging | 38 | 20 | 14 | 9 | 8 | 24 |
| Boring | 19 | 36 | 36 | 64 | 75 | 33 |
| Old-fashioned | 27 | 56 | 11 | 2 | 4 | 27 |
| Difficult to understand | 16 | 23 | 27 | 27 | 21 | 22 |
| Depressing | 3 | 8 | 12 | 36 | 25 | 8 |
| Irrelevant | 3 | 3 | 8 | 18 | 17 | 4 |
| Total number (100%) | 271 | 437 | 112 | 11 | 24 | 855 |
| Average of positives | 52 | 40 | 34 | 29 | 15 | 42 |
| Average of negatives | 14 | 25 | 19 | 29 | 28 | 19 |
| Positive ÷ negative 'score' | 3.8 | 1.6 | 1.8 | 1.0 | 0.5 | 2.2 |

and uplifting,' he said.[19] Indeed, that survey showed that highly-committed churchgoers thought church services were enjoyable and encouraging.[20] This factor of commitment was important with the RAKT Study, as shown in Table 29.

The 'score' shows the large difference between those strongly committed, those positive but not strong, and those not positive at all. It is derived by dividing the average of the positive percentages by the average of the negatives. Thus in the first column 52 ÷ 14 = 3.8. The difference between this 3.8 and the 'scores' in the other columns is very large. Those not sure if they are a Christian do not find services so enjoyable, lively, modern or challenging. Those no longer a Christian find them even less so, but massively boring, depressing and irrelevant. Those who have never been a Christian find very few positive features compared to the rest and again find services boring, depressing and irrelevant. It is very interesting that by far the highest percentages for services being old-fashioned came from the two committed groups!

Which parts of the service are enjoyed most? (Several wags wrote, 'The end'!) Answers are given in the Table 30.

There is no doubt that singing modern hymns and songs are highly popular with teenagers—more so by far than any of the other features. The lack of modern hymns was felt by some to be a sign of lack of friendliness, liveliness, and enjoyment in the churches. Is this another reason why youth services are so popular because they have their own, and certainly modern, music? Of the four most popular items three are music, and the Holy Communion/Mass/Eucharist ranks third only because of the high emphasis on mass by the Roman Catholic church. Exclude the Catholics, and this item becomes fourth most popular.

New/House Church services are enjoyed for their personal testimonies and prayers, but not for their Bible reading (is this an area of weakness with them?) Baptist and Other Independent services are enjoyed especially for their modern singing and personal testimonies also. Anglican, Methodist

*Table 30: Parts of service most enjoyed, by denomination*

| Part of service | Anglican % | Methodist % | Baptist % | New/House Church % | Other Independent % | Other Free % | Roman Catholic % | Overall % |
|---|---|---|---|---|---|---|---|---|
| Singing modern hymns/songs | 66 | 69 | 89 | 84 | 71 | 70 | 43 | 67 |
| Other musical items | 35 | 29 | 32 | 40 | 31 | 44 | 12 | 32 |
| Holy Communion/Mass/ Eucharist | 30 | 33 | 19 | 9 | 7 | 15 | 57 | 27 |
| Singing traditional hymns | 26 | 17 | 27 | 2 | 25 | 17 | 29 | 23 |
| Personal testimony | 15 | 24 | 27 | 37 | 36 | 20 | 8 | 19 |
| Sermon | 20 | 21 | 17 | 21 | 20 | 18 | 15 | 19 |
| Bible reading | 14 | 12 | 17 | 9 | 19 | 15 | 25 | 16 |
| Prayers | 15 | 16 | 20 | 28 | 22 | 11 | 15 | 16 |
| Total number (100%) | 300 | 58 | 106 | 43 | 59 | 170 | 134 | 870 |
| Average | 28 | 28 | 31 | 29 | 29 | 26 | 26 | 27 |

and Other Free church services achieve average scores for enjoyment—and are in some ways therefore those by which others are judged. Every denomination has its own traditions but the two factors which teenagers enjoy particularly are singing modern hymns/songs and personal testimonies. Perhaps denominations which have less of these should introduce more of them if they are going to reach and keep young people. It was through the sermon and personal testimony that the service was judged to be challenging or not. Testimonies and sermons were generally understood by young people and thought to be lively.

The Youth Officers interviewed agreed that young people enjoyed exuberant worship, partly because they could be involved in such worship. Andy Hickford of Stopsley Baptist Church said they also enjoyed items which are short or different, and cited drama, visuals and personal testimony. Tony Campolo, an American sociologist and dynamic preacher, once said, 'If you assume one minute's attention span for every year of their age—you assume too much!' He made a five-minute rule—change the item then to be fast moving and to involve your teenage audience. Mark Landreth-Smith of the Coign Church also mentioned the after-service refreshments which gave the opportunity to talk.

Had teenagers helped with church services in any way at least once every six months? Most had read the lesson or taken the Bible reading (29%), taken the collection (25%) or participated in dance or drama (24%), or the music group (18%). These all involved between one in three and one in five young people. The next group, involving one in eight to ten, were welcoming visitors (13%), serving refreshments (13%), teaching in Sunday School (12%), particularly the older teens, helping with creche (11%), or singing in the choir (10%). The final group of activities involved fewer still. These had led prayers (9%), served at the altar (8%), led worship (6%), rung the bells (3%) or preached (1%). Even so about a quarter (22%) had not been involved at all.

How does this list of activities compare with teenagers at school who had left the church but who had been involved? This group's experience of church was when they were a few years younger on average than those now in the church, but even so the comparison is interesting. It shows:

- Far fewer young teens had been involved (58% against 78%)
- Far fewer had helped with the creche, led worship, welcomed visitors, acted in dance/drama, taught in Sunday School, led prayers, played in the music group or read the lesson. Virtually all these are age related.
- Far more younger teens sang in the choir (17% against 10%)—and these had left the church. Could singing in the choir have put them off? The percentages suggest so.
- About the same proportion of lapsed and 'stayed on' had rung the bells, served at the altar, or served refreshments, that is, helped where they could.

This suggests the importance of using young people wherever possible in church services, and the more the better, apart from the formality and perhaps unwelcomed commitment of a church choir. As mentioned earlier, however, this is no guarantee they will stay.

### Teenage experience and the Church

Were church teenagers involved with activities in the church? Two-thirds (64%) attended the youth group, one in five (19%) belonged to a home group or Bible Study group, one in six (16%) a music group, one in twenty (5%) a prayer group, one in fifty (2%) an evangelistic group, and one in eight (13%) some other kind of group, such as confirmation classes, drama groups, Girls' Brigade, Boys' Brigade, Girl Guides, bell ringing, choir and practice, Sunday School teachers' meetings, Corps Cadets, Pathfinder Club, Campaigners Bible Club, Holiday Bible Club, Scouts, Healing team, Badminton and even the Parochial Church Council. These percentages were not very different from those who had once attended church when allowances were made for age. So it is not church involvement, or lack of it, which is likely to be a key motivator. Of those involved with a home group, 5% had felt like stopping going to church at sometime but 95% had not.

In the schools, half (50%) the strongly committed teenagers currently attended a youth group, against only a fifth (19%) of those who were Christian but not very committed. The youth group is clearly a key focus area for some youth, but there are substantial numbers of church teenagers and highly committed Christian young people who are not involved. Church youth groups vary in age of attendance and gender ratios. The results of a 1991 survey showed the following:[21]

*Table 31: Average age and gender ratios of church youth, by denomination 1991*

| Denomination | Average age (years) | Male: Female Ratio |
|---|---|---|
| Church of England | 15.9 | 44 : 56 |
| Baptist Union of Great Britain | 16.0 | 50 : 50 |
| Methodist | 16.0 | 50 : 50 |
| Baptist Union of Scotland | 16.4 | 55 : 45 |
| Church of Scotland | 16.5 | 43 : 57 |
| Elim Pentecostal | 16.8 | 53 : 47 |
| Salvation Army | 17.0 | 42 : 58 |
| Assemblies of God | 17.7 | 42 : 58 |
| Overall | 16.6 | 46 : 54 |

## Religious experiences

The questionnaire suggested eleven types of religious experience and gave room for an open twelfth. Not everyone who has had some kind of experience necessarily knows what kind it was.

Asked if they had had any religious experience, 47% of the

church sample and 26% of the school sample agreed they had, as did 66% of the strongly committed, putting both groups together. 'No' said 15% of the strongly committed and the remaining 19% did not know. One might have expected more than two-thirds of the strongly committed to have had a religious experience.

36% of not very committed Christians had had a religious experience, again putting both groups together, 15% of those who were not sure, 17% of those who said they were no longer a Christian and 11% of those who said they had never been a Christian but were members of another religion (who amounted to 3% of the school teenagers). The church group had a much higher proportion of experience (as might be expected), as follows.

*Table 32: Church group's religious experience by Christian commitment*

| Religious experience | Strong % | Weak % | Unsure % | No longer % | Overall % |
|---|---|---|---|---|---|
| YES | 58 | 27 | 13 | 14 | 26 |
| NO | 19 | 31 | 43 | 68 | 35 |
| Don't know | 23 | 42 | 44 | 18 | 39 |
| Total (=100%) | 100 | 449 | 222 | 50 | 821 |

Two-fifths of the school teenagers questioned did not know whether or not they had had a religious experience and of the three-fifths who did know 43% were affirmative and 57% were negative. The uncertainty factor is real, and highest for the one group who said they were 'not sure', though not much above those who felt they were not strong Christians. Clarity of experience is not the hallmark of most teenagers!

Assuming that the school sample reflected teenagers in Britain, then the general religious experience of teenagers, by strength of their commitment to Christianity can be as shown in the following table, which is based on the previous one but expresses all the figures as a proportion of the overall total. Table 33 is illustrated in Figure 17.

*Table 33: Religious experience of teenagers by Christian commitment*

| Religious experience? | Strong % | Weak % | Unsure % | No longer % | Overall % |
|---|---|---|---|---|---|
| YES | 7 | 15 | 3 | 1 | 26 |
| NO | 2 | 17 | 12 | 4 | 35 |
| Don't know | 3 | 23 | 12 | 6 | 39 |
| Total | 12 | 55 | 27 | 6 | 100 (=821) |

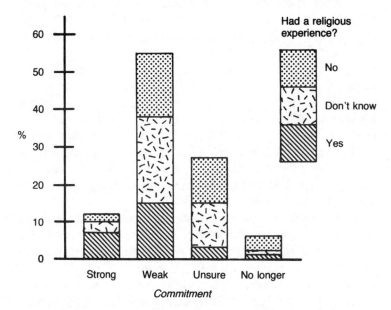

Figure 17: Religious experience by Christian commitment

This suggests that at best 12% of teenagers would say they have a strong commitment to Christianity but overall 26% have had a religious experience. Just over half of these (15%) puts them in the Christian camp, though not strongly. A further 7% are strongly committed.

In the church sample 47% had had a religious experience, an overall figure comparable to the 26% in the school sample. It was made up of 88% in the New/House Churches, 65% Other Independents, 54% Baptists, 46% Other Free Churches, 45% Anglican, 38% Methodist and 30% Roman Catholic.

## Types of experience

All those who had had some kind of experience were asked to try and pick one of the types suggested, and, for simplicity, the experiences of those at school and church have been combined in the tables and discussion that follow. Some could have more than one type of experience simultaneously, or consecutively. This aspect was not covered in the questionnaire, nor how long each took. The details of type of experience are given in Table 34.

The experiences fall into three groups: (a) that of God's presence, peace and becoming a Christian; (b) someone speaking to you (trying to communicate, visions/dreams, conversion or healing), and (c) an external other. Although some, perhaps many, might equate 'a conversion experience' with 'becoming a Christian', it is clear that these teenagers in many cases did not, since there were only 25% converted but 58% became a Christian. Perhaps the terminology is used differently by different groups.

Averaging the relevant percentages, about 52% of teenagers experienced type (a), 25% or 165 teenagers type (b), and 13% or 83 teenagers type (c). Adding these together, those who could affirm an experience total 602 teenagers, of whom 59% are type (a), 27% type (b) and 14% type (c). The occurrence of these three groups of affirmative experiences by various categories is given in Table 35 and illustrated in Figure 18.

*Table 34: Religious experience, by type and whether or not teenagers had had one*

| Type of religious experience | YES % | Not sure % | NO % | Total (=100%) |
|---|---|---|---|---|
| Becoming a Christian | 58 | 34 | 8 | 653 |
| A feeling of peace | 53 | 35 | 12 | 657 |
| The presence of God | 50 | 37 | 13 | 654 |
| Feeling as if somebody/something were trying to communicate with you | 30 | 52 | 18 | 654 |
| Visions/voices/dreams | 26 | 60 | 14 | 655 |
| Conversion | 25 | 60 | 15 | 652 |
| To do with healing | 20 | 69 | 11 | 652 |
| To do with nature | 15 | 71 | 14 | 649 |
| Beyond description | 14 | 72 | 14 | 642 |
| Some other spiritual/supernatural force | 14 | 71 | 15 | 644 |
| Something else | 9 | 87 | 4 | 608 |
| Overall | 28 | 59 | 13 | 647 |

*Table 35: Religious experience by various categories*

| Category | Type of experience | | | |
|---|---|---|---|---|
| | Becoming a Christian % | Someone speaking % | External Other % | Total (=100%) |
| Overall | 59 | 27 | 14 | 602 |
| **Christian commitment** | | | | |
| Strongly committed | 59 | 29 | 12 | 272 |
| Not strongly committed | 62 | 24 | 14 | 271 |
| Unsure if Christian | 46 | 37 | 17 | 29 |
| No longer Christian | 39 | 45 | 16 | 9 |
| **Gender** | | | | |
| Males | 55 | 27 | 18 | 275 |
| Females | 60 | 27 | 13 | 342 |
| **Age** | | | | |
| 11,12 | 53 | 31 | 16 | 88 |
| 13 | 58 | 27 | 15 | 122 |
| 14 | 63 | 25 | 12 | 94 |
| 15 | 57 | 29 | 14 | 90 |
| 16 | 61 | 24 | 15 | 78 |
| 17 | 61 | 27 | 12 | 66 |
| 18 or over | 58 | 30 | 12 | 63 |
| **Denomination** | | | | |
| Church of England | 61 | 26 | 13 | 139 |
| Methodist | 66 | 22 | 12 | 20 |
| Baptist | 67 | 24 | 9 | 62 |
| House Church | 58 | 29 | 13 | 49 |
| Other Independent | 63 | 28 | 9 | 44 |
| Other Free Churches | 62 | 30 | 8 | 77 |
| Roman Catholics | 58 | 20 | 22 | 35 |
| **Religion** | | | | |
| Christians | 56 | 28 | 16 | 147 |
| Other Religions | 37 | 33 | 30 | 14 |
| No religion | 19 | 44 | 37 | 23 |

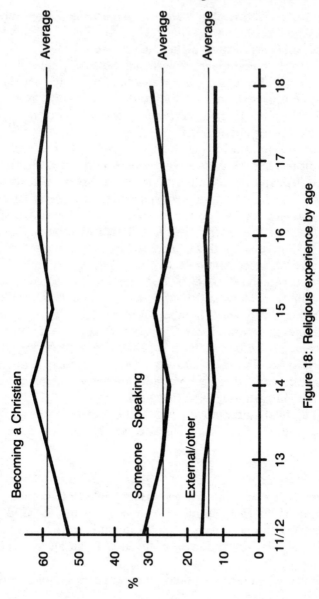

Figure 18: Religious experience by age

Table 35 shows the reality of experience, especially of 'Becoming a Christian'. Those who have some commitment, weak or strong, scored higher than those without.

Females scored higher than males reflecting other findings that more females are converted—here a greater percentage have a positive relationship. Maybe the male average experience is less precise, an external other experience, which perhaps means less, or endures less.

The proportion having definite experience increases with age from 11 to 14, falls at 15 and slowly declines thereafter. Type (b) experiences rather than Type (c) seem to take over, suggesting that the religious experience for some older teenagers is not totally specific and clean cut. There was some evidence of this in the 1983 Luis Palau Mission to London which showed a slightly higher percentage of teenagers coming forward for re-dedication than for salvation.[22]

Baptists and Methodists had the highest percentage of 'Becoming a Christian' experiences, although the latter is based on a very small number. Interestingly it is the Roman Catholics and New/House Churches which have the smallest percentages here, but type (b) is the second strongest for New/House Churches and type (c) for Roman Catholics. Anglicans and Other Independent churches are about average: for the church group type (a) average is 62%.

The final alternative was 'other experiences'. What were these? The following are actual quotes from the forms:

'The Holy Spirit'  'Being slain in the Spirit'
'Something evil in my dreams'  'Being able to tell others'
'Filling of the Holy Spirit'  'Calling to work for God'
'Being confirmed'  'Being at one with God'
'Sudden great joy and love of God'  'Feeling I can always turn to God'
'Felt sad when Grandad died'  'I saw the Holy Spirit enter a
'Renewing my life with Christ'  person'

| | |
|---|---|
| 'Bad dreams of devil and myself' | 'Seeing God's power in others' |
| | 'An immense feeling of awe' |
| 'Felt comfortable at Spring Harvest' | 'I felt the devil come inside me' |
| | 'Saw a ghost' |
| 'Answered prayer' | 'Forgiveness' |
| 'Deliverance' | 'Tongues' |
| 'God gave me a Bible verse' | 'Feeling of love and purpose' |

Perhaps the most interesting was 'A small poltergeist, not very lively'!

Other studies of teenagers have classified their religious experiences differently from the specific—personal—general types employed here. One study of the YWCA in 1991[23] used the categories Mystical, Continuous Awareness and Numinous, which might approximate with the three used here. What they found was that 35% in all had such an experience, 17% had two of the three types, and 22% claimed all three. (The remainder had no such experiences.)

### The Church for the teenager

What are some of the practical outworkings from this chapter? It is clear that many teenagers are leaving the church. 13% of English teenagers attended church in 1979, only 9% were doing so in 1989. We dare not be complacent. The average number of teenagers in any one church is small, and since teenagers are frequently keen to do things together and be involved, this argues for youth work across churches. In Selby, North Yorkshire, for example, six churches banded together to form one youth group called 'King's Arms'. This example could be followed elsewhere.

A sixth of all teenagers going to church in England in 1989 went to an Independent church—average 15 per church, enough for a 'gang'. Just over a fifth of all teenagers going to church went to an Anglican church—average four per church, not enough to 'get lost'. Two-fifths went to Roman Catholic churches—average 35 per church. The point is obvious.

The key factor determining a teenager's attendance at church is personal commitment to being a Christian, which varies especially by denomination and age. Certain denominations attract more teenagers than others. What can be learnt from them? This question was posed to the Youth Officers interviewed. The suggestions were the emphasis on relationships, lively worship, relevant activities, and a strong sense of identity and belonging. Patrick Harrison of the Diocese of Arundel and Brighton indicated the associated commitments to the family. The church needs to be interested in all aspects of young people's lives: physical, emotional, intellectual and spiritual.

Andy Hickford of Stopsley Baptist Church cited the Dallas church which increased its teenager numbers 400% in a single year because each adult invited two teenagers to stay with them for a whole weekend. As a consequence, teenagers made meaningful contact with church members, felt they were being treated as adults, were wanted, and stayed. They were able to share the life of the church which gave them a sense of belonging. They were part of the team, not a sub-section of it.

It has to be recognized that teenagers change with age (we all do!). A 13 year old is very different from a 16 year old, in turn very different from a 19 year old. Church activities, sermons, worship, involvement, responsibility need to reflect these changing ages. The main reason for teenagers stopping going to church was that the worship service was boring. The second reason was that there were few other people there of their own age. Boredom and loneliness are correctable problems! It is often the lack of willingness to delegate downwards or introduce modern hymns or songs or to trust others to do a job as well as we are doing it that creates the hesitation. These are essentially management skills, and training to help with them is readily available!

Not every teenager has as clear an understanding of their religious experience, judging from their answers, as perhaps they could have or should have. One church in Hayes, Kent has developed a Bible School for young people which teaches basic doctrines, and the Scriptures, and helps people to learn the key elements of Christian life, belief and practice. Could others do the same?

### Summary

- Only four teenagers are identified as such in the Bible—Ishmael, Joseph, Uzziah and Jehoiachin.
- 49% of those aged 10–19 attending church in 1979 had left 10 years later.
- The New/House Churches and Roman Catholics have well the above average number of teenagers per church—15 and 35 respectively.
- Weekly church attendance increases with commitment, decreases as teenagers get above 15 years old.
- Lapsed teenagers were more likely to be from Anglican and Methodist churches than attending teenagers.
- They stopped attending because of boredom, loneliness and lack of relevant activities.
- Lapsed teenagers had attended church for nearly four years on average before giving up.
- 79% of teenagers attend one of three denominations, Roman Catholic, Anglican or Independent churches. The Independent churches attract more, especially from Other Free churches.
- 72% of church services were deemed 'friendly' but only 45% 'enjoyable'. Modern hymns/songs was the part most enjoyed.
- 26% of teenagers have had a religious experience. For 59% this was to 'become a Christian', but for over half of these their commitment was not strong.

# 4

# *Motivations for Church Attendance*

Nick, a 17 year old Anglican, attends church because he 'believes in God and, therefore, should worship Him.'

Kathy, an 18 year old Catholic, sees the church as 'a place where people go to pray and get comfort.'

'The church doesn't offer anything I want. There is no future in the church for people my age.'

'I changed to another church which has positive and relevant teaching, good music. It's relevant to my life, not so theological. It strengthens my faith. I've made friends there and feel encouraged and supported.'

'I moved when I was about 14 and never became part of the new congregation. I tried the youth group but never felt welcome.'[1]

These are all Australian examples, but they could easily be British. The sentiments are all similar. 'Why did you choose to come to this particular church?' we asked our church interviewees. 'I enjoy the fellowship,' said one 18 year old Methodist. 'I like the people,' said a 16 year old New/House Church lad. Another 16 year old New/House Church lad said, 'Because it's mad!' Three 12 year old non-churchgoing boys all from the North were asked what would make them go to church. They had a simple answer: 'Girls!'

Some churches are highly popular with young people. The 9pm Sunday service in the Plymouth Elim Church draws an average of 1,100 young people per week. They must have some reason for going! This chapter identifies some of those reasons.

## Reasons for going/not going

A government survey on young people in the early 1980s[2] looked at youth involvement with churches, among other things. 22% of white youth claimed to be involved, as did 40% of the West Indians. Why were they involved? Five reasons were given:

*Table 36: Reasons for church attendance 1982*

| Reason | % |
|---|---|
| Meeting other young people | 33 |
| Participating in church activities | 25 |
| Doing something useful/helpful | 19 |
| Having fun/enjoyment | 15 |
| Pursuing of religious knowledge | 12 |

*Churchgoers reasons for going*

Altogether 891 forms were completed by church teenagers in our survey. 139, or 16%, did not answer the question of why they went to church, but the remainder did, with every eighth person giving two reasons. These reasons were:

*Table 37: Churchgoers' reasons for church attendance 1992*

| Reason | % |
|---|---|
| To worship God | 26 |
| To learn more about God | 22 |
| To go with parents | 20 |
| To have fun/enjoyment | 19 |
| To meet others | 15 |
| Duty | 4 |
| To do something useful/helpful | 4 |
| To pray | 3 |
| To participate in church activities | 2 |

This is a very different list from the earlier survey. Three key phrases were employed again and again 'To worship God', 'To learn more', 'I enjoy it.' Worship—learn—enjoy. These words are almost a mini-theological course! They accounted for the reasons why over two-thirds of church youth currently attend church (including prayer with worship). The two other main reasons were their parents (several testifying 'I was made to go, but now enjoy it') and to meet their friends. The first of these was not mentioned in the 1980s list, and the second came top, but now was the fifth reason. Learning about God, which had been the bottom reason, appears now as second.

Worship—learn—enjoy are essentially 'personal' or spiritual reasons. Parents—friends—church activities are corporate 'fellowship' reasons. Personal reasons totalled 70%, fellowship reasons 37%; do present youth reckon it's twice as important to go for personal reasons rather than social reasons?

## *Ex-churchgoers reasons for going*

Of 1,131 school group respondents used for analysis, 49% had at some stage attended a church at least once a month and of these, just over half still did so. Why had those who stopped gone in the first place? Their reasons are as follows, and the list is deliberately in the same order as the last table to aid comparison. Some gave two reasons, so the figures total more than 100%.

*Table 38: School groups' reasons for church attendance*

| Reason | % |
|---|---|
| To worship God | 2 |
| To learn more about God | 8 |
| To go with parents | 51 |
| To have fun/enjoyment | 9 |
| To meet others | 7 |
| Duty | 2 |
| To do something useful/helpful | 2 |
| To pray | 1 |
| To participate in church activities | 22 |

This list is also very different from either of the previous lists. The key phrases used here were 'my parents made me' and 'I had to go with the Brownies/Guide Church parade.' In other words there was a considerable amount of coercion. It must be remembered that these reasons are those given by teenagers now aged 12 or 14 or 16 who have stopped going to church, and who by and large are replaying the reasons why they went when 8 or 10 or 12.

The reasons are very different, however. The worship—learn—enjoy reasons account for 20%, including prayer. Parents—friends—activities account for 80%, four times as much. Whereas the personal/fellowship ratio was almost 2:1 for current church youth, it was ¼:1 for lapsed youth. The first group largely want to go, the latter group largely had to go—and stopped when they had the chance. The implication is obvious—force children to do something they do not really want to do for a long time and many will react against it later. Many, but not all as noted earlier. Perhaps one in eight will continue and enjoy it, possibly because they come into a more personal experience for themselves, and this then provides the motivation. Coercion clearly does not work for the majority.

## Non-churchgoers reasons for going

The school questionnaire went on to ask 'Why do you think young people go to church?' to which 13% did not answer, and 7% did not know. Only 155 currently went to church weekly, so 86% of the answers came from those who did not do so. Only 170 currently attended a church youth group. Of the remainder answers are given in Table 39, on page 131 again using the same order as before.

This list comes somewhere between the two previous lists. All three lists are illustrated in Figure 19.

The worship—learn—enjoy motives this time total 45% and the parents—friends—activities 48%, very similar proportions. In other words many who do not go to church recognize that many who do go to church go either because they believe or

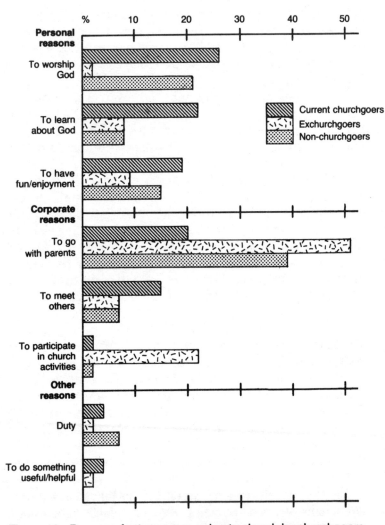

Figure 19: Reasons for teenagers going to church by churchgoers, exgoers and nongoers

Table 39: Reasons assumed for others' church
attendance by non-churchgoing school teenagers

| Reason | % |
|---|---|
| To worship God | 21 |
| To learn more about God | 8 |
| To go with parents | 39 |
| To have fun/enjoyment | 15 |
| To meet with others | 7 |
| Duty | 7 |
| To do something useful/helpful | 0 |
| To pray | 1 |
| To participate in church activities | 2 |

because they have to accompany their parents. They do not consider the need to learn about God to anything like the extent of churchgoers (indicating a lack of awareness), and overestimate parental influence considerably, partly perhaps reflecting coversations with others. They also underrate the importance of fellowship.

A few who indicated that they thought churchgoers went to church because they had 'nothing else to do', 'had no lives', 'are bores', were excluded.

How typical are these results from this carefully selected sample of churches and schools? In addition to the questionnaires a different sample of 100 teenagers were interviewed, some who went, some who had been, and some who largely had never gone to church. The results were *broadly in line*, confirming the above conclusions. The results may thus be summarized, each totalling over 100% as some gave more than one answer, and are given in Table 40, illustrated in Figure 20.

The overall figures are simply arithmetical averages and do not mean very much as the variations are wide. Although corporate reasons outweigh personal overall, they do so because of those outside the church, not those inside, for

*Table 40: Summary of churchgoing reasons*

|  | Churchgoers % | Ex-churchgoers % | Non-churchgoers % | Overall % |
|---|---|---|---|---|
| *Personal* Worship-learn-enjoy | 70 | 20 | 45 | 45 |
| *Corporate* Parents-friends-activities | 37 | 80 | 48 | 55 |
| *Other reasons* Duty/To do something | 8 | 4 | 7 | 6 |

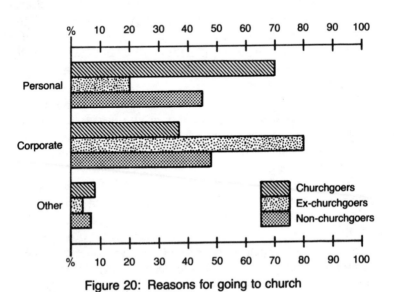

Figure 20: Reasons for going to church

whom personal reasons are the most important. If others assess churchgoers as going for corporate reasons they could well judge that as they have a different, non-religious, circle of friends, they don't need religious ones. This, however, is far too simplistic. Ex-churchgoers who remember being made to go when younger may assume that tradition or rule still applies to those who go as adults. They are seen as not having broken free from their parental influence. Those without that experience give more weight to 'believe in God'. They recognize that churchgoers do believe in God (and said so, many times), and that such belief entails going to church. This might sound rather naïve, but these are still teenagers' opinions of other teenagers. Ask the same questions ten years later and you will probably get different answers.

## Churchgoers reasons for not going

Churchgoing teenagers were asked why they thought others do not go to church. Answers varied significantly with age, and an asterisk (*) in Table 41 indicates statistically significant variation.

The main perceived reason is boredom, well ahead of the nearest other reason. Perhaps this reflects the personal experience of teenagers who do go, or comes from media portrayal of churchgoing. Boredom rises slowly to a peak at 14, and moderates thereafter. The second reason, that going to church isn't the 'done' thing, also rises to a peak, this time at 15, and then subsides. Five out of every eight teenagers thought this unacceptability a major barrier. The third most common reason, lack of belief in God, also peaked at 15.

The fourth reason, that none of their friends go, declines in importance with age. Although reckoned to account for half the teenagers in practice, loneliness mattered more to younger teenagers. The fifth reason, lack of parents' encouragement, also declines with age (and says something incidentally for parental comments made above). The sixth reason, having better things to do on a Sunday, didn't vary significantly with age, but generally decreased with importance after the age of 13.

*Table 41: Churchgoing teenagers' assumptions for others' non-attendance, by age*

| Reason | 11,12 % | 13 % | 14 % | 15 % | 16 % | 17 % | 18 or over % | Overall % |
|---|---|---|---|---|---|---|---|---|
| 1) They think it is boring | 83 | 91 | 94 | 87 | 92 | 82 | 85 | *88 |
| 2) Going to church isn't the 'done' thing | 52 | 62 | 65 | 71 | 60 | 64 | 56 | *62 |
| 3) They don't believe in God | 56 | 53 | 62 | 67 | 54 | 60 | 44 | 57 |
| 4) None of their friends go | 64 | 60 | 50 | 51 | 49 | 34 | 27 | *50 |
| 5) Their parents don't encourage them to go | 57 | 51 | 47 | 42 | 40 | 35 | 32 | *45 |
| 6) They've got better things to do on a Sunday | 43 | 53 | 47 | 44 | 42 | 42 | 41 | 45 |
| 7) They think it is irrelevant | 18 | 25 | 23 | 36 | 41 | 44 | 49 | *32 |

*Table 41: Continued*

|  |  |  |  |  |  |  |  |
|---|---|---|---|---|---|---|---|
| 8) They don't know what happens at church | 25 | 28 | 22 | 31 | 22 | 26 | 38 | 27 |
| 9) They feel out of place | 20 | 22 | 20 | 27 | 31 | 23 | 36 | 25 |
| 10) They don't like the moral teaching | 8 | 16 | 7 | 14 | 16 | 20 | 19 | *14 |
| 11) They don't know anyone at church | 17 | 17 | 12 | 11 | 14 | 17 | 7 | 14 |
| 12) They don't feel welcome | 12 | 12 | 6 | 11 | 14 | 6 | 18 | 11 |
| 13) They don't like the people who do go | 12 | 8 | 7 | 10 | 8 | 8 | 7 | 9 |
| 14) They don't like the minister/leader | 4 | 3 | 1 | 0 | 5 | 3 | 0 | 3 |
| 15) Other reasons | 7 | 6 | 6 | 10 | 8 | 13 | 8 | 8 |
| Total number (100%) | 139 | 155 | 140 | 132 | 134 | 95 | 73 | 868 |

Only two other factors varied significantly with age, both broadly increasing with importance the older the teenager. The first was that some felt the church was irrelevant, and the second that they disagreed with its moral teaching.

This is a very interesting list of reasons which might be divided into two groups, one relating to the church and one to themselves as follows:

*Church factors*

1) Boredom (ignorance of services)
7) Irrelevance (ignorance of teaching)
8) Ignorance of activities
10) Dislike of morals (?ignorance of teaching)
11) Knowing no-one (ignorance of people)
12) Feeling unwelcome (ignorance of fellowship)
13) Dislike of people (ignorance)
14) Dislike of leader (ignorance)

*Personal factors*

2) Unacceptable (for their peers) (feeling)
3) Disbelief in God (knowledge)
4) Loneliness (feeling)
5) Not being encouraged
6) Priorities
9) Feeling out of place

Of the 14 specific factors, 8 relate to the church, and all indicate ignorance of some aspect of its people, activities, or teaching. Of the six personal factors, three relate to feelings either with themselves or vis-à-vis peers. Of the remaining three, one would be seen as lack of knowledge, one lack of parental support, and one lack of time.

It should be possible to overcome ignorance with appropriate learning, given a suitable opportunity. This shows the importance of the church going out to teenagers, welcoming every opportunity to meet with them, generally sharing their faith. So ministers taking a school assembly, for example, could form one way of the church moving out into the world.

The church teenagers ticked five boxes each on this list on average, in total percentages:

|  | % |
|---|---|
| Ignorance of church activities (factors 1,7,8,10) | 161 |
| Situational factors (factors 3,5,6,15) | 155 |
| Bad feelings (factors 2,4,9) | 137 |
| Ignorance of church people (factors 11,12,13,14) | 37 |

Ignorance of church people (if a true perception) is very well down the list. It is not the people who put teenagers off but ignorance of the church's activities, situational factors (the title taken here as a single word summary for the factors given), and bad feelings, all to much the same extent, but in that order. Intellectual, personal/psychological/spiritual, and emotional—a fairly well rounded set of reasons! Dividing these into two age bands we get as average percentages (ignoring the people factor altogether):

|  | *14 or under* | *15 or under* | *Overall* |
|---|---|---|---|
| Ignorance | 147 | 171 | 161 |
| Situation | 163 | 149 | 155 |
| Feelings | 138 | 136 | 137 |

This shows ignorance has more importance for older teenagers, their personal situation for younger teenagers, and their feelings in respect of churchgoing much the same whatever their age. How these three factors vary with other questions is given in Table 42.

These factors are remarkably uniform. They hardly vary by gender or churchmanship, or denomination (except Catholics do not think bad feelings are quite as important as non-Catholics). They do vary by strength of commitment: those who are not sure whether they are a Christian score much the same as those who are committed, but those no longer

Table 42: Factors for not going to church, by various categories

| Category | Ignorance % | Situation % | Feelings % |
|---|---|---|---|
| Overall | 161 | 155 | 137 |
| Male | 164 | 155 | 133 |
| Female | 157 | 156 | 140 |
| Christian commitment | | | |
| Strong | 164 | 151 | 134 |
| Weak | 158 | 159 | 139 |
| Unsure | 163 | 156 | 137 |
| No longer | 164 | 201 | 91 |
| Never | 156 | 108 | 184 |
| Evangelical | 162 | 157 | 144 |
| Non-Evangelical | 159 | 151 | 126 |
| Anglican | 152 | 154 | 142 |
| Free Churches | 168 | 156 | 142 |
| Roman Catholic | 160 | 154 | 110 |

committed regard situational factors much more seriously than others, and those no longer a Christian put the feelings of non-going teenagers high.

These factors did not vary according to whether teenagers have felt like stopping going to church, whether or not they attended Sunday School (though those who had were less inclined to positive bad feelings), what they thought of Sunday School (though those who had been encouraged to attend rated situational factors less important), whether or not they had had a religious experience, or what type it was, whether they had been involved in any form of occult activity, whatever their picture of God, who they thought Jesus Christ was, or what makes a person a Christian.

Church teenagers were asked to indicate what other reasons there might be for not going to church. These included:

- 'They're not normal but stupid.'
- 'Need to keep up street cred.'
- 'Can't be bothered.'
- 'They think it's old-fashioned.'
- 'They think it's steggy.' (sic)
- 'Their friends make fun of them.'
- 'It's what old people do.'
- 'They think it's the same every week.'
- 'Church is full of self-righteous people.'
- 'Feel God won't help them in life.'
- 'They can be good without going.'
- 'Think they'll be posh if they go.'

and so on. These mostly fall into the ignorance or situational factors.

### Non-churchgoers reasons for not going

A similar question was also asked on the school questionnaire where the majority (86%) did not go to church as frequently as once a week. The results, given in Table 43, are presented in the same way as the churchgoers' for ease of comparison.

This table is more homogenous than the previous one (there are only three significant differences instead of six). That one's friends do not go is less important as teenagers get older (as it was with church teenagers also). That church is thought to be irrelevant becomes more important with age, as does dislike of the church's moral teaching as the reason why some do not attend. Church teenagers had the same trends.

There is, however, quite a difference in the order of importance. Boredom stays well ahead as the main reason, having something better to do rates second and that none of one's friends would go is third. That it was considered not the 'done' thing or that teenagers didn't believe in God were not rated as highly as by churchgoing teenagers.

Table 43: School teenagers' explanations of why teenagers don't go to church by age

| Reason | Age of school teenager | | | | | | | | Overall | |
| | 11,12 % | 13 % | 14 % | 15 % | 16 % | 17 % | 18 or over % | School % | Church % |
|---|---|---|---|---|---|---|---|---|---|
| 1) They think it is boring | 90 | 90 | 93 | 89 | 90 | 84 | 84 | 89 | *88 |
| 2) Going to church isn't the 'done' thing | 40 | 40 | 47 | 43 | 40 | 33 | 28 | 40 | *62 |
| 3) They don't believe in God | 49 | 42 | 44 | 45 | 38 | 50 | 48 | 45 | 57 |
| 4) None of their friends go | 77 | 56 | 65 | 58 | 55 | 39 | 40 | *61 | *50 |
| 5) Their parents don't encourage them to go | 35 | 39 | 46 | 37 | 40 | 38 | 38 | 38 | *45 |
| 6) They've got better things to do on a Sunday | 64 | 59 | 62 | 67 | 60 | 63 | 56 | 62 | 45 |
| 7) They think it is irrelevant | 19 | 17 | 14 | 31 | 30 | 44 | 36 | *24 | *32 |
| 8) They don't know what happens at church | 15 | 16 | 15 | 20 | 20 | 13 | 16 | 17 | 27 |

Table 43: *Continued*

| Reason | Age of school teenager | | | | | | | | Overall | |
|---|---|---|---|---|---|---|---|---|---|---|
| | 11,12 % | 13 % | 14 % | 15 % | 16 % | 17 % | 18 or over % | | School % | Church % |
| 9) They feel out of place | 25 | 25 | 25 | 33 | 30 | 30 | 26 | | 27 | 25 |
| 10) They don't like the moral teaching | 11 | 12 | 9 | 18 | 18 | 33 | 38 | | *16 | *14 |
| 11) They don't know anyone at church | 21 | 23 | 14 | 16 | 16 | 20 | 18 | | 19 | 14 |
| 12) They don't feel welcome | 16 | 13 | 3 | 11 | 11 | 11 | 12 | | 12 | 11 |
| 13) They don't like the people who do go | 17 | 11 | 12 | 15 | 11 | 9 | 8 | | 13 | 9 |
| 14) They don't like the minister/leader | 5 | 3 | 5 | 7 | 2 | 4 | 2 | | 4 | 3 |
| 15) Other reasons | 2 | 2 | 3 | 5 | 6 | 1 | 2 | | 3 | 8 |
| Total number (100%) | 277 | 263 | 125 | 201 | 89 | 80 | 50 | | 1085 | 868 |

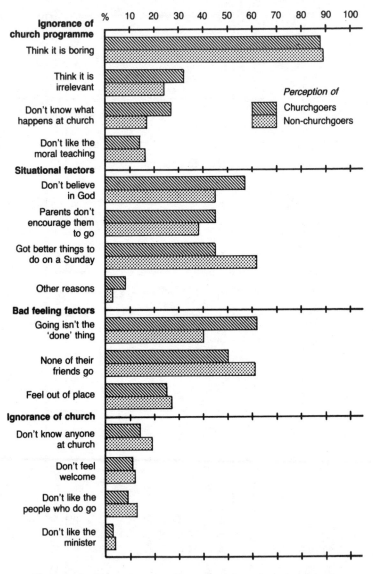

Figure 21: Reasons why teenagers do not go to church

But these differences apart, the four categories are much the same for both groups, and the overall factor scores from the school group are, respectively for ignorance, situation and feelings, 146%, 148% and 128%. These are all less than for churchgoing teenagers, with those on ignorance the biggest drop. The order of the first two is also reversed, though only just. In other words non-churchgoing teenagers estimate they are not quite as ignorant of the church as churchgoing teenagers reckon they are!

Other factors influence these overall conclusions.

*Table 44: Factors for not going to church by various categories*

| Category | Ignorance % | Situation % | Feelings % |
|---|---|---|---|
| Overall | 146 | 148 | 128 |
| Christian | 141 | 145 | 132 |
| Other religions | 168 | 119 | 117 |
| No religion | 153 | 161 | 121 |
| Males | 154 | 150 | 123 |
| Females | 137 | 147 | 132 |
| *Marital status of parents* | | | |
| Married | 145 | 148 | 127 |
| Separated | 157 | 154 | 110 |
| Divorced | 142 | 155 | 141 |
| Unmarried | 139 | 145 | 121 |
| Widowed | 159 | 129 | 138 |
| *Christian commitment* | | | |
| Strong | 153 | 142 | 126 |
| Weak | 137 | 145 | 139 |
| Unsure | 150 | 152 | 123 |
| No longer | 192 | 150 | 120 |
| Never | 147 | 157 | 114 |

As with the church teenagers, the school teenagers' reasons for not going to church were remarkably uniform. However, there were some important variations:

- The ignorance of those of other religions was put higher, but their situation and feelings much lower.
- Females reckoned other teenagers less ignorant of Christianity than males.
- Those whose parents were not married rated the situation higher; those with a widowed parent much lower.
- For those with separated parents, feelings about Christianity were very low; but divorced or widowed parents' children rated it highly.
- Ignorance was reckoned to be much higher for those no longer a Christian. Church youth put their situation higher (because in greater tension?)
- Those never a Christian had lower feelings, the opposite for church young people.

What other reasons were given by the school group for teenagers not going to church? Only a few answered the question, with comments such as:

- 'After childhood there is no more meaning to churchgoing.'
- 'They think they are big and trendy.'
- 'I can't get up early.'
- 'They think their friends will tease them.'
- 'The church hasn't got my interest.'
- 'Only gay people go to church.'
- 'There is no such thing as God.'
- 'The church is outdated.'
- 'I think church is rubbish.'
- 'It doesn't look good to go to church.'

These go across all three factors, whereas the church teenagers tended to give ignorance or situational factors. In other words, school teenagers also gave feelings as a reason why teenagers do not attend church.

Non-churchgoing teenagers (defined as those going less than once a month) were asked how frequently in fact they went to church: 27% went several times a year, and 15% once or twice a year. One of those who said he never went nevertheless went to weddings etc. So three in seven 'non-going' teenagers still go occasionally. We must not assume that a non-churchgoing teenager therefore is strictly that. Some still come sometimes.

## *Youth Officers' assessment of teenagers' reasons for not going to church*

What reasons did the Youth Officers interviewed give for teenagers not going to church? 'We do not take Christian kids seriously,' said Steve Chalke, Director of Oasis Trust. 'We are happy for them to teach in the Sunday School, but assume they are not mature enough to be listened to in the church meeting. When God wanted to give His Son a mother He chose a teenager. We on the other hand don't find it easy to give the young responsibility. This even tends to be true of the New/House Churches, though not at first when all the leaders were in their twenties! And the same principle is true of things like Spring Harvest, which was started by young radicals but now struggles to give those under 30 the same kind of responsibility or opportunity.'

Andy Hickford, of Stopsley Baptist Church, said that young people have a media stereotype of the church and the church has a media stereotype of young people. That church stereotype is of young people as 'violent, untrustworthy, sporty, likely to be involved in an accident, intimidating old people.' The church will find a youth leader and then say they can't use the church building (because of the potential violence)!

Ian Vallance, a Scripture Union Schools Worker, felt churches were scared of a big influx of young people. Many had never even been invited to a church. The church services generally alienated young people, and it is hard to find youth leaders. 'When we do, so often they are not adequately trained.'

Patrick Harrison, of the Diocese of Arundel and Brighton, again mentioned the negative stereotyping, largely because it stemmed from the national press for whom only scandal was newsworthy. The local press was much more favourable to young people but, of course, its area of influence was that much less, though it can still be quite significant. He also spoke of the key tussle: 'The "win at all costs" success competition image is a direct counter to the faith community which seeks to put others first.'

Nick Aiken, of the Diocese of Guildford, spoke of alien values in the church as far as young people were concerned, and Mark Landreth-Smith, of the Coign Church, felt sometimes their parents' dour brand of 'Christianity' did not enthuse them to attend church.

Is the cultural barrier really as great? We asked the non-churchgoers if they knew other teenagers who did go to church: three-quarters did. How did they get on with them? Five-sixths said: 'Fine', 'Okay', 'Alright', 'They are the same as everyone else', 'It's their own individual thing'. The other sixth said: 'No, churchgoers were bullied', or they were 'lonely', 'arrogant', or 'only ever talked about church'. The culture gap doesn't seem too wide. Three-quarters of the quarter who did not know any churchgoing teenagers knew churchgoing adults. That leaves 7% of this sample of non-churchgoing teenagers, or one in every 13, who did not know *any* churchgoers at all.

## Why churchgoers stopped going to church

Teenage churchgoers were asked whether they had ever felt like not going to church any more. Over half (53%) had. This percentage did not vary by gender, environment, denomination, geographical part of the country, or even by age. It did vary by churchmanship (48% evangelicals against 58% non-evangelicals) and, of course, by Christian commitment. Only 37% of those strongly committed had felt like stopping, 58% of those whose commitment was not strong, 62% of those unsure if they were a Christian, 63% of those never a Christian and 91% of those who were no longer a Christian.

However of the 53% who had felt like stopping, only 21% (11% of the total sample), reckoned they actually would! It is interesting that a significant number of those who had enjoyed going to Sunday School were less inclined to give up going to church, and those who had found Sunday School boring, were more likely to.

'Do you think you will stop attending church in the future?' YES said 14%, and 9% didn't know, leaving 77% saying NO. 10% of the evangelicals gave an affirmative answer, and 19% of non-evangelicals. 20% of those who found Sunday School irrelevant reckoned they would stop going too, as did 24% whose perception of God was of an 'old man', 33% who thought of Jesus as very wise, and 59% who considered Jesus an ordinary human being (concepts discussed in the next chapter).

What were some of the reasons why church teenagers felt like not going to church anymore? Here are the most frequently cited examples (though not in order):

- 'It does not help with everyday life.'
- 'Church is boring after Sunday School.'
- 'I find it boring—it's the same every week.'
- 'Sometimes it means getting up early.'
- 'I don't know many of the folk who go.'
- 'I can be close to God in my own way.'
- 'I don't act as a Christian at school.'
- 'Nothing happens to me spiritually when I go.'
- 'I get teased at school when I go.'
- 'I blame God for Grandad's death/my cat's death.'
- 'The hockey club train on Sunday mornings, so it clashes.'
- 'I feel I'm not wanted at church.'

Without doubt the word used most was 'boring'. Virtually every other or every third comment said the services were boring. Next came the fact that so many teenagers are tired and dislike getting up early. After that it was the sheer irrelevance of the whole process that daunted them. These are real teenagers, struggling to keep on worshipping God, and finding it tedious. Their sense of duty, their previous commitment, their memories of enjoyment make them continue going, but some time some day that will tail off. We have GOT TO WAKE UP! The above statements are a shameful indictment for any church, and are typical of thousands in our land. Peter Drucker, the guru of modern management, once remarked 'Good management of a person is the effective use of their strengths.' How effectively are we using the strengths of our teenagers?

But perhaps these comments are exaggerated. Are services really boring? 'Yes,' said one Youth Officer we interviewed, 'Church services *are* boring. I'm bored stiff myself!' What is boring about the services? Virtually no participation. 'We're into maintenance Christianity,' he continued, 'Only certain jobs for certain people. It's a spectator sport.' Also the repetition week after week. And the lack of relevancy is counted as 'boring' by teenagers.

'We have to use contemporary language,' said another. In 1986 the Inter-Church Process produced a series of Lent discussions based on the book *What on Earth is the Church For?* which very quickly became extremely popular. No less than 57 local radio stations (three-fifths of all those in Britain) invited responses on prepared questionnaires. The 100,000 returned were subsequently analysed and published in a booklet *Views from the Pews*.[3] What did people say? One key conclusion was summarized as 'Jesus hidden by jargon'.[4] It seems that not every church has listened to what so many grass-roots people were saying. The Youth Officers merely applied it especially to teenagers!

'Boredom' is a fair word to use for young people not used to sitting, not used to listening to long sermons, not used to music not relevant to their culture, not used to adult subjects.

Churches need to consider the needs of the people who attend, was the remedy put forward, especially where these are teenagers. 'You have to have a vision of seeing young people being won for Christ, a willingness to have time to enable youth work to happen.' Ah, but that says it all!

Will young people stop attending? Some said YES, some said NO, and these are the reasons given.

| *Yes I will stop* | *No I won't stop* |
|---|---|
| • 'I will grow out of it.' | • 'I feel strongly about my faith.' |
| • 'I will not have the time.' | |
| • 'I will leave the Scouts.' | • 'It is partly habit, partly routine.' |
| • 'I am going to University.' | |
| • 'I have too much homework.' | • 'As a Christian it is important to go.' |
| • 'I was forced to go by my parents.' | |
| • 'I will leave the choir.' | • 'I love learning about God.' |
| • 'I have more fun without going.' | • 'I go to church for God, not the people.' |
| • 'It's boring and depressing.' | • 'I have made friends at church.' |
| • 'My family will be more important.' | • 'I play the clarinet at church so I have to.' |
| | • 'I enjoy it, it's something to look forward to.' |
| | • 'Joining the church has reborn me.' |
| | • 'I will want my children to learn about God.' |

The book *Falling from the Faith*[5] presents a series of essays on various facets of the subject. One helpfully analysed dropouts, and although these were developed from an analysis of Catholic data, they are applicable more widely:

|  | Percentage 22 or under % | Percentage 23 or over % |
|---|---|---|
| 1) Family-tension Dropouts (rebelled against both family and the church) | 54 | 2 |
| 2) Weary Dropouts (found church boring and uninteresting) | 24 | 44 |
| 3) Lifestyle Dropouts (objected to moral teaching of the church) | 20 | 28 |
| 4) Spiritual-need Dropouts (spiritual needs not met by the church; some changed churches) | 2 | 12 |
| 5) Anti-change Dropouts (objected to liturgical change) | 0 | 14 |

Another article recounted the experience: 'Disengagement was most closely linked to reaching young adulthood among those reared in the Mormon tradition and to relatively recent affiliation among converts, while return was associated with marriage and family formation.'[6] So losing young people is not just something associated with traditional and orthodox Christian churches. Nor is it something just relevant for Britain. 'One Lutheran church leader from Germany summarized: "Last generation we lost the working class. This generation we are losing our young people."'[7]

*More science, less Christianity*

Professor Leslie Francis, first Mansel Jones Fellow at Trinity College, Carmarthen, has done a formidable amount of research among young people with about 200 papers and 20 books published. In one study of 6,000 secondary school pupils in Scotland between 11 and 15,[8] he found that their attitude towards Christianity deteriorated with age, and that this decline was linked to a corresponding increase in their faith in the power of science and the prevalence of the belief that to be a Christian it was necessary to believe God created the universe in six days. One in three pupils believed that Christians were committed to accept creationism. The study was summarized as showing 'that scientism and creationism inhibit pupils from developing positive attitudes to both science and Christianity.'[9]

A 1991 survey of 700 16–18 year olds in Scotland demonstrated a significant negative correlation between attitude towards Christianity and interest in science. 'Two key factors which help to explain this apparent negative relationship are the perception of Christianity as necessarily involving creationism and the view that science attains to absolute truth (scientism).'[10]

Many papers have been written on these broad subjects mostly from a sociological perspective. One from a psychological perspective suggested that the critical factor was how far young people achieved 'complementarity', that is, the ability to co-ordinate conflicting statements and arrive at synoptic points of view.[11]

In a major book, *The Contours of Christian Education*, published in 1992,[12] Leslie Francis argues that 'regular (teenage) churchgoers are no less likely than non-churchgoers to believe that Christians have to accept the Biblical account of creation. At the same time, regular churchgoers are no less likely than non-churchgoers to believe that science disproves the Bible account of creation. Secondly, regular churchgoers are less likely than non-churchgoers to argue that scientific laws make miracles impossible.'

### Reasons for starting

'What made you start going to church?' we asked in the teenage interviews. 'The toys box' wrote one! But more generally, of those who still currently attend, half said their parents. A quarter said their brother/sister or friends. One came because she started with the Girls' Brigade (and 'through that Sunday School and then the church'), one in eight came because 'they had nothing else to do' and 'did not know anyone', and one person because they 'gave my life to God and felt I should come'.

Those who have since left the church nevertheless started going for much the same reasons. Rather more (at most three-quarters) went because of their parents. 'Mum took me', 'Mum made me' were frequent comments alongside 'Parents'. Fathers never featured, although a grandfather did for one person! Friends were important in 8% of cases. The rest went because of church organizations (like The Boys' Brigade and The Girls' Brigade), of church activities (like the choir, confirmation classes or the linked school).

### Conversion

Of the 56 teenagers directly asked why they started going to church only one 16 year old New/House Church boy specifically mentioned his conversion. It might be thought this would be a major reason! But this begs the question, when are teenagers converted?

A 1968 survey of 4,000 people on conversion experience[13] showed that 17% were converted under the age of 12, 59% between the ages of 12 and 19, and the remaining 24% at 20 and over. Of these conversions, 69% were 'definite' (that is, the exact day of conversion could be recalled) and 31% were 'indefinite' (a specific conversion experience but the precise day was unknown).

The prime immediate reasons for conversion for teenagers were the local church context (30%), occasional activities like summer camps or missions (24%), personal witness (14%), large scale meetings with professional evangelists (13%), and regular youth work, including Sunday School (11%). Key past influences had been personal witness outside the home (31%), within the home (26%), the local church (15%), internal sensation (13%), and Christian teaching during youth (10%).

The average age of conversion was 14 years 9 months. Males were slightly older (15 years 0 months) than females (14 years 7 months). Those coming from a Christian home were slightly younger (14 years 5 months) and those having a 'definite' conversion slightly older (14 years 11 months). The average age of conversion increased during the 1960s as Figure 22 shows.

Did the average age continue to rise in the 1970s and 1980s? A much more recent detailed survey by Canon John Finney (now Bishop) on how 500 people of 16 or over came to faith[14] unfortunately does not analyse their findings by age or year when it happened. However, it is clear that sudden and gradual conversion percentages varied markedly from those given above, as the following table from his study illustrates:

*Table 45: Coming to faith*

| Category | Gradual % | Sudden % |
|---|---|---|
| Those who knew they once were not Christian | 62 | 38 |
| Those who had always been Christian, though less committed | 60 | 20 |
| Evangelical | 63 | 37 |
| Non-Evangelical | 80 | 20 |

Coming to faith took an average of about 3 years 8 months.[15] The main factors were former family (33%), friends (19%), the minister (16%) or church/evangelistic events (6%). For women these proportions were, 24, 27, 17 and 13% respectively. In a Singapore study in 1979,[16] 18% of conversions were influenced by the family, 18% by friends, 36% by the church, and 6% by special evangelistic meetings, showing the greater dominance of the church in coming to faith.

Supporting factors in John Finney's study were given for men as friends (54%), family (49%), the minister (42%) and

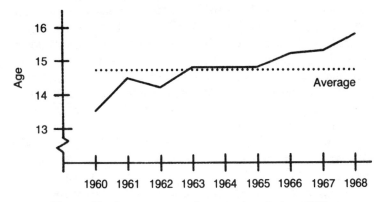

Figure 22: Average age of conversion during 1960s

church/evangelistic events (36%), these totalling over 100% as more than one factor was supportive. For women these percentages were 49, 52, 43 and 54% respectively.[17]

These results are important, but the qualification expressed in the *Church of England Newspaper* leader is valid: 'Most of the people being reached with the gospel in Britain today are already on the fringes of the church, people who already have personal contact with believers.'[18] This reflects the findings of a survey of 400 Christians in 1991 by the Churches Together in England Evangelism Research Project, based on work by John Finney between 1982 and 1985, where '75% of people who become Christians had some sort of Christian upbringing.'[19]

This study also suggested 'the peak age for conversion is the late 20s', but other studies suggest the teenage years. Some earlier in the century put people making their 'first personal religious commitment' at a mean age of 16 or 17. 'A 1928 study of 1,200 people found that religious "awakenings" usually began at 12, but clear-cut conversion experiences occurred at a mean age of 16. The modal age of Billy Graham converts in America in 1954 was 15.'[20] The same author found the modal age of conversion to Roman Catholicism to be 20.

The campaigns of Luis Palau in 1983 and 1984 (Mission to London) and Billy Graham in Britain in 1984 and 1985 (Mission England) all put the highest responses for salvation in the teenage years. In the 1983 Mission to London 65% of those accepting Christ were under 18,[21] and in 1984 64%.[22] The Billy Graham 1984 Mission England events over six cities recorded an average age of 18 for the 64% of those going forward for salvation.[23]

An American poll of several thousand churchgoers[24] found that '85% said they had responded to the Gospel before they were 18 years old'. How great is the urgency then to preach to teenagers!

Two Canadian surveys investigated conversion.[25] A church survey of 6,000 people found 42%'s main influence on their decision was their Christian upbringing and a further 25% someone's personal witness. An evangelism study put family as the main influence for 31% and a friend at 29%. This study covered only those over 15 years of age, and found the average age of conversion was about 30 in the 1980s. Maybe the 1980s did herald a significant change in the age of conversion—but this study and John Finney's both omit the many coming to Christ as children and early teens.

There is, however, one study,[26] unfortunately with a very small sample, which looks at the age of conversion since 1960. 'Did it rain the day you were saved?' is particularly important in this respect, and Figure 23 comes from the report.

This certainly suggests an increase in the age of conversion in Britain in the 1980s, supported by John Finney's study and the Canadian work. In the 1960s, perhaps 70% of conversions were in the teenage years. In the 1970s it was about the same proportion but, in the 1980s this fell to about a third. The average age of conversion in the 1960s and 1970s was mid-teens, but in the 1980s it was about 30. Why this should have occurred is not clear, unless it reflects the loss of teenagers in the church.

Not all the evidence points to a lengthening of the age of conversion, however. Every three years, immediately after

Christmas, The Evangelical Missionary Alliance (TEMA) holds a Congress on the Continent attended by thousands of young people across Europe, both East and West (as they were). A contingent attends from the United Kingdom also, and have subsequently completed a form indicating their reactions. These forms have included questions from which the age they came to faith may be deduced. Nearly 600 such forms have been analysed for 1986, 1989 and 1992. The sample of those attending is entirely self-selected but is random across gender and denomination. In each of these three years, 68% came to faith between the ages of 11–20 (inclusive) and 90–92% between the ages of 6 and 25. The median age (by which 50% came to faith) has consistently remained at 15 years. These figures are given in the Reports *What UK delegates thought* for Mission 87, Mission 90 and Mission 93 analysed by MARC Europe or the Christian Research Association.

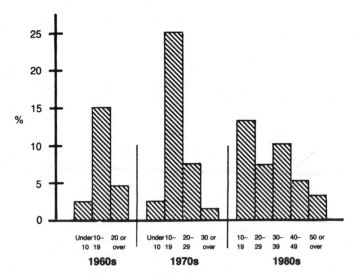

Figure 23: Age of conversion 1960–90

## Baptism

Is infant baptism a motivation for churchgoing? It could be, judging from the church teenagers in the RAKT project. 82% overall had been baptized or christened, 88% who were strongly committed Christians, 83% who were Christians, but not very committed, 65% of those who were unsure if they were Christian, 78% of those no longer a Christian, and 65% of those never a Christian. These results were statistically highly significant, as were the proportions of those confirmed or admitted to adult membership of their church—overall 39%, and then respectively, 48, 39, 24, 22 and 12%.

Non-evangelical teenagers were more likely to be baptized than evangelicals (88 against 75%) and also confirmed (51 against 29%). Having been baptized did not vary with age, but being confirmed did, as might be expected. 24% had been confirmed under the age of 15, but 54% of 15 year olds and above. Rather more had been confirmed in the North of England in our sample than elsewhere. More had been confirmed in rural areas (45%) and council estates (43%) than those attending city centre churches (39%) or suburban ones (32%). The figures also varied greatly by denomination, with fewer Independent, New/House Church and Baptist teenagers than other churches (59% against 88% baptized, and 15% against 46% as adult members). They did not differ by gender.

Did being baptized make you a Christian? YES said 38% who had been baptized against 19% who hadn't, with similar figures for 'leading a good life'. Did knowing Jesus as your personal saviour make you a Christian? YES said 59% who had been confirmed against 71% who hadn't! So much for confirmation classes! Did believing the Bible is true make a person a Christian? YES said 49% of confirmees, against 62% who had not been! Virtually identical results emerged from the schools sample. Those who had stayed on in a church group till over 15 were much more likely to have been confirmed.

Did being baptized make you more likely to stay at church? Analysis of those we interviewed showed 56% of current churchgoing teenagers to have been baptized against 65% who had left—no significant difference.

Did being confirmed or admitted into adult membership make you more likely to stay on? Of current churchgoing teenagers 88% were confirmed/admitted against 61% of those not staying—a significant difference, with age making no difference. This suggests that those taking the step of commitment into adult membership are more likely to continue going to church. It is interesting that, whereas the proportion of all babies being christened has steadily fallen since the mid-1940s, the proportion of christened babies being confirmed 15 years later has been remarkably similar since the 1970s.[27]

## Faith development

Professor James Fowler, of the Center for Research in Faith and Moral Development at Emory University in Atlanta, Georgia, United States lectured on 'Faith, liberation and human development' in 1974. A number of other papers and books appeared on the same subject in the 1970s, and further research has been done on his basic proposition that an individual's faith develops and that the steps of knowing, valuing and committing may be outworked in an explicit or implicit coherent image of ultimate reality.[28]

How does this help our study of teenagers going to church? Simply, that he breaks down faith development into six stages and suggests how this varies with age. The implications of his concepts are very helpfully explored in the excellent little book *How Faith Grows*.[29] The editors translate Fowler's terminology into easier phrases. The six steps are given below with the first title from *How Faith Grows*, and the second that of Fowler.

1) *Impressionistic faith* [Intuitive-projective faith] (early childhood): Imagination not yet controlled by logical thinking combines with perception and feelings to create long-lasting images which can protect or threaten.

2) *Ordering faith*  [Mythic-literal faith] (childhood or beyond): A developing ability to think logically helps order one's world, enter the perspectives of others and capture life meaning in stories.

3) *Conforming faith*  [Synthetic-conventional faith] (adolescence and beyond): New cognitive abilities require an integration of diverse self-images. A personal and largely unreflective synthesis of belief and values evolves to support identity and to unite one in emotional solidarity with others.

4) *Choosing faith*  [Individual-reflective faith] (young adulthood and beyond): Critical reflection on one's beliefs and values; understanding of the self as part of a social system; the internalization of authority and the assumption of responsibility for making ideological and lifestyle choices opens the way to relationship commitments and vocation.

*Table 46: Distribution of the stages of faith by age*

| Stage | Age in years | | | | | | | | Percentage of total sample in each stage % |
| | 0–6 % | 7–12 % | 13–20 % | 21–30 % | 31–40 % | 41–50 % | 51–60 % | 61+ % | |
| --- | --- | --- | --- | --- | --- | --- | --- | --- | --- |
| 1 | 88 | 3 | – | – | – | – | – | – | 6 |
| 1–2 | 12 | 7 | – | – | – | – | – | – | 1 |
| 2 | – | 73 | 4 | 1 | – | – | 6 | – | 7 |
| 2–3 | – | 17 | 12 | 5 | – | – | – | 2 | 5 |
| 3 | – | – | 50 | 18 | 37 | 9 | 35 | 24 | 24 |
| 3–4 | – | – | 29 | 33 | 8 | – | – | 15 | 17 |
| 4 | – | – | 5 | 40 | 21 | 56 | 29 | 27 | 25 |
| 4–5 | – | – | – | 3 | 19 | 22 | 6 | 14 | 8 |
| 5 | – | – | – | – | 15 | 13 | 24 | 16 | 7 |
| 6 | – | – | – | – | – | – | – | 2 | 0 |
| Total number (= 100%) | 25 | 29 | 56 | 90 | 48 | 32 | 17 | 62 | 359 |

5) *Balanced faith* [Conjunctive faith] (early mid-life and beyond): An alertness to paradox, embracement of polarities, and the need for multiple interpretations. Symbol, story, metaphor and myth are newly appreciated as vehicles for expressing truth.

6) *Selfless faith* [Universalizing faith] (mid-life and beyond): Beyond paradoxes and polarities, individuals are grounded in a oneness with the power of being. Visions and commitments free them for a passionate but detached spending of the self in love, for justice.[30]

Professor Fowler's research has led him to suggest the proportions of these steps that might be seen at different ages. These are indicated in Table 46.[31]

This table shows that teenagers cover a wide variety of faith, from types 1–4, from the ordering faith, through conforming faith to choosing faith. As we ponder how to reach and keep teenagers it's worth using the findings here of the different stages teenagers will be in and passing through, perhaps quite rapidly.

Table 46 could suggest that those leaving the church are not necessarily disenchanted with conventional religion or its leaders. As Reginald Bibby says of Canadians, 'Few people, young or old, are "mad" at the churches.'[32] In Canada,[33] as in Europe,[34] belief in God increases with age. What no-one can tell is whether the existing faith belief, faith development, or faith understanding across different ages will be similar as the present generation ages. In other words, how static are these perceptions? This uncertainty is part of the challenge of the vision of extending God's Kingdom.

*Emulation*

Both church and school teenagers were asked if they could think of a famous sportsman/woman, pop star or celebrity who is a Christian. They gave the following list:

Table 47: Prominent Christians teenagers could name

|  | Church % | School % |
|---|---|---|
| Cliff Richard | 49 | 22 |
| Kriss Akabussi | 22 | 5 |
| M C Hammer | 6 | 2 |
| Amy Grant | 5 | – |
| Roy Castle | 4 | – |
| Andre Agassi | 4 | 2 |
| Simon Mayo | 3 | – |
| Glen Hoddle | 3 | 2 |
| Cyril Regis | 1 | – |
| Madonna | – | 4 |
| David Icke | – | 3 |
| Hulk Hogan | – | 2 |
| Harry Secombe | – | 1 |
| Others | 26 | 18 |

At school, those under 13 were much more likely to be unable to name anyone than those older (29% against 54%), and boys were more ignorant than girls (51% against 45%). Much more interestingly, Christians were *more* likely to be unable to name anyone than those of other religions or none (52 against 33 and 39% respectively)! That included strongly committed Christians! The same comments were true of the church sample, though the percentages were different.

## Reasons for continuing

### *Responsibility*

Does giving young people appropriate responsibility make them more likely to continue coming to church? There is not much evidence, but three-quarters of the churchgoing teenagers interviewed said that young people were given responsibility in their church. That was identical to the proportion who had left their churches. Should they be given responsibility? 100% of churchgoers and 90% of ex-churchgoers said YES, which does not suggest that giving responsibility is a vital factor for retention. However, several ex-churchgoers said responsibility made you feel more involved, and more interested in going and staying. Several said 'It encourages them.' 'It makes you feel part,' said a couple.

All the Youth Officers agreed that young people should be given responsibility, but carefully, sensitively and in a manner which stretched them a little but not too much. They leave the church not because they are not given responsibility but because there is 'no opportunity to think through questions of faith and doubts in an accepting environment' (Patrick Harrison), because 'church does not give kids answers.' (Steve Chalke).

Steve went on to comment, 'Some church leaders say teenagers are apathetic. But apathetic teenagers don't joyride in other people's Porsches. That's not apathy, it's frustration.'

## Youth services

There is no doubt that properly run youth services are extremely popular (for teenagers!) and successful in attracting congregations. Take the St Thomas Crookes NOS Service (as it is called, standing for Nine O'clock Service) in Sheffield or the Elim in Plymouth, examples previously cited. Not all such services are by evangelicals. St Mary and St John, a high Anglican church in North Oxford, runs a 'Joy' service at 10 pm on Sundays. 'There are no pews, no hymn books, no altar. But there is an abundance of energy.' One A-level student attender said of it, 'This feels real, it's relevant.' The atmosphere owes much to the dance floor, but tradition is not ignored. Prayers written by members of the congregation are read over 'house' music while everyone sits on the floor, 'hymns' are phrases of the liturgy accompanied by a rock band, and the 'reading' follows Gospel stories but is in colloquial language.

'The journey towards Bethlehem had been a pig,' is how one reporter summarized it.[35]

But although this may be a popular service it does not attract anything like the response at St Thomas's. Nor should its particular style be assumed to be similar to others held. The 700 who attend the evening service at Holy Trinity, Brompton, for example, would have quite a different experience —improvised, charismatic, bearing no resemblance to the official Anglican liturgy, and no old-fashioned language. Damian Thompson, the religious correspondent of the *Daily Telegraph*, said that its most important feature is not that they are Anglican, nor 'their exuberant worship, but their evangelical theology.' Almost certainly true, even if St Mary and St John are the exception which proves every rule. But, Mr Thompson warns, 'if conventional Christians imagine they can win back the young simply by adopting the charismatic evangelical youthful style, they will be gravely disappointed.'[36] Perhaps.

A major conference for over 800 young people over a weekend in November 1992 recognized that boring services is certainly one reason why young people drop away from the church. But they also indicated this is only one part of the total problem. 'Poor pastoral care and teaching, attitudes to young people within the church, over-zealous Christian parents' can deter young people,[37] as well as all the pressures outside the church. They also debated youth congregations—are they God's strategy or a divisive diversion?

What did the young people themselves say to youth services? 84% of current churchgoing teenagers said a loud clear YES, as did 94% of the ex-churchgoing teens and 72% of non-churchgoing young people. Here are a 100 teenagers chosen at random from different denominations, backgrounds, parts of the country. Overall 83% are saying YES to special youth services, five out of every six. It would be foolish to ignore such a response, even if it is based on a small number.

Why would such services be popular? The key reasons given were as follows:

- 'It would give a better, clearer, understanding of Christianity.'
- 'It would stimulate involvement, which creates interest and retains commitment.'
- 'The formal language so often used is a barrier.'
- 'Many more young people would be attracted.'
- 'Youth services would be seen as exciting, more relevant than ordinary services.'
- 'It's time young people heard about God and Jesus!'
- 'To have up-to-date music would be super—not that old organ!'
- 'I see normal services by grown-ups as being *for* grown-ups.'
- 'Young people could actually enjoy themselves in church.'

Not all churches have the willingness, premises, leaders and resources to provide them. In any case, some are against youth services. Why? Some, mostly non-churchgoers, said people wouldn't go anyway. Some felt that it was good to have a mix of ages ('a community shouldn't be broken up into bits'). One felt it would be 'patronizing'. But the best reason given by a non-churchgoer was, 'Some young people if they go might believe'! Precisely.

## Attracting young people

How do pubs attract young people? The advertisement[38] reproduced as Figure 24 shows how one brewing company tried to attract trainee pub managers. Firstly the type faces varied, obviously quite deliberately. They wanted to attract attention. Secondly, they knew what they wanted—a packed and buzzing group. Thirdly, they recognized the difficulties—competition, changing needs and tastes, not every manager's gift. Fourthly, they knew what type of person they wanted—a person in control, quick on the uptake, with charisma, willing and able to respond to a challenge. Fifthly, they promised to put the necessary

Figure 24: Advertisement for a successful pub manager

resources behind them—training, support and advertising promotion.

Just ask, what do you want in your church in respect of young people?

- What would be your characteristics for an exciting youth involvement?
- What difficulties do you face?
- What kind of leaders do you need?
- What resources would you put their way?
- What opportunities do you have?
- How much attention do you want to attract?
- In short, what is your vision of success?

The Diocese of Salisbury experimentally appointed an 18 year old straight from A levels, David Bouskill, as a Youth Officer for a year. His brief? 'To commend the Christian faith to young people, helping them to live and share their faith with those around them.'[39] A room was designated as a meeting place and drop-in centre, dedicated as 'The King's Arms'. Events were then organized—a weekend in Torquay, a pilgrimage to Lincoln Cathedral, a visit to Minehead Spring Harvest, to special events in Salisbury Cathedral, Glastonbury, and to concerts. It was so successful that the year became two years, and although David went off to college then, the work is continuing.

How would young people make church services more attractive? We asked them and got the following replies:

- Have facilities to attract youth, eg a snooker room
- Have new style lively music; more joyful songs
- Let young people join in the services, and give their views
- Make the services learning times
- Have less formality, a friendlier atmosphere
- Be more positive, and more welcoming
- Discuss modern issues; be relevant
- Have quizzes, drama, activity, discussion, sketches, that is, greater variety
- Have a break in the services
- Don't have 'all the costumes'

- Have shorter sermons, shorter services. Let a young person preach?!
- Be brighter—have colours? Posters to invite people in.

The Youth Officers would probably have agreed with most of these. In addition they suggested the importance of involving young people in planning as well as participation. They all stressed the importance of actual involvement. Is that why the new House Churches and Roman Catholics are more successful than other denominations in keeping their teenagers? New/House Churches involve them with the music provision and testimonies. Roman Catholics use boys for altar service.

One Youth Officer stressed the importance of having *good* musicians with modern instruments. Another stressed the importance of being visual, in every way possible.

### Challenge

Sandra Kimber, the Youth Officer with the Evangelical Missionary Alliance, is conscious that many churches are emphasizing mission less and less to their young people. She also knows that many Missionary Societies lack the resources and trained personnel to take full advantage of such opportunities as exist. But far from being discouraged she insists: 'We have the most exciting challenges to offer them.'[40] So 'Shout about it. Don't apologize for mission!' she says.

The same attitude is true for other aspects of youth work. Yes, a tremendous challenge. But if young people are working with you, challenge these young people with the challenge. Use books like *Creative Ideas for Youth Evangelism*,[41] 'that takes a lot of the hard work out of motivating young people to get involved.' In the late 1950s Rev Fred Pizzey, a vicar in South London, slipped a disc just after Christmas. There was no-one else to take the evening service, so he took it despite enormous pain. He could not stand to preach, as it hurt too much, so he just knelt down and poured his heart out. One teenager present couldn't remember a word he said afterwards but could not forget his sheer guts in taking the service at all. 'Christianity is a man's religion, after all,' he said and gave his life to Christ. He met the challenge—and is still working for the Lord forty years later. I know—for it was me!

### Summary

- Key reasons given for going to church were to worship God, to learn about God and to have fun.
- Accompanying parents, meeting others, and participating in church activities were also important.
- Main reasons for not going were boredom, irrelevance, lack of knowledge, and dislike of moral teaching.
- Other reasons included disbelief in God, lack of encouragement by parents, and other priorities.
- Emotional reasons included feeling awkward with their peers, loneliness when there, and being totally out of place.
- Drop-out reasons include family tension, weariness with services, and changing lifestyle.
- The average age of conversion seems to have moved from the teens in the 1960s and 1970s to the twenties in the 1980s.
- Infant baptism made no difference to teenage church attendance but the commitment of confirmation did.
- Teenagers experience a crucial range of faith development stages.
- Cliff Richard was by far the best known Christian to teenagers.
- Teenagers want responsibility, youth services, an attractive environment and challenge.

# 5

# *The Influence of School, Sunday School and Home*

This is a true story. An emergency fire door in a school became unsafe, and one of the teachers complained to the local London Borough Council. She wrote several times, but got no response. In desperation she called personally and asked if it was possible for someone to come and help mend it. 'I marked the letter 'urgent',' she said. 'That's no good,' said the Council official. 'If you want anything done here it has to be marked 'Urgent, Urgent'. In fact, if you want something done today it has to be marked 'Urgent, Urgent, Urgent'. Otherwise no action is taken!'

The school situation with regard to Christianity is now such that we need to write everywhere 'Urgent, Urgent, Urgent'!

## School

In 1993 there were almost 4,000 secondary and special schools in the United Kingdom and a further 2,300 independent schools, many of which will have teenage pupils.[1] Of these secondary schools 231 were for boys only, 260 for girls only, and 3,485 (88% of the total) co-educational. There were almost 3 million pupils at these schools, together with just over half a million more at the independent schools, an average of 745 and 245 pupils in each respectively. There were just over 200,000 secondary and special school teachers, and a further 50,000 at the independent schools, an average respectively of

15 and 11 pupils per teacher. 4% of the secondary schools were Anglican in 1986, and 9% were Roman Catholic.[2]

## Readiness for religion

A 1979 survey report on 'The Curriculum Influence on the Attitudes of Government-sponsored School Children in Religious Education'[3] in part reflected the doctoral thesis of Professor Leslie Francis' findings on children's readiness for religion. It was the beginning of a life work of research on young people. His findings can be summarized as follows:

- There is a constant and persistent deterioration in a child's attitude towards religion with increasing age.
- The root of this deterioration lies in the primary school (and any corrective action therefore needs to be based in the primary school that is, pre-teen).
- There is an increasingly hostile attitude which occurs among pupils in their fifth year of secondary school (now year 11).
- There is a high positive correlation across all ages between a child's attitude to religion and a combination of church attendance, private religious practice and a feeling of being involved in religious things. Favourable attitudes are primarily due not to the influence of school, but the influence of home, church and friends.

## Attitude to Christianity

What difference does a school make to a pupil's attitude to Christianity? Or, more reasonably, what are school pupils' attitudes to Christianity? Leslie Francis has found a deterioration with age. Others have found a deterioration over time, most marked with age.[4] Females show a more positive attitude to Christianity than males[5] (except in Northern Ireland),[6] starting at least in junior school,[7] but positive attitudes towards Christianity has declined for both genders.[8]

Every four years since 1974 Leslie Francis has asked 500 secondary school pupils whether they agreed or disagreed with

*Table 48: Agreement with statements 1974–90*

| Subject | Statement | | 1974 % | 1978 % | 1982 % | 1986 % | 1990 % |
|---|---|---|---|---|---|---|---|
| Bible | 'I find it boring to listen to the Bible.' | – | 33 | 34 | 40 | 49 | 48 |
| | 'I think the Bible is out of date.' | – | 20 | 21 | 30 | 30 | 24 |
| Church | 'The church is very important to me.' | + | 27 | 19 | 13 | 15 | 13 |
| | 'I think going to church is a waste of my time.' | – | 26 | 30 | 37 | 39 | 31 |
| | 'I think church services are boring.' | – | 39 | 49 | 53 | 56 | 54 |
| Prayer | 'Saying my prayers helps me a lot.' | + | 36 | 29 | 24 | 18 | 20 |
| | 'Prayer helps me a lot.' | + | 36 | 29 | 22 | 19 | 22 |
| | 'I think praying is a good thing.' | + | 55 | 47 | 40 | 37 | 40 |
| | 'I believe that God listens to prayers.' | + | 47 | 37 | 33 | 29 | 36 |
| | 'I think saying prayers in school does no good.' | – | 36 | 37 | 41 | 41 | 40 |
| | 'I think people who pray are stupid.' | – | 11 | 6 | 11 | 11 | 8 |
| Jesus | 'I know that Jesus helps me.' | + | 42 | 30 | 22 | 23 | 20 |
| | 'I want to love Jesus.' | + | 39 | 34 | 26 | 23 | 18 |
| | 'I know that Jesus is very close to me.' | + | 36 | 28 | 20 | 20 | 18 |
| | 'I believe that Jesus still helps people.' | + | 49 | 49 | 36 | 38 | 40 |
| | 'Jesus doesn't mean anything to me.' | – | 16 | 17 | 21 | 23 | 20 |

*Table 48: Continued*

| Subject | Statement | 1974 % | 1978 % | 1982 % | 1986 % | 1990 % |
|---|---|---|---|---|---|---|
| God | + 'God helps me to lead a better life.' | 39 | 33 | 27 | 29 | 27 |
| | + 'I believe that God helps people.' | 59 | 58 | 44 | 42 | 26 |
| | + 'I like school lessons about God very much.' | 32 | 28 | 23 | 21 | 13 |
| | + 'God means a lot to me.' | 39 | 31 | 28 | 24 | 25 |
| | + 'God is very real to me.' | 41 | 33 | 26 | 22 | 25 |
| | + 'The idea of God means much to me.' | 40 | 33 | 28 | 25 | 27 |
| | + 'I know that God helps me.' | 42 | 34 | 27 | 25 | 28 |
| | − 'I find it hard to believe in God.' | 36 | 40 | 43 | 50 | 41 |
| Average | − Eight negative statements | 27 | 29 | 35 | 37 | 33 |
| | + One positive on Church | 27 | 19 | 13 | 15 | 13 |
| | + Four positive on Prayer | 44 | 36 | 30 | 26 | 30 |
| | + Four positive on Jesus | 32 | 35 | 26 | 26 | 24 |
| | + Seven positive on God | 42 | 36 | 29 | 27 | 24 |
| | + 16 positive statements | 39 | 35 | 28 | 26 | 25 |

24 statements about aspects of Christianity.[9] Table 48 lists the five main areas they cover and shows how they have varied since 1974.[10] The statements have been whittled down from 110 that were originally formulated; that some on some subjects do not seem balanced (for example the two Bible statements are both negative) is just how reactions to them were made.

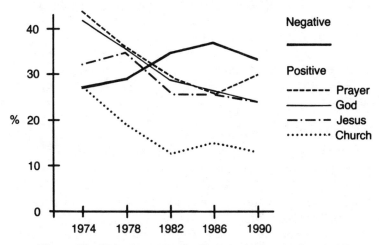

Figure 25: Attitudes towards Christianity by pupils 11–16

Negative concepts of Christianity have increased since 1974, although the 1990 figure reversed the trend. Positive concepts have continuously decreased, however, though that on prayer improved in 1990. Attitudes have clearly declined since 1974, more rapidly between 1974 and 1982 than between 1982 and 1990. The 1980s show an average negative score of 35%, an average positive score on prayer, Jesus and God of 27% and an average positive score on the church of 14%. These attitudes changed little during the 1980s. One third of teenagers may be negative, but a quarter are positive on three key attributes, though not very positive about the church. It is not Christianity teenagers reject so much as the church.

The individual attitudes making up the positive statements are a mix of personal and objective. The personal statements average, respectively for the years measured, 33, 29, 23, 22 and 22%. The objective statements average, respectively, 46, 41, 33, 31 and 29%. Both have declined, the objective statements most and continuously, the personal statements less so during the 1980s. Does this suggest that there are groups of pupils whose faith holds despite external change? Is it too far-fetched to begin to see here two groups emerging—those with faith and those with interest only?

A subsequent paper by John Greer and Leslie Francis concluded that the 'naming of personal religious experience is associated with the formation of more positive attitudes toward Christianity.'[11]

*Attitude towards the church*

Another Leslie Francis survey, of over 500 year 10 (fourth year) pupils in a county and a Church of England voluntary secondary school,[12] revealed that the Church of England (at least in this particular school) had no influence on its pupils' religious practice, belief or attitude! It also showed that there were four main factors in a pupil's attitude towards the church (the numbers reflect the values of a number varying between ±1, one of a number of ways of determining statistical significance. The factors mentioned are the only significant ones):

Personal belief in God (+0.33)
Mother's church attendance (+0.14)
Personal church attendance (+0.12)
Gender (+0.10)

Their own church attendance depended highly on their mother's church attendance, which in turn depended negatively on their mother's social class (−0.14). Their personal belief in God also depended on their mother's church attendance (+0.13). So their mother's practice (and beliefs and attitudes presumably), were critically important for the pupil's attitude towards the church since it influences the other factors. John Finney found that church schools had a higher influence on attitudes to Christianity than state schools (45 against 18%),[13] contrary to what Leslie Francis found above.

The Eysenck Personality Inventory has been a key and well tried psychological test since the early 1960s. Eysenck found 'religion belongs to the domain of tender-minded social attitudes.'[14] T J Mark[15] however found 'that a positive attitude to institutional religion need not be associated with tender-minded attitudes to other people.' This might be paraphrased: If there is a relationship between religious youth and inward looking thinking (introversion) that does not prevent a healthy respect for the church (even if in practice it is rarely there).

Prayer rose slightly in importance between 1986 and 1990 among secondary school pupils. 'Among 16 year olds the influence of church is stronger and the influence of parents weaker than among 11 year olds in determining both the attitudinal predisposition to pray and the practice of prayer.'[16] But another study found that 'only half of those who regard themselves as practising members . . . prayed during the past week, and three-quarters within the past month. This means that one in every four of those who regard themselves as practising Anglicans or Roman Catholics understand prayer to be a completely unimportant aspect of their religious commitment.'[17]

## Attitude towards school

In a fascinating study of 3,800 11 year old pupils in the South of England, Leslie Francis found that pupils' 'religiosity', as measured by their self-reported frequency of church attendance and personal prayer, was 'found to be a significant predictor of positive attitudes towards school and towards English, music, maths, religious education and assemblies, but not games lessons.'[18] This study now needs to be replicated with older pupils in secondary schools to see if similar motivational responses arise.

## Roman Catholic schooling

The Roman Catholics pour huge resources into secondary school education, and account for one secondary pupil in 11,[19] and about three-quarters of all teenage Catholic pupils.[20] In a study of 1,023 Roman Catholics in 1978—the biggest and most comprehensive study so far in England and Wales—there was high agreement (76%) that 'it is really up to parents rather than the school to give children the basis of their religious education'[21] and (65%) that 'there is more discipline in Catholic schools than in non-Catholic schools.' 32% who chose a Catholic school for their children said they did so because it 'grounds them in the faith.'[22] However this might be, adult religious practice owed far less to Catholic schooling than to personal belief and occupation.[23] Perhaps this explains why in the English Church Census 8% of all Roman Catholics attending mass were teenagers, one of the highest percentages (after the Independents, Pentecostals and Afro-Caribbeans),[24] and equivalent to their proportion in the general population, whereas their percentage of attenders aged 20–44 was lower than the population proportion.

Are the benefits of Catholic schooling still apparent today? Leslie Francis and John Greer, from a study of 1,079 pupils in Years 7–10 (ages 13–16) in Northern Ireland, found 'that pupils in Catholic schools hold more strongly to traditional moral values than pupils in Protestant schools.'[25] These findings about Catholic pupils are consistent with other research.[26,27,28] However, 'Roman Catholic secondary schools have no direct influence on their pupils' attitudes towards prayer, after allowing for the influence of home and church.'[29]

In one particularly important piece of research by Leslie Francis and Josephine Egan, a member of the Community of the Daughters of the Holy Spirit, 1,204 questionnaires were returned from four schools in North-East United States in the late 1980s.[30] This examined mass attendance of pupils and the religious practice of their parents. Where both parents regularly attended mass, mostly their child did also. Where neither parent regularly attended, nor did their child. Where one parent regularly attended, sometimes their child did and sometimes he/she didn't. The difference was caused by the non-practising parent. If he/she had never attended mass the child would nevertheless often attend; if he/she had stopped attending, so did the child. In other words, the child followed their parents' belief system. If the child had parents with different systems (one religious, one not) the child coped knowing that these two systems had different behavioural patterns which were logical. It was when one parent renounced his or her faith that the child had problems. The belief system supposedly followed was in disarray. This is important and follows the comments in the previous chapter where non-churchgoing teenagers expected teenagers who 'believed in God' to go to church. This was the anticipated consequential behaviour. Furthermore to 'believe in God' was not deemed to be transitory but permanent. When therefore (to return to the American study) a parent denies what is perceived as a permanent belief not so much in words necessarily but in practice (stops going to mass) their teenage child faces confusion, uncertainty and (in behavioural terms) stops going to church also.

Keeping our teenagers in church partly depends on keeping their parents—and in the reverse order. We need to examine therefore why adult people are leaving our churches. This is not the subject for this book, though some light comes from the comments of some teenagers interviewed. 'We moved home and my mum and dad decided to go to church no more' (and the teenager didn't go either). Moving house is a critical time—one of growth for some churches who reckon on visiting all newcomers within a month of arrival. The opting-out of church can particularly affect Catholics.[31]

## The church school as a community

Church schools are a positive influence in village communities. Many such schools are Anglican, and research shows they are likely to increase the number of confirmation candidates under 14 years of age.[32] In urban communities such schools increase the numbers of 14–17 year olds through church youth groups,[33] as well as giving opportunity for young people to serve the adult (worshipping) community by joining the choir or acting as altar servers. The study giving these findings was undertaken to help the 1988 General Synod Report *Children in the Way*.[34] 'Anglican young people enjoy a higher level of well-being than those who do not belong to a church.'[35] There is also 'a series of bonds' that constitutes 'the basis for identification and participation in Catholicism: belief, spiritual experiences, community, identity, tradition, and family solidarity.'[36]

## Religious education

'We are convinced that most people—certainly most parents— have a strong hope and expectation that school religious instruction should be based upon, and principally feature, Christian teaching. Other religions can and should be taught but educationally this is best done on the basis of a firm grounding in our historic 'home' religion. . . . To provide by statute that religious instruction should be 'predominantly Christian' can only strengthen, not undermine, the local agreed syllabus machinery, which is in many cases weak in a number of areas.' So wrote nine Diocesan Bishops to *The Times* in 1988 before the introduction of the Education Act 1988.

Not that everyone agrees. A Margaret Newson, writing in the *Yorkshire Post* in October that same year, said 'Religious indoctrination stunts the mind, blunts the reason, and destroys sound judgement; that is why it is imperative that good, honest grounding in philosophy and ethics is implemented, therefore storing up a more concerned and caring adulthood.'

What in fact is taught? In the agreed RE syllabus for Bromley Borough Council (as with many other such syllabuses in the country), Christianity accounts for half the lessons, and other religions the other half. As a study in one school in that Borough found, however, not all parents feel this is right. 'Too much time is spent on other religions,' they said. 'More emphasis should be put on Christianity.' The Religious Education syllabus of course covers topics like honesty, morality, family values, Third World concerns, societal care, justice and racial equality. These are taught from a Christian perspective, and therefore form part of the lessons devoted to Christianity. But this reduces the amount of classroom time given to explaining exactly what that religion is: the time available to study the Old and New Testament, the miracles and teaching of Jesus, key church leaders, and the many forms of church, mission and faith today. Another school in the Borough makes visits to Hindu temples, Jewish synagogues, Muslim mosques, but rarely to Christian churches. So parents complain, 'There is not equal emphasis placed on learning about Christianity.'

'How important are RE lessons for teenagers and their image of Christianity?' we asked the Youth Officers interviewed. Potentially of great importance, they replied, but in reality of little importance, and it can be very negative. 'Christianity is frequently portrayed simply as Church of England—high and traditional,' said one. Andy Hickford said that Religious Education taught properly could help teenagers enquire as to the nature of truth and ultimately expose as illogical that all paths lead to God. Patrick Harrison said, 'Understanding Christianity involves encountering people whose lives are affected by their Christian faith—and that could be the science teacher or the caretaker.'

'How important are RE lessons for teenagers and their image of the church?' we also asked. There was potential for confusion here, they said. 'You cannot teach people to believe.' The media portrayal was felt to be crucial, often conflicting with what a Christian teacher would say. Ultimately, the church is expressed in people, and the teenagers see the faith of the church at work in their friends or hear through speakers at Assembly.

So what is the influence of the school on the average teenager? As a 'faith community', Anglican church schools have some marginal impact. Catholic schools have greater weight, especially on traditional moral values. But the impact of personal belief and the authentic behavioural manifestations of faith are much greater than school values or RE lessons. 'The majority of young people who do not themselves belong to a church are far from hostile to the church.'[37] They may not actively support churches, but by no means do they totally lack their goodwill either.

## Sunday School

The English Church Census showed 82% of Free Church children in Sunday School, and 64% of Anglican children under 15 years of age, a total of virtually 600,000.[38] At the same time there were 210,000 teenagers attending these churches. Although fewer children were born in the 1970s (and there were therefore fewer teenagers in the 1980s) it is clear that the decline between Sunday School and church cannot be accounted for solely by demographic variation. Even if one argues that Sunday School children span 10 years (5–14) and teenagers five (15–19) there is still a significant fall. So how important is Sunday School?

The figures given above, and disregarding Roman Catholics who have no Sunday School comparable to Anglican and Free Church classes, still amount to 7% of the children in England in 1989. In 1985 it had been 8%. In 1885 it had been 18%, and, apart, from a slight pause in decline during the years of the Welsh revival, has been steadily falling since then.[39] Professor David Martin of the London School of Economics estimated that 'in 1957, 76% of those aged over 30 had at some time attended Sunday School.'[40] The proportion in 1992 would probably be about half that, 41%, many of whom would now be over 50.

A Welsh Church Census in 1982 revealed a curious finding—so curious that it was initially thought to be a random statistical fluctuation. It was noticed that denominations whose child attendance was increasing were precisely the ones which had the smallest proportion of children in Sunday School![41] The Scottish Church Census which followed in 1984 found the same thing.[42] It was not totally surprising to find a similar state of affairs in England in 1989![43] In writing this finding up for one Report, a delightful misprint occurred: 'The Census showed in general terms that denominations whose children wee most in Sunday School tended to be the ones who were losing children fastest.' There may be truth in that also!

This general observation has since been corroborated in other, more local studies. These have found that churches where children share in the adult service to some extent (and the extent varies from church to church) are much more likely to grow than ones where there is no contact with the main body of worshippers. The growing churches were drawing their Sunday School children in to the main adult worship service at least for part of the time. Do Sunday Schools therefore have any influence? Leslie Francis, in a study of rural Anglicans, concluded 'Where Sunday Schools exist, they lose their pupils after the age of nine.'[44] So should there be Sunday Schools?

Had the teenagers interviewed in the RAKT Project ever regularly attended Sunday School (that is, at least once a month)? They did in the proportions shown in Table 49 where 'Sunday School' is taken to mean any similar youth group meeting.

These are substantial numbers of young people, many more than given in the statistics above. This in turn suggests one or other is incorrect. They may be. The RAKT figures, for example, give no suggestion of rural decline as suggested by Leslie Francis (the figures for rural churches are respectively 64, 66, 59 and 31%). But the forms did not ask how long or how continuously they attended, and it may be that they didn't stay long! (The Sunday School figures quoted earlier would tend to be average Sunday attendance.)

*Table 49: Age when teenagers attended Sunday School*

| Age at time of attending | School % | Church % | Overall % |
|---|---|---|---|
| 5,6 | 34 | 57 | 44 |
| 9,10 | 32 | 62 | 46 |
| 13,14 | 12 | 55 | 32 |
| 15 or over | 3 | 30 | 15 |
| Total number (100%) | 1,055 | 876 | 1,931 |

What was the teenagers' reaction to Sunday School? This is given below:

*Table 50: Reactions to Sunday School*

| Reaction | School % | Church % | Overall % |
|---|---|---|---|
| 'Enjoyable' | 37 | 64 | 52 |
| 'An opportunity to learn a lot' | 29 | 51 | 41 |
| 'An encouragement to attend church' | 22 | 42 | 33 |
| 'Boring' | 32 | 17 | 24 |
| 'Irrelevant' | 13 | 7 | 10 |
| 'A waste of time' | 27 | 6 | 15 |
| Total number (100%) | 589 | 755 | 1,344 |

Sunday School teachers should take encouragement from these figures! It is clear that the overall impression was favourable. Over half enjoyed it, two-fifths reckoned they learnt a lot, and a third were encouraged to come to church—and these figures include 86% of the school teenagers who are not committed to the church! On the other hand, a quarter found it boring, one in six a waste of time, and one in ten irrelevant. Such experiences are not likely to encourage youngsters to come on to church. The average of the positive percentages is 42%, and the negative 16%. There is no question that for the majority of children (looking back as a teenager) Sunday School was a positive experience, informative and encouraging. No suggestion here they should be closed down! Quite the reverse, in fact.

Sunday School was especially important for the Methodists (76% attended at 9 or 10 years of age), Other Free Churches (76%) and Baptists (72%), and, apart from the Catholics, least for Anglicans (64%). Reactions, however, did not vary by denomination. All were equally well favoured!

Girls tended to go more at 9 and 10 than boys, 66 against 58% – was Sunday football too great a temptation? Girls reckoned they learned more than boys (54 against 46%), and enjoyed it more (68 against 58%).

There was no significant difference between present Christian commitment and Sunday School attendance. In other words, going to Sunday School was an educational process, maybe an encouragement to keep going to church but not the place of challenge to commitment.

There was a complete contrast, however, between evangelical and non-evangelical churches, as Tables 51 and 52 indicate.

Clearly Sunday School was enjoyed by children more in evangelical churches than in others. The average of the positive statements for evangelicals is 57%, but only 44% for non-evangelicals. The negatives average 9% and 11% respectively, showing it is the positive attributes which are the more important. In addition it should be noticed that 476 evangelical and 390 non-evangelical teenagers answered the question on age recorded in Table 51. 29 of the evangelicals declined to complete the question on reactions recorded in Table 52, but 92 non-evangelicals!

It was also significant that children who had gone to Sunday School were much more likely to have had a religious experience: 59% against 42% who had not. What kind of experience? Not a conversion experience—that was the same for both groups, but 'becoming a Christian' did vary—70% for those who went to Sunday School against 59% who had not. In all 41% of

*Table 51: Sunday School attendance by age and churchmanship*

| Age at time of attending | Evangelical % | Non-evangelical % | Overall % |
|---|---|---|---|
| 5,6 | 63 | 49 | 57 |
| 9,10 | 71 | 51 | 62 |
| 13,14 | 65 | 43 | 55 |
| 15 or over | 36 | 22 | 30 |
| Total number (100%) | 476 | 390 | 876 |

*Table 52: Reactions to Sunday School by churchmanship*

| Reaction | Evangelical % | Non-evangelical % | Overall % |
|---|---|---|---|
| 'Enjoyable' | 70 | 55 | 64 |
| 'An opportunity to learn a lot' | 57 | 40 | 51 |
| 'An encouragement to attend church' | 45 | 36 | 42 |
| 'Boring' | 16 | 19 | 17 |
| 'Irrelevant' | 6 | 8 | 7 |
| 'A waste of time' | 6 | 6 | 6 |
| Total number (100%) | 447 | 298 | 755 |

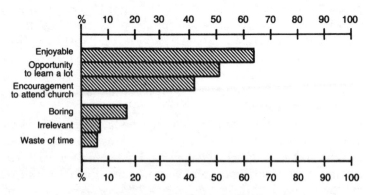

Figure 26: Sunday School attendance

those who went to Sunday School became a Christian against 25% who didn't. Yes, going to Sunday School makes a considerable difference!

Age made no difference to these figures, and interestingly, nor did the marital status of the teenager's parents. Being baptized made a small difference overall—70% against 60% who were not baptized. It made a greater difference for those attending at 5 or 6 years of age (74 against 57%). But Sunday School attendance had a very great effect on confirmation. 23% of those who went to Sunday School were confirmed/ received into adult membership at the time of the survey, against only 8% who did not. Those who had been to Sunday School also, by and large, had a more positive attitude to church. They viewed church as more friendly (39 against 31% who hadn't attended Sunday School), more enjoyable (19 against 12%), more modern (10 against 7%), more challenging (12 against 5%), more lively (14 against 8%), easier for strangers to join in (29 against 22%), and less boring (54 against 62%)!

In the light of so many positive outcomes it is clear that Sunday School like certain beers, does you good, and reaches parts that others don't! Martyn White, Managing Director of Scripture Press, in a recent interview told of one of his former Sunday School pupils who became a Christian while visiting Australia. When she returned she deliberately sought out Mavis, her old Sunday School teacher, who had sown the seed.[45]

In a study on the influence of Sunday Schools among 4,000 teenagers in Scotland,[46] Leslie Francis concluded 'that they demonstrate a positive contribution' to the religious development of adolescents and indicated that this contribution is both unique and additional to influences exerted through church attendance and parental example. 'Through their Sunday School work churches appear to be achieving something which they would not be achieving without them. This may be particularly encouraging in the light of the sustained criticism to which Sunday Schools have been subjected during the past two decades . . . They (also) demonstrate the marginal nature of the positive contribution made by Sunday Schools to the religious development of adolescents after taking into account the sizable influence of contemporary church attendance. Unless Sunday School attendance during childhood leads into teenage membership of the church congregation, the impact of the Sunday School on adolescent religious development is marginalized. This indicates that churches which invest heavily in Sunday School work need to give equal attention both to the pastoral care of those who are out-growing Sunday School attendance and to assuring that there is adequate opportunity for children and young people to grow into a welcoming worshipping community.'

Steve Chalke was anxious to update some 1957 research which showed only 2 to 5% of Sunday School children becoming adult churchgoers. The RAKT survey shows that 51% of teenagers currently going to church went to Sunday School, with two-fifths saying that the experience encouraged them to attend. How many of these churchgoing teenagers will stay on as adult churchgoers remains to be seen but it is highly likely to be over 5%.[47] In an inner London borough like Newham where churches try to reach young people by every way possible (and touch in the process 6% of teenagers aged 14 to 18),[48] Sunday School still draws more youngsters than uniformed organizations, young people's fellowships or open youth clubs. It can only be because they are effective!

### The influence of the home

'The young people of today think of nothing but themselves. They have no reverence for parents or old people. They talk as if they alone knew everything and what passes for wisdom with us is foolishness to them. As for girls, they are forward, immodest, unwomanly in speech, behaviour and dress.' Sound familiar? You will probably not guess who wrote this or when!

It was penned by a wandering ascetic who helped to launch the First Crusade, a man called Peter the Hermit. And the year? 1098—almost nine hundred years ago. Perhaps things haven't changed as much as we have thought!

The March for Jesus event in May 1992 asked a random sample of 2,300 young people a few quick questions. One of them was: 'What is the most important thing in your life?' Of all those answering, 32% said 'Family'.[49] In the RAKT survey over 850 churchgoing teenagers were asked who they went to church with: 75% said family, 15% said friends and 10% went by themselves; 35% then sat with their family, 61% with their friends, and 4% by themselves. Among the school teenagers, 280 attended church at least once a month, of whom 67% went with their family, 30% with friends and 3% by themselves. 47% sat with their family, 51% with their friends, and 2% by themselves. Such simple figures make it very clear that the average teenager values his or her family.

## Role models

Why does a teenager need a family? Parents (and youth club leaders, school teachers and other 'loco parentis' where necessary) at least theoretically:[50]

- Set an example (role model)
- Act as a listener and confidant
- Give affirmation and encouragement
- Provide information and teaching
- Show support for them.

In the RAKT study of 2,000 teenagers, the parents of 87% of churchgoing teenagers and 77% of school teenagers were married; 2 and 4%, church and school respectively, were separated; 7 and 13% were divorced; 1 and 3% were unmarried and 3% of both groups were widowed. Rather more churchgoing teenagers have a more traditional family background, and in both cases, a good majority does, 90% and 80% (including the widowed parents in this context). These percentages are almost identical to those in the comprehensive Canadian study, *Canadian Youth 'Ready for Today'*.[51]

The 13% of churchgoing teenagers without married parents lived with their mother (10%), father (1%) and with others (2%). The 23% of school teenagers in the same circumstances lived with their mother (15%), father (3%), two adults (4%) and 1% with others. The dominance of the mother in single-parent families is typical of the country as a whole, and the percentage of broken families with teenage children was also similar to the national picture—for school families. More churchgoing teenagers had a traditional home background. Most of the fathers had jobs too, 86% for school teens, and 92% for church teens. Church teens' families were, as many church families, dominantly middle class.

'Over many years, many feminists have maintained that the male role model is not altogether necessary in raising male children. However, faced with the shocking results of 20 years of liberation from traditional ideals of the male role model, experts and feminists alike in the USA are now coming round to a stark realization. Young men without fathers are not going to draw a male identity from their mothers, but rather will seek out a strong male influence they can emulate.

'To put it bluntly,' writes the Australian evangelist John Smith, 'they are looking for a father substitute, but the type of father they get on the streets is a shadowy reflection of the loving, patient protector a father ought to be. Unfortunately these father-family substitutes are available in ample supply in the ghettos. They provide protection, security, a sense of belonging, and a warped male identity, to the insecure. They are known as gangs.'[52]

## Families at work

What makes a family tick? 1,700 church youth were asked in a survey by Agapé, formerly Campus Crusade for Christ, about their relationships with their parents.[53] The results were as follows:

Table 53: *Occurrence of parental/teenage interactions*

| Nature of interaction | Father % | Mother % |
|---|---|---|
| Feel proud of your . . . | 40 | 42 |
| Feel your . . . shows his/her love | 36 | 54 |
| Seek advice from your . . . | 23 | 54 |
| Show your love to your . . . | 20 | 33 |
| Do something special with your . . . that involves just the two of you | 9 | 17 |
| Talk with your . . . about your personal concerns | 7 | 36 |
| Wonder whether or not your . . . loves you | 6 | 5 |

The significance of the mother figure is very clear from this table. Every situation occurs more often with the female parent. The crucial importance of involvement, sharing, interaction is clear. This is a two-way process. 56% of the same teenagers felt their parents were frequently really interested in what they, their teenage children, were doing, and 43% said their parents often spent time with them, the teenager. As for parents' relationships with others, 41% of the teenagers said their parents frequently showed they really loved each other, and 18% frequently admitted it when they were wrong or mistaken.[54] Teenagers therefore are perceptive about the marriage relationship in their family. As a consequence, 57% said that their 'home is a place where I feel secure and loved.'[55]

What did this mean in practice in talking about things that really matter with their parents? Unlike listening to music or watching television, which accounted for hours a day, talking with parents was measured in minutes a week! On average mothers got 38 minutes a week and fathers 23! Daughters in both cases got more (46 and 25 minutes respectively) than sons (29 and 21 minutes).[56] If parents were judged to be 'very close' to the teenager these times increased to 50 and 37 minutes respectively! Still less than an hour a week in the best of situations, and, often, if certain personal experience is allowed, usually after midnight! As someone once said, 'The greatest illusion about communication is . . . that it has been achieved.'

Perhaps there is greater communication when relaxing on holiday? Ah no, another study showed that families with children between 10 and 15 are more likely to take holidays which rate as 'fun and excitement' rather than 'relaxation'.[57]

No wonder it is difficult! The Zadok Institute for Christianity and Society in Australia have published a Reading Guide for Parents;[58] perhaps someone should do the same in this country. But it is critically important: Don Posterski, Canadian researcher, summarizes it precisely, 'Even with day care, school and the baby sitter all having some influence, parents of pre-adolescents are the primary gatekeepers between their children and our culture.'[59] And not just pre-adolescents!

*Time . . . and time again*

The same issue of *Context*[60] published a table (see Table 54) of findings from these different studies looking at parents who effectively pass on their values to their teenaged children.

Parents whose styles are closest to the left hand set will consistently have greater success in ensuring their adolescent children maintain the essentials of the family's religious values.

What are the parents' domains? This is clear from the answers to the question, 'Who do you find yourself most likely to turn to when you are making decisions in . . . ?' in a Canadian study,[61] given in Table 55 on page 192.

Although the low level for 'having fun' is rather embarrassing there are a number of strengths in the data from this study.

Table 54: An effective parenting mix

| Parenting models: | Authoritative | Permissive | Authoritarian |
|---|---|---|---|
| | • Stresses Control<br>• AND support | • Stresses support<br>• NO control | • Stresses control<br>• NO support |
| Parent-teen relationship model: | Companionship | Extreme affection | Extreme control |
| | • Open communication between parents and children<br>• Fair discipline | • Suffocating affection<br>• Youth is afraid independence will hurt parent | • Little emotional connection between generations<br>• Poor communication with strong discipline |
| Family type: | Translucent | Transparent | Opaque |
| | • Integrated with society but with own distinctions<br>• Parents interpret outside world fairly<br>• Not hostile to other values | • Conforms to general social values<br>• Parents offer no interpretation of outside world<br>• No distinctive family values | • Completely separated from society<br>• Self-righteous, all outside sources are considered 'fallen' or evil<br>• Ascribes faith only to those who fully conform |

*Table 55: Areas in which parents and friends are consulted*

| Area | Parents % | Friends % |
|------|-----------|-----------|
| Spending money | 48 | 18 |
| Career | 48 | 10 |
| Right and wrong | 45 | 22 |
| School | 45 | 20 |
| A major problem | 31 | 41 |
| Sex | 8 | 55 |
| Relationships | 7 | 75 |
| Having fun | 3 | 81 |

Time also needs to be given to the issue of language. Canadians also found that what adults think adolescents mean by certain phrases differs.[62] Consider:

| *Adolescent says . . .* | *Adults think they mean . . .* |
|---|---|
| 'Let me learn.' | No rules |
| 'Let me make some real decisions.' | Licence |
| 'Give me the right to voice an opinion.' | Recklessness |
| 'Accept me.' | Lawlessness |
| 'Trust me.' | Irresponsibility |
| 'Treat me as an adult.' | Destructiveness |
| 'Grant me independence.' | Disaster |

Time is also required to get an appropriate balance. It is all too easy to make a major issue over an item of minor importance. The Canadian authors of *Teen Trends* suggest two simple principles: 'As few rules as necessary and as many choices as possible' and 'Major on the majors and minor on the minors'.[63] As examples of the kind of items that might fall into these last two categories, they suggest:

| Major | Minor |
|---|---|
| Sexual promiscuity | Consistent refusal to tidy bedroom |
| Taking illicit drugs | Spending too much time on the phone |
| Pathological lying | Wearing earrings |
| Abusive language | Hair-styles |
| Violent behaviour | Wearing too much makeup |
| Unrelenting disrespect for other family members | Disagreements about spending money |
| Disregard of curfews and other agreements | Arguments while negotiating curfews and other agreements |
| Getting picked up for drunk driving | Getting a ticket for speeding |

Distinguishing between majors and minors will lead to an easier home life. Items will vary from one family to another. Does it work out in practice? Two American economists tried to find mathematical equations linking household allocation of time to religious duties and participation in these of husband and wife.[64] Their model suggested that as wages increased individuals would move to less time-intensive forms of religious activities, and that as individuals earn more as they get older, they will spend less time on religious activities either by moving to less time-consuming denominations or by giving more money but less time to an existing denomination.[65] Both trends seem sensible (and to some extent are observable from casual contact and conversation), but not everyone agrees with this kind of prediction. Few would feel it works as mechanistically as this model suggests.

But that it works empirically seems without question. Where the study of UK church youth found that overall 18% had experienced sexual intercourse only 16% of teenagers 'very close' to both parents had experienced it compared to 32% 'not close' to either parent.[66] Of those coming from a Christian home, 80% received Christ before they were 12, 50% while in their teens and 40% when older, against overall norms of 17, 59 and 24% respectively.[67] In *Finding Faith Today*[68] John Finney says that the general family background of the 500 or so Christians interviewed was 80% Christian, 19% Nothing and 1% Other Faiths.

It may be worth pausing to consider how, in the light of these principles and practices, your own family or your church situation, could be improved.

## Moving into adulthood

Teenagers are moving towards adulthood. Indeed Jews recognize their 13 year old sons as adults in their Bar Mitzvah ceremony. Teenagers can reason like adults even though they are less mature. Communication should therefore treat teenagers with respect.[69] Subsequently in late teens or early twenties they have a time when they want to feel independent of their parents. 'This crisis is necessary and normal. Before he attains adult maturity, the young man must first go through this time of storm and stress when he has to subject everything to question. The day will come when he will discover again many of the treasures of his childhood, when he will return to the faith in which he grew up and the principles which were inculcated in him.'[70] These are the comments of Paul Tournier, a well-known Christian psychologist. They help us to understand Solomon's wisdom, 'Train a child in the way he should go, and when he is old he will not turn from it.'[71]

Part of our difficulty is that we sometimes appear to communicate the following: 'You are fully adult when you have finished your education, are holding down a full-time job, paying taxes, and are preferably married with at least one child. When all these criteria are met, maybe by the time you reach 30, you are accepted by the older generation as fully adult.'[72] Others might define adulthood as the period when a person begins to act responsibly in his/her social obligations and maturely in his/her relationships.

Teens are a time of 'whole-life stewardship' as futurologist Tom Sine puts it. 'Whole-life stewardship certainly means helping young people wrestle with some of the most important questions that are likely to shape their future: (1) What is ultimately important? (2) What is the good life? and (3) Where are we likely to find it?'[73] At present few churches seem to provide answers to such questions.

How do we help young people? The pastor of Trinity Lutheran Church in Roselle, Illinois, Charles Mueller, says simply, 'Pray and Persevere'. 'Keep on reaching out. Parents have to reject fear. Remember accurately, teach carefully, model as best as they know how, and pray with fervour.'[74] Reginald Bibby and Don Posterski, the Canadian researchers, put it as 'the almighty power of friendship'.[75]

What are young people wanting of their parents? The initials ATTIRE can sum up the four key things: (1) They want to be Allowed Trust. Give them some responsibilities. Yes, they may fail, but are you perfect? (2) Time. Give them quality time, to talk, think, pray if they wish. Often they want to talk when it is inconvenient to us, but part of looking after teenagers is last minute adaptation, which some parents find difficult. (3) Interest in their friends, their work, their hopes and fears, but not intrusion into their privacy. One of our sons said to us, 'I hate your barrage of questions.' He was right. (4) Reasonable Expectations. They may not get six GCSEs or 3 A grades at A-level. But they might help you in a family project. When my wife was a teenager she literally helped her builder father build the bungalow they all lived in.

ATTIRE is really an alternative way of spelling 'friendship'. Jesus said, 'I have called you friends.'[76] We have primarily to be friends, 'signs of hope' as the Salesian Sisters of St John Bosco said when identifying how they wanted to be in their relationships with the many young people they help.

## The final result

As part of the Europeans Value Systems study up to 1,000 people were interviewed in 1981 in nine European countries. Professor Kerklofs of the Catholic University of Louvain chaired the Steering Committee. Pro Mundi Vita subsequently published in 1984[77] a summary of some of the results as they applied to young people. Table 56 relates to churchgoing and Christianity across all denominations and teenage years. The table was initially given for Mother and Father but the final figures are so close as to be insignificant. So long as one parent is a churchgoer (and it doesn't matter which) the average outcome is as shown in Table 56. This may be interpreted as follows:

- Across Europe a quarter (24% in the final column) of families have at least one churchgoing parent (the degree of regularity was not stated), a quarter (25%) are nominal (saying they are Christian but not actively involved), and half (51%) are not churchgoing at all.
- Of the families where one parent is a churchgoer, half the children (first line, 12% is half of 24%) end up going to church regularly, just over a quarter (7 out of 24%) end up as nominal Christians, and just under a quarter (5 out of 24%) end up as total non-churchgoers.
- Of the nominal families, half their children end up as nominal churchgoers also (second line, 12 out of 25%). One in eight (3 out of 25%), however, goes to church regularly, and three in eight (10 out of 25%) do not go to church at all.
- 80% of non-churchgoing families have non-churchgoing children (third line, 40 out of 51%). One in 17, or 6%, (3 out of 51%) however, end up as regular churchgoers and the remaining 14% (8 out of 51%) as nominal churchgoers.

There is hope and challenge for all of us in such findings, and such outcomes. The figures are illustrated in Figure 27.

*Table 56: Churchgoing of children from churchgoing parents*

|  | Children have become | | | |
| Parents are: | Nominal Churchgoers % | Non-churchgoers % | Churchgoers % | Total % |
|---|---|---|---|---|
| Churchgoers | 12 | 7 | 5 | 24 |
| Nominal churchgoers | 3 | 12 | 10 | 25 |
| Non-churchgoers | 3 | 8 | 40 | 51 |
| Total | 18 | 27 | 55 | 100 |

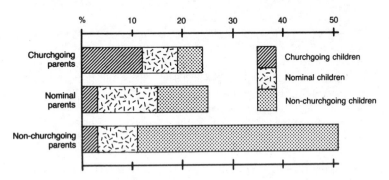

Figure 27: Churchgoing of children from churchgoing of parents

### Summary

- At school, negative attitudes to Christianity have increased since 1974.
- At school, positive attitudes about prayer, Jesus and God have decreased but were holding steady in the 1980s.
- At school, attitudes towards the church were the least positive but also steady in the 1980s.
- At school, a pupil's personal belief in God is the key religious issue, largely reflecting their mother's church attendance.
- Pupils from Roman Catholic schools hold much more to traditional moral values.
- RE lessons have much potential. Most teenagers are not hostile to the church.
- Churches whose Sunday School children are not integrated into the main worship services have declining numbers of children.
- Substantial numbers of young people attending Sunday School find it helpful and enjoyable, and find it an encouragement to go to church.
- Evangelical Sunday Schools are more attractive to children than non-evangelical ones.
- Most teenagers regard their family as the most important element in their life.
- Parenting models vary, but spending time with teenagers, taking an interest in their activities, allowing them trust, and having reasonable expectations of them are key.
- Half the children of churchgoing families throughout Europe end up going to church regularly.

# 6

# *Teenage Beliefs and Values*

One question was 'Do you believe in God?' One boy answered, 'The devil believes in God—does that make him a Christian?'

The teenager in the cartoon stood before his youth group to give this summary: 'And so, to conclude my report on the beliefs of 400 different denominations, I can only say that in my opinion somebody goofed.'[1]

It is always a difficult question. Many well wishing adults frequently ask it especially of middle range teenagers. Replies vary from the absurd, extravagant and outrageous to the more frequent 'I don't know.' The question? Very simple: 'What are you going to do?' Evaluating strengths and weaknesses and projecting these into an actual job is not easy for most teenagers. Implicit within their thinking and discussions in these years are also their basic aspirations ('I want to marry a nice rich man'), and their beliefs and value systems. The RAKT study did not look at these in great detail, but mention must be made here of such findings as did emerge.

### Aspirations

The researcher, Roy Langmaid, was asked to talk to groups of young lads in a research project for the Army. They wanted to recruit more people, and wanted to find out what kind of person young men wanted to become. Roy's method was to take a handful of youngsters and talk to them for 90 minutes. Eventually he would ask, 'What kind of man do you wanna be?' The answers that emerged are an impressive list of the qualities to which they aspired:

- Confidence
- Decisiveness
- Pride
- Maturity
- Responsibility
- Strength
- Trustworthiness
- Sociability
- Being one's own man
- Independence
- Caring
- Generosity
- Honesty
- Being respected by self, family and friends[2]

As it happens most of these qualities fit the Army very well. Most of these qualities would fit Christian youth also, and most employers and institutions (apart from, say, the Mafia!). Doubtless many would fit young women also, but their aspirations were not part of this study.

In the church youth groups survey undertaken for Agapé,[3] young people were given a list of characteristics and asked which of these described themselves. We scored them on a point system from −2 for 'not at all accurate' to +2 for 'very accurate'. The top five characteristics[3] were:

- Kind          1.2
- Intelligent   0.7
- Popular       0.6
- Religious     0.6
- Lonely        0.6

These perhaps are surprising. Yet young people are very close to their friends and would see themselves as being kind to them on most occasions. They are generally very kind to animals, and to the environment. In that sense, young people are 'green'. So putting kindness as their foremost attribute is a fair reflection on how they see themselves. They saw themselves as religious because they were church youth, after all! This kind of listing is important, and gives insight to those wanting to reach young people. How did Jesus show His kindness? What did He have to say to the intelligent? The popular? The religious? The lonely? How does what He said then help us in our approach today?

## Beliefs

### *Religious belief*

In an attempt to ascertain teenagers' understanding of what being a Christian is, Leslie Francis surveyed 202 sixth form pupils taking Religious Studies A-Level. They were aged from 16–19. 38% attended church weekly, a further 11% at least once a month, 33% attended from time to time, and 18% never attended.[4] 36 descriptions were used, divided into four main topics, as given in Table 57.

Public practice plays a very small part in older teenagers' definition of being a Christian. They put far more weight on belief, consistent with earlier findings. Those going to church weekly are of the same opinion. Christianity is seen essentially as private, not public. That privacy of belief is weaker by far in those who never go to church. That might be expected except that the descriptions used are very basic, and follow traditional lines. Here again there is a glimpse, as we have seen once or twice before, of a fundamental belief gap between regular churchgoers and others. It is not that belief is relegated as unimportant, but it is that key Christian doctrines—heaven, resurrection, deity of Jesus—are rated very low.

Table 57: Criteria for 'Being a Christian' by topic and church attendance

| Topic | Description | Percentage endorsing % | Percentage rating 'essential or very important' who attended church | |
|-------|-------------|------------------------|--------------------------------------------------------------------|---|
| | | | Weekly % | Never % |
| Religious belief | Believes that God exists | 82 | 87 | 84 |
| | Believes in Jesus | 74 | 86 | 61 |
| | Loves God | 69 | 77 | 58 |
| | Believes that Jesus is the Son of God | 62 | 78 | 47 |
| | Believes that Jesus is worthy of worship | 61 | 74 | 47 |
| | Finds God in Jesus | 53 | 70 | 36 |
| | Follows God's word | 53 | 66 | 47 |
| | Believes in the resurrection of Jesus | 53 | 75 | 25 |
| | Believes he/she will enter heaven through Christ | 50 | 64 | 17 |
| | Average | 62 | 75 | 47 |

| | | | | |
|---|---|---|---|---|
| Personal morality/ relationships | Forgives other people | 53 | 62 | 42 |
| | Tries to lead a good life | 43 | 47 | 44 |
| | Is considerate of others' feelings and views | 37 | 40 | 43 |
| | Helps others | 37 | 36 | 31 |
| | Tries to treat people equally | 36 | 43 | 31 |
| | Is a good person | 32 | 28 | 36 |
| | Is friendly | 22 | 27 | 14 |
| | Is hopeful | 19 | 25 | 22 |
| | Orients his/her life towards the needs of others | 15 | 15 | 11 |
| | **Average** | 33 | 36 | 30 |
| Personal spirituality | Prays to God (individual prayer) | 38 | 51 | 27 |
| | Has committed his/her life to Christ | 34 | 48 | 14 |
| | Allows the Spirit to change his/her life | 24 | 45 | 8 |
| | Has received the Holy Spirit | 24 | 42 | 14 |
| | Believes he/she has been saved | 23 | 40 | 6 |
| | Seeks to know God better through reading the Bible | 16 | 23 | 8 |
| | Reads the Bible | 16 | 25 | 8 |
| | Tells other people about Christianity | 16 | 30 | 8 |
| | Is humble | 13 | 18 | 11 |
| | **Average** | 23 | 36 | 12 |

Table 57: *Continued*

| Topic | Description | Percentage endorsing % | Percentage rating 'essential or very important' who attended church | |
|---|---|---|---|---|
| | | | Weekly % | Never % |
| Public practice | Is baptized | 16 | 29 | 0 |
| | Goes to a place of worship | 14 | 24 | 8 |
| | Encourages his/her children to attend church/Sunday School | 13 | 27 | 0 |
| | Attends church at Christmas | 12 | 23 | 6 |
| | Frequently receives communion | 10 | 23 | 3 |
| | Regularly receives communion | 9 | 22 | 0 |
| | Supports church activities | 7 | 12 | 0 |
| | Is a regular churchgoer | 6 | 12 | 3 |
| | Supports the church financially | 2 | 5 | 0 |
| | Average | 10 | 20 | 2 |
| Overall average | | 32 | 42 | 23 |

The other area of wide difference is that of personal spirituality. Those who never go to church hardly begin to appreciate what spirituality is or might be. There's a simple Biblical explanation for that in that 'the God of this world has blinded the minds of the unbelievers.'[5] At best, only a quarter of non-churchgoing teenagers perceive the importance of private prayer, with far lower levels of acceptance of the features of spirituality.

There is, however, a much closer agreement between regular and non-churchgoers on the importance of relationships in the definition of a Christian. Indeed the two features where non-churchgoers outnumber churchgoers are in this section. More non-churchgoers than churchgoers agree that a Christian 'is a good person'. Likewise that a Christian 'is considerate of others' feelings and views' is believed by more non-churchgoers.

This study identifies four features of teenagers' understanding of what it means to be a Christian. Beliefs are seen as far more important than practice. Non-churchgoers' understanding is deficient in most areas, but especially in belief in basic doctrines, spirituality and practice. Their perception of the importance of relationship gives a clue as to how teenagers might be reached—the bridge so to speak over which to walk. This study might be summed as: Teenager non-churchgoers reckon Christians believe in God and are 'good' people. They do not expect 'good works' though.

## Belief in God

Belief in God seems an appropriate key pre-requisite for being a Christian. Not only did it get the highest endorsement, but even non-churchgoers see it as a cardinal element in Christianity. In the Gallup European Values Study, 76% of British people said they believed in God, but only 59% of those aged 18–24.[6] In 1989 in Australia '66% of young people affirmed a belief in God.'[7] In the RAKT Survey, we asked those in school (but not those in church) if they ever thought about the existence of God. 78% did, and 67% said they believed in

Him. Those thinking about God did not vary significantly with age, gender, part of the country lived in or marital status of parents. It did vary by Christian commitment, with those not very committed or not sure if they were a Christian thinking about Him much more—85% did so. Three-quarters (76%) of those who were no longer Christians said they thought about Him, as did two-thirds (66%) of those who had never been Christians.

As might be expected, those of other religions thought about the existence of God too (the same as the Christians, 83%). But even those who had no religion (66%) still thought about Him. There is a continuing searching, and wondering, and even such a simple question reveals that many teenagers ponder eternal realities.

67% of school teenagers believed in God, which did not vary significantly either except for the two factors already mentioned, and for gender. 70% of females believed in God against 62% males. 70% of Christians believed in God as did 89% of adherents to other religions. Only 31% of those with no religion believed in God—almost a contradiction in terms. Likewise strongly committed Christians were more likely to believe in Him (93%—surprisingly not 100%) than less committed (84%) or unsure (63%). Only a quarter (26%) of those no longer a Christian believed, as did a third (33%) who had never been a Christian.

To the question 'Do you believe that we can know God personally?' 32% said YES. 41% of Christians replied in the affirmative and so did 41% of those in other religions. Only 10% of those with no religion felt the same way, though 82% of strongly committed Christians believed we could know God personally, but only 41% of less committed, 23% of the unsure, 14% of those no longer Christians and 11% of those who had never been Christians. Commitment makes the crucial difference here.

## Picture of God

What is God like? Nine suggestions were made and multiple answers were allowed so the percentages in Table 58 total over

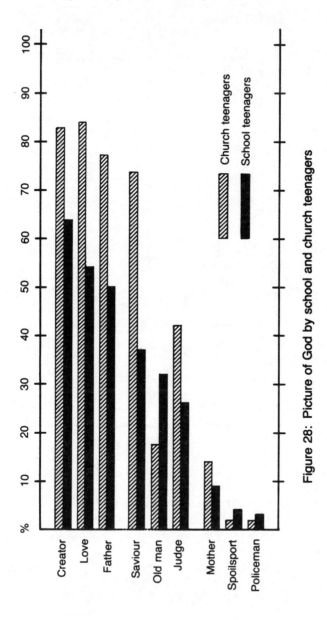

Figure 28: Picture of God by school and church teenagers

*Table 58: How God is pictured by different groups in schools*

| Picture | 11,12 % | 13 % | 14 % | 15 % | 16 % | 17 % | 18 % | Male % | Female % | Overall % |
|---|---|---|---|---|---|---|---|---|---|---|
| Creator | 67 | 68 | 68 | 50 | 53 | 66 | 72 | 62 | 65 | 63 |
| Love | 57 | 62 | 57 | 47 | 45 | 54 | 42 | 47 | 62 | 54 |
| Father | 56 | 55 | 58 | 45 | 39 | 39 | 32 | 48 | 52 | 50 |
| Saviour | 36 | 44 | 42 | 29 | 19 | 37 | 24 | 32 | 38 | 35 |
| Old man | 34 | 29 | 36 | 32 | 42 | 27 | 40 | 36 | 29 | 32 |
| Judge | 24 | 29 | 25 | 24 | 24 | 27 | 38 | 30 | 22 | 26 |
| Mother | 11 | 10 | 7 | 10 | 10 | 1 | 4 | 9 | 9 | 9 |
| Spoilsport | 6 | 2 | 7 | 3 | 6 | 0 | 2 | 6 | 2 | 4 |
| Policeman | 3 | 3 | 4 | 2 | 3 | 1 | 4 | 5 | 1 | 3 |
| Other | 8 | 6 | 13 | 8 | 16 | 11 | 12 | 10 | 9 | 9 |
| Total number (100%) | 277 | 263 | 125 | 200 | 89 | 79 | 50 | 541 | 555 | 1,114 |

*Table 58 (Cont): How God is pictured by different groups in schools*

| Picture | Christian commitment | | | | | Christian % | Other religions % | No religion % | Overall % |
| --- | --- | --- | --- | --- | --- | --- | --- | --- | --- |
| | Strong % | Weak % | Unsure % | No longer % | Never % | | | | |
| Creator | 72 | 76 | 62 | 37 | 46 | 71 | 65 | 45 | 63 |
| Love | 76 | 66 | 50 | 31 | 35 | 63 | 63 | 32 | 54 |
| Father | 78 | 59 | 44 | 29 | 33 | 58 | 43 | 32 | 50 |
| Saviour | 62 | 43 | 31 | 18 | 21 | 42 | 37 | 19 | 35 |
| Old man | 20 | 27 | 39 | 35 | 41 | 30 | 17 | 42 | 32 |
| Judge | 32 | 28 | 28 | 31 | 18 | 28 | 29 | 20 | 26 |
| Mother | 16 | 8 | 9 | 6 | 6 | 9 | 12 | 7 | 9 |
| Spoilsport | 0 | 3 | 5 | 0 | 7 | 3 | 2 | 6 | 4 |
| Policeman | 3 | 2 | 3 | 8 | 3 | 3 | 5 | 4 | 3 |
| Other | 9 | 8 | 7 | 33 | 12 | 8 | 8 | 14 | 9 |
| Total number (100%) | 100 | 449 | 222 | 49 | 233 | 734 | 65 | 315 | 1,114 |

Table 59: How God is pictured by different groups in the churches

| Picture | Evangelical % | Non-evangelical % | Christian commitment | | | | | | Male % | Female % | Overall % |
| | | | Strong % | Weak % | Unsure % | No longer % | Never % | | | |
|---|---|---|---|---|---|---|---|---|---|---|---|
| Creator | 87 | 79 | 94 | 83 | 70 | 55 | 50 | 83 | 84 | 83 |
| Love | 87 | 81 | 94 | 85 | 73 | 46 | 59 | 79 | 89 | 84 |
| Father | 83 | 71 | 88 | 77 | 67 | 55 | 36 | 76 | 78 | 77 |
| Saviour | 78 | 67 | 84 | 74 | 54 | 18 | 46 | 68 | 76 | 73 |
| Old man | 15 | 21 | 9 | 20 | 26 | 46 | 27 | 19 | 16 | 17 |
| Judge | 45 | 38 | 50 | 42 | 24 | 64 | 36 | 47 | 38 | 42 |
| Mother | 12 | 15 | 18 | 11 | 15 | 0 | 5 | 11 | 16 | 14 |
| Spoilsport | 1 | 2 | 0 | 3 | 2 | 9 | 0 | 2 | 2 | 2 |
| Policeman | 1 | 2 | 2 | 2 | 2 | 9 | 0 | 2 | 1 | 2 |
| Other | 14 | 15 | 19 | 12 | 14 | 9 | 18 | 13 | 16 | 14 |
| Total number (100%) | 474 | 401 | 269 | 436 | 111 | 11 | 22 | 381 | 487 | 868 |

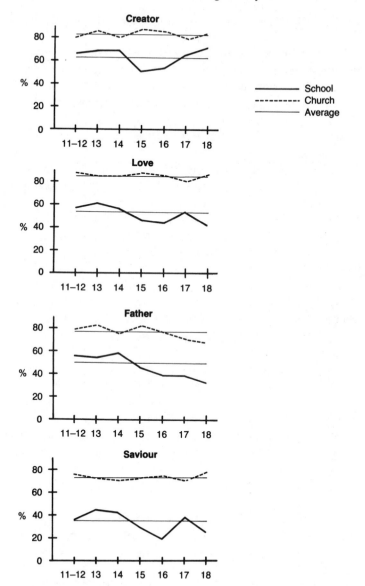

Figure 29: Top four pictures of God as they vary by age of teenagers

100%. Details in Table 58 are for school teenagers, and in Table 59 for church teenagers.

Most teenagers' picture of God is as a Creator, Love and Father, whether they be school or church teenagers. These three pictures dominate for both groups, even though 86% of the school teenagers were not regular churchgoers. The fourth picture is much more important for church youth than school youth—that of Him as Saviour. Putting both groups together 72% picture God as Creator, 67% as Love, 62% as Father, and 52% as Saviour. All other pictures have few subscribers. That this is how He is mainly pictured by both groups gives opportunities again for reaching teenagers. All are thoroughly Biblical. It is very interesting that God as Creator dominates and underlines the comments about science that were expressed earlier. This is an issue much more important to teenagers than to many older Christians.

It is also interesting that this question was answered so seriously. The caricatures of God as spoilsport and policeman included in the question were dismissed out of hand. More school teenagers pictured Him as an old man than church teenagers—with a combined percentage of just 25%.

The significant variations in these figures are also interesting. The school figures varied rather more than the church ones. In both, however, commitment and gender were important variables. Age was important at school but not at church, as the graphs of Figure 29 make clear. The change in school teenagers was invariably at the age of 15 and 16 when the picture declined, but at 17 or above generally recovered. This again agrees with earlier findings that 15 is the critical age for belief change with teenagers.

The church figures did not vary much by denomination except that 28% of Methodist teenagers thought of God as Mother and 65% of Catholic teenagers considered God as Saviour. There is an otherwise remarkable degree of conformity, which can only be helpful for the future. Beliefs did vary by churchmanship, however, with the five substantive pictures (the fifth is God as Judge) all being more widely accepted by evangelicals than non-evangelicals.

Respondents were asked to give other, personal, pictures of God. These are examples from the two samples:

| *School teenagers* | *Church teenagers* |
|---|---|
| • Eternal force of the Universe | • A King |
| • Spirit/higher source | • Everything good |
| • A blob of light | • Positive force of creation |
| • Forgiver | • Preacher |
| • Helper | • Ruler over all the world |
| • Listener | • Good listener |
| • Decision maker | • Ultimate form of supreme being |
| • Person who cares for me | • Protector |
| • Friend (many gave this) | • Friend (many gave this) |
| • Someone extremely powerful | • Lion/element of fear involved |
| • Onlooker | • Teacher and guide |
| • Adviser | • Someone who's always there |

So many who wrote anything wrote 'Friend' or 'my best friend'. How true is the verse, 'There is a friend who sticks closer than a brother,'[8] and it may well be this is a text likely to be specially powerful for reaching teenagers. I personally know one young man who found Christ as Saviour through this verse. The friendship of God is therefore a very appealing characteristic for teenagers. Phil Moon, head of CYFA, part of the Youth and Children's Division of CPAS, wrote, 'Give them responsibilities and treat them as your friends, because that's what we want to develop,'[9] and suggests one positive way of encouraging this is to go away with them for a weekend or a holiday.

Unlike an Australian study where the 'idea of God as redeemer had little appeal to the under 18 year old group yet they strongly identified Jesus as Saviour'[10] this study suggests

God as Saviour is high in teenage belief with the need to know Jesus as Saviour less strong.

## Picture of Jesus

The questionnaire also asked teenagers 'Who do you think Jesus Christ is/was?' Answers were very correct:

- 68% said 'He is the Son of God'
- 14% a 'very wise human being'
- 7% an 'ordinary human being'
- 7% 'Someone who never existed'
- 2% a 'spaceman'
- 2% didn't know.

These were the school answers, which did not vary by age of pupils. Girls more than boys were inclined to say Jesus was the Son of God (72 against 63%). As might be expected, answers varied by religion: 78% of Christians said Jesus was the Son of God, and a surprisingly high 57% of other religions agreed, as did 44% of those with no religion. 21% of other religions said Jesus was 'a very wise human being' and 14% 'an ordinary human being'.

Church answers were 92, 4, 2, 1 and 1% respectively with no-one saying they didn't know. These did not vary by denomination, but evangelicals more than non-evangelicals said Christ is the Son of God (95 against 90%). These answers are consistent across all ages, both genders, and all areas and environments too.

Both school and church teenagers gave varying answers to the majority view that Jesus is the Son of God by the strength of their commitment, as in Table 60.

Four out of five teenagers take the orthodox view that Jesus is the Son of God. Fifteen out of every sixteen who are strongly committed Christians do so too. Those who have renounced the faith are those who disagree most, closely followed by those who have never been a Christian. This suggests two things:

Table 60: Agreement that 'Jesus Christ is the Son of God', by Christian commitment

| Christian commitment | Church teenagers % | School teenagers % | All Teenagers % | Total number (100%) |
|---|---|---|---|---|
| Strong | 98 | 89 | 93 | 368 |
| Weak | 95 | 79 | 86 | 880 |
| Unsure | 82 | 67 | 74 | 329 |
| No longer | 55 | 29 | 41 | 60 |
| Never | 55 | 46 | 50 | 250 |
| Overall | 92 | 68 | 79 | 1,885 |

- We should be able to build on this solid foundation when explaining the gospel to teenagers
- We need to help the small number of the strongly committed who do not yet accept Christ's deity.

The proportion of school teenagers who believed that Jesus Christ is the Son of God is similar to the 70% Leslie Francis found in a study on 'Believing without belonging.'[11] He found, however, that some practising teenagers did not always agree with the basic tenets of the faith, something that is confirmed as we look at answers to the question on how to become a Christian.

### Understanding of Christian commitment

We have looked already at Leslie Francis' work based on a sample of 200 sixth formers. In the RAKT study we have answers to a related question by about the same number of sixth formers, but augmented by many younger teens in the schools selected. Answers given are in Table 61.

The table reveals a woeful ignorance of basic theology. As the lad quoted at the beginning of the chapter said, the devil believes in God too. That four out of five teenagers make this the criterion leaves much to be said both for the church

*Table 61: Opinions on what makes a person a Christian?*

| What makes a person a Christian? | School % | Church % | All % |
|---|---|---|---|
| Believing in God | 75 | 83 | 79 |
| Believing the Bible is true | 59 | 57 | 58 |
| Knowing Jesus as personal Saviour | 34 | 67 | 49 |
| Being baptized/christened | 43 | 34 | 39 |
| Going to church | 41 | 33 | 37 |
| Leading a good life | 26 | 30 | 28 |
| Being born in the UK | 8 | 1 | 5 |
| Something else | 7 | 8 | 7 |
| Don't know | 11 | 2 | 7 |
| Total number (100%) | 1,051 | 857 | 1,908 |

teaching as well as RE lessons. The second criterion, and the only other to command a majority among all teenagers, relates to the Bible—is it true?

The third criterion, knowing Jesus as personal Saviour, is accepted by two-thirds of church teenagers and a third of school teenagers, amounting to virtually half the teenagers. It is the one criterion which separates church and school teenagers strongly. Being baptized and going to church are acceptable as criteria to almost two in every five. The importance of leading a good life reflects (at similar percentages) the finding found earlier that being a Christian means being 'a good person'. This underlines the random selection of schools for the RAKT study; they had no special bias.

How did the answers vary? Not very much by age: 13 and 14 year olds at school felt believing the Bible more important than other age groups (67 against 52%), and those aged 11–14 felt going to church more important than older teens did (45 against 31%). School boys more than school girls put being born in the UK as a criterion (12 against 5%), knowing Jesus as personal Saviour (37 against 30%) and also leading a good life (29 against 23%). Believing in God was important for

Christians (76%) but less so for those of other religions (62%, of which the largest group, the Muslims, put 54%). Those of no religion scored 69%. Those who had had a religious experience were more inclined to define a Christian as knowing Jesus as personal Saviour (46 against 29%) as were those who believed we could know God personally (51 against 25%). Answers varied by commitment also but similarly as for church teenagers.

Church teenagers were similar to school ones at the younger ages. Those who went to church every week were likely to say knowing Jesus as personal Saviour makes a person a Christian (69 against 53% for less regular attendance). The church teenagers figures did vary however by other factors as shown in Tables 62 and 63, and Figure 30.

The main variations in opinions of what makes a person a Christian are:

- New/House church strength and Roman Catholic weakness in knowing Jesus as personal Saviour

- Roman Catholic strength in leading a good life and being baptized/christened

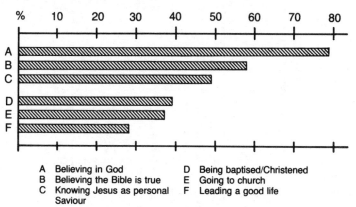

|   |   |   |   |
|---|---|---|---|
| A | Believing in God | D | Being baptised/Christened |
| B | Believing the Bible is true | E | Going to church |
| C | Knowing Jesus as personal Saviour | F | Leading a good life |

Figure 30: Criteria for being a Christian

*Table 62: Criteria for Christianity, by denomination*

| What makes a person a Christian? | Anglican % | Methodist % | Baptist % | New/ House Church % | Other Independent % | Other Free % | Roman Catholic % | Overall % |
|---|---|---|---|---|---|---|---|---|
| Believing in God | 88 | 85 | 75 | 67 | 77 | 85 | 84 | 83 |
| Believing the Bible is true | 62 | 60 | 56 | 50 | 59 | 61 | 43 | 57 |
| Knowing Jesus as personal Saviour | 61 | 81 | 85 | 95 | 85 | 71 | 34 | 67 |
| Being baptized/christened | 34 | 24 | 27 | 26 | 30 | 31 | 56 | 34 |
| Going to church | 34 | 38 | 21 | 14 | 44 | 38 | 40 | 33 |
| Leading a good life | 26 | 22 | 21 | 7 | 21 | 34 | 60 | 30 |
| Being born in the UK | 1 | 2 | 0 | 0 | 0 | 2 | 1 | 1 |
| Something else | 7 | 9 | 4 | 17 | 3 | 7 | 10 | 8 |
| Don't know | 2 | 2 | 2 | 0 | 0 | 1 | 2 | 2 |
| Total number (100%) | 302 | 58 | 103 | 42 | 61 | 167 | 134 | 867 |

Table 63: *Criteria for Christianity, by commitment and churchmanship*

| Picture | Christian commitment | | | | | Evangelical % | Non-evangelical % | Overall % |
| | Strong % | Weak % | Unsure % | No longer % | Never % | | | |
|---|---|---|---|---|---|---|---|---|
| Believing in God | 77 | 88 | 77 | 100 | 88 | 81 | 84 | 83 |
| Believing the Bible is true | 57 | 60 | 43 | 82 | 67 | 61 | 53 | 57 |
| Knowing Jesus as personal Saviour | 79 | 59 | 62 | 82 | 71 | 78 | 52 | 67 |
| Being baptised/ christened | 33 | 38 | 27 | 37 | 21 | 31 | 39 | 34 |
| Going to church | 31 | 34 | 28 | 46 | 58 | 31 | 38 | 33 |
| Leading a good life | 27 | 32 | 29 | 36 | 42 | 21 | 42 | 30 |
| Being born in the UK | 0 | 1 | 1 | 0 | 0 | 1 | 1 | 1 |
| Something else | 11 | 6 | 9 | 0 | 4 | 8 | 7 | 8 |
| Don't know | 1 | 1 | 7 | 0 | 0 | 1 | 2 | 2 |
| Total number (100%) | 271 | 438 | 113 | 11 | 24 | 465 | 402 | 867 |

- Other Independent strength and New/House Church weakness in going to church
- Evangelical strength in knowing Jesus as personal Saviour
- Non-evangelical strength in leading a good life
- Those not sure if they are a Christian being weaker generally in what makes a person a Christian
- The strength by those no longer Christian in believing in God, believing the Bible is true and knowing Jesus as personal Saviour
- Those never a Christian emphasizing going to church and leading a good life.

The question asked if there were other things that could make a person a Christian. The following is a sample of answers from the different samples.

*School teenagers*

- Being prepared to aid others
- Being brought up as Christians
- Giving life to Jesus
- Believing in oneself
- Trying to do all God wishes
- Believing there is only one God
- Being nice and helpful to other people
- Having no set rules for being a Christian
- Realizing people matter, not material wealth
- Being brought up in a Christian society
- Speaking about God
- Believing that Jesus is your Lord and ruler

*Church teenagers*

- Trusting God to take away your sins
- Not ignoring God the rest of the week
- Asking for forgiveness from sins
- Having a strong faith in God
- Believing Jesus died and rose to help us
- Believing God is the only way to eternal life
- Loving life, caring for all
- Trying to live as Jesus did
- Believing Jesus rose from death
- Believing in creation
- Helping through charities
- Accepting Jesus as Lord

58% of teenagers think that believing the Bible is true makes a person a Christian. We did not directly ask a question about the Bible as such—there was no room to cover everything—but this question comes as close to it as we can. In a sample of 1,013 American respondents, George Barna found that 65% agreed that the 'Bible . . . is totally accurate in all that it teaches,'[12] a percentage similar to ours.

## Belief in heaven and hell

The teenagers who were interviewed were asked if they believed in God, heaven, hell, reincarnation and Jesus, and they gave the answers (in Table 64).

This shows that the further teenagers are away from the church the less they believe in God, Jesus, heaven or hell. They increasingly believe in reincarnation, however. Also a growing proportion say they believe in none of these five at all. It is interesting that three churchgoers, one ex-churchgoer and two non-churchgoers believed in all of them, despite the inherent illogicality in the list. Small numbers of teenagers may believe in reincarnation, but that any do at all is a worrying feature. The overall percentage believing in God is similar to the proportion of school teenagers (78%) who similarly believed, mentioned earlier.

The percentages for heaven, hell and reincarnation compare with the Gallup surveys in 1986: of those aged 18–24 in that study 46% believed in heaven, 23% in hell and 29% in reincarnation,[13] lower than we found for heaven and hell, but our sample is small, and their age range is higher.

The chapter on church attendance referred to Fowler's work on faith development. Teenagers cover stages 2–4 in his model. An assessment among Roman Catholics based on this work covers changes in belief in such items as we have been considering over these stages. Of course stages 2–4 are not confined to teenagers, but it is interesting that those opting for literal belief in God at stage 2 were 92%, stage 3 95% and then fell to 85% at stage 4. Likewise the divinity of Christ

*Table 64: Belief in God, Jesus, heaven, hell and reincarnation*

| Belief in . . . | Church goers % | Ex-church goers % | Non-churchgoer % | Overall % |
|---|---|---|---|---|
| God | 100 | 88 | 63 | 79 |
| Jesus | 100 | 83 | 65 | 78 |
| Heaven | 100 | 88 | 60 | 78 |
| Hell | 63 | 49 | 26 | 41 |
| Reincarnation | 19 | 22 | 40 | 29 |
| None of these | 0 | 5 | 19 | 10 |
| Total number (100%) | 16 | 41 | 43 | 100 |

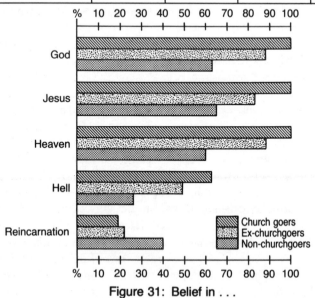

Figure 31: Belief in . . .

scores respectively 88, 91 and 78%, and a belief in the afterlife 57, 57 and 48%.[14] Our figures are broadly comparable to these, even though the interviewees were too few to justify an analysis by age.

An earlier study of 1,085 young people staying at London Central YMCA included asking about their beliefs.[15] Of those aged 16 to 21, 28% believed in reincarnation, 61% in God, and 48% that Jesus Christ is the Son of God. The first figure is almost identical to our findings (29%). The second is similar to the 67% we found among school teenagers (at beginning of this section), but the 68% found believing that Jesus Christ is the Son of God is higher than in the YMCA sample. The question was not asked identically. The YMCA asked specifically about belief; our question was simply 'Who do you *think* Jesus Christ is/was?' Believing and thinking are not necessarily the same.

Finally, a study based on teenagers in the South West of England[16] found that 80% believed Jesus is the Son of God, just one figure from extensive interviews, but again in similar order of magnitude to the others.

These studies all confirm in different ways, at different times and in different places that the bulk of teenagers take an orthodox view of Jesus Christ, well over the majority believe in God, a slight majority believe in the after life/heaven/hell, and a minority, just over a quarter, accept reincarnation.

This is not the theology of people likely to be converted next week, but it is the theology of the large number of nominal and notional Christians in England today—who number 55% of the population.[17] In other words, what we have found, to put it in grandiose terms, is that the belief system with which most teenagers leave school fits them for the nominal/notional Christianity which is, and has been, so much part of the English Christian scene. It used to be said that 'Nominal Christians are dying off'—literally! This survey, however, indicates the rise of a new generation of nominal Christians, perpetuating the lifeless faith of their predecessors. It is important to know that the pool of notional Christianity, static during the 1980s, is likely to continue the same in the 1990s. We are turning out nominal Christians (who still believe in God), with little strategy at a national level to reach them and patchy effort at local level.

## Values

The forms used included no direct question on teenagers' values, but it may be helpful to indicate briefly a few sources of such information for those interested. 'Values, if they are regarded as something outside the world of what we call facts, are expressions of the will. They are things that we desire, not rock solid realities on which we can either build or be wrecked'[18] said Bishop Lesslie Newbigin introducing 'The Gospel and our Culture' consultation in 1992.

Archbishop George Carey in the same consultation went on to say,[19] 'The connection between morality and religion is no longer self-evident to many people. So much so that an exploration of the connection between goodness and godliness is likely to be misunderstood. Not for a moment would I suggest that atheists cannot be good or that Christians have a monopoly of goodness. Rather, we may ask why it is that so many human beings—atheists, agnostics and believers alike—go beyond self interest in their behaviour. Is our capacity to be good in ways that go beyond our self-interest a sign of God's presence in the world? Since Christians believe that all humankind is made in God's image, we have no difficulty in recognizing that image of God's goodness in the life of atheists as well as believers. Atheists can hardly be expected to agree, but can certainly not ask Christians to restrict our world-view so as to exclude them.'

The book, *Teenage beliefs*[20] includes many incidents reflecting the new values of teenagers who had become Christians as well as their beliefs. 67 were interviewed between 1985 and 1988 in England and Wales; questions included ones on the difference being a Christian made to them and the way they now behaved as a result.

The annual British Social Attitudes Report[21] covers many issues. Two control questions always include age and frequency of religious attendance and/or denomination. Some years they probe issues like honesty. For example, the 1988 study asked whether you would keep £5 you found: 87% of those aged 18–24 said they would. For £20 69% in the same age group said YES and for £100 32% affirmed they would. Older people were less likely to keep any money they found. It is possible to get from the researchers, Social and Community Planning Research, computer tables breaking down variations by both age and religious observance.

Some of Leslie Francis' work looks specifically at values. In his YMCA study[22], for example, he gives the following results:

Table 65: Those agreeing values

| Value | 16–21 % | 22–23 % |
|---|---|---|
| Friends | 95 | 95 |
| Appearance | 89 | 89 |
| Moral values | 77 | 84 |
| Saving money | 74 | 68 |
| To own my own home | 73 | 74 |
| What other people think | 70 | 72 |
| Politics | 42 | 52 |
| Having a good time | 36 | 29 |
| Religion | 35 | 28 |

He found 'an important relationship between age and value ascribed to religion, morals and politics'. The values of religion declined, as did having a good time, whereas the values of politics and morals rose.

Occasional surveys among Christians or from a Christian perspective include Arkle Bell of Scripture Union's MA dissertation[23] on beliefs and values of young people and reviews of texts on this subject, including John Benington's *Culture, Class and Christian Beliefs*[24] and Roger Mitchell's *Searching for Values.*[25]

Research studies exploring teenage values with no reference to a Christian dimension include a Trustee Savings Bank study by the Research Business in April 1992,[26] which found that 'the traditional teenage preoccupations of pop music, fashion and junk food were ousted by concern for family, friends, health, world peace and animal welfare' from the 600 young people they interviewed. As with the Gallup study of 14–16 year olds[27] they found a concern among younger teens about 'the need to achieve good examination results to get good jobs.'[28]

Christian studies from other countries include the Canadian *Teen Trends*[29] already cited which found that 'people who go to church place a greater value on those virtues which enhance collective living. People who "love their neighbours" are forgiving, generous and ready to work hard for others. But most Canadians, including the vast majority of our young

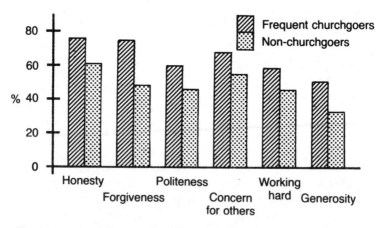

Figure 32: Canadian value differences between churchgoers and others

people, don't go to church. The consequences are alarming. We are headed in the direction of becoming less honest, polite and concerned for others.'[30] They give the results in Figure 27.

Another frequent researcher in North America is George Barna who publishes an enormous amount of material. Some of this relates to values and is broken down by age-group. Here are some examples from one recent volume:[31]

Table 66: Value beliefs by age

| Value | Percentage who agree | |
|---|---|---|
| | 18–26 % | 27 or older % |
| 'My free time is important to me.' | 95 | 92 |
| 'My career is important to me.' | 89 | 78 |
| 'My community is important to me.' | 88 | 92 |
| 'Government and politics are important to me.' | 67 | 78 |
| 'Abortion is morally wrong.' | 54 | 59 |
| 'Lying is sometimes necessary.' | 51 | 33 |
| 'The values and life-styles shown on music videos generally reflect ways most people live and think these days.' | 38 | 34 |

These show similar differences in the importance of a career for young people as observed in Britain, but slightly less concern for the community. They show a much greater willingness to lie!

### Summary

- Church youth see themselves primarily as kind, intelligent, popular, religious but lonely.
- Being a Christian is perceived primarily as religious belief, and least by public practice.
- 67% of school teenagers believe in God, a percentage widely supported by other studies.
- God is primarily seen as Creator, Love and Father. Churchgoing teens add Saviour.
- 68% of school teens and 92% of churchgoing teens regard Jesus as the Son of God.
- A Christian is taken as a person who believes in God, believes the Bible is true and who knows Jesus as their personal Saviour.
- 78% of teenagers believe in heaven, 41% in hell and 29% in reincarnation.
- Friends, appearance, free time and career are all especially important for young people.

# 7

# *Reaching and Keeping Teenagers*

Sir, I have much sympathy for my fellow non-Christian, the imam, who is said to pray that the British would start to honour the name of Jesus again (Clifford Longley, May 2nd). Only last week I was told by a class at a supposedly Church of England School that the Last Supper was the final meal before a nuclear war!

It benefits none of the other faiths that the level of Christian knowledge and religious awareness is so poor in this country. One result is that moral imperatives are lacking and society loses much of its coherence and stability.

Another result is that religious toleration declines, for usually there is little respect for the beliefs of others who do not value their own religious heritage.

Amen to the imam's prayer.

> Yours faithfully
> Rabbi Jonathan Romain
> in a letter to *The Times*[1]

The motivation behind the research which led to this book was the simple fact which emerged from the 1989 English Church Census: 91% of those aged 15–19 in England did not go to church, an increase over ten years from the 87% of 1979. How then do we reach—and keep—our teenagers, reaching them for the church, for the Gospel, for Christ? Keeping them for a life of commitment, discipleship and service?

91% is a considerable number of young people. Yet we have hardly looked at some of the hardest cases—those with unstable families, the lowest social backgrounds, those caught up in cults, those who are involved in drugs, crime and violence. Yes, of course, they are part of the 91% and as desperately need to become Christian just as much as any other. Many work with such and that is fine. But whatever percentage they may add up to—and that depends on your definition to some extent—they are still in the minority. Yes, they need help but we must be careful not to assume that because of that the majority do not need help too. They need it just as much and if we concentrate here on the more 'normal' teenager who isn't yet a drug addict, hasn't got caught by the police, is not normally violent, that is simply because we need to reach the majority of our teenagers and to think through workable ways of doing so. By all means then let's adjust these methods, or develop new ones, for the 'tougher' young people, but let's rescue as many as we can while we can. Going for what might seem the softer underbelly is a perfectly reasonable strategy, although some will immediately say that it is not any easier in so doing! What then are some of the strategies and implications that emerge from this research project, if we are to be faithful to its main purpose? I would like to suggest seven.

## 1. Strengthen commitment to the under 12s

It was very clear that Sunday School exerts a profound influence on young people. It not only gives them a better framework of understanding about the Bible and its teaching, but it gets them used to the idea of church and what it means. They are introduced to God, Jesus and the Holy Spirit in some way.

The term 'Sunday School' is used to include the various youth organizations working in a Christian context with young people. The Boys' Brigade, the Girls' Brigade, the Campaigners, the Covenanters, Crusaders, the Salvation Army youngsters are all included where these work in conjunction with a local church or churches as so many do. Not that the monthly church parade seemed to help very much—that very often put youngsters off more than on—but the church contact outside parades is helpful.

Leslie Francis' research has shown conclusively that the religious stirrings of young people emerge in the primary school ages. Even pre-school church contacts can aid in the teenage years.[2] Infant baptism is too early to make any decisive influence but religious formation happens in the years up to 10. Contact with the church then can yield considerable dividends, sometimes well beyond the years of adolescence. The testimony of Mrs Doreen Irvine, who attended a Salvation Army Sunday School when she was young for just two weeks and was given a hymn book which later helped her find Christ despite being involved in witchcraft in this country at the highest level is testimony to the power of Sunday School movements.[3] Rev Robert Raikes, the founder of the Sunday School movement, founded an institution whose influence has been wide and strong.

The Welsh, Scottish and 1989 English Church Censuses make it clear that Sunday School *must* be integrated within the larger church family to be successful. This is not just an organizational link but a spiritual link also. Sunday School is not an isolated activity for children but a specialist activity for part of the church, and it must be seen that way. Effective integrated Sunday School work lays a valuable foundation on which to build in the teenage years.

Integration, of course, needs to go hand in hand with effective teaching. Project work is a popular approach to Bible teaching. Following through young people's concerns (such as with the environment) is critical also.

'Understand that the crux of the spiritual war today is over children; that the focus of strategy of the enemy is for little minds and hearts; that the Dragon waits by the Woman not to kill her, but her baby.'[4,5]

## 2. Hold specialist youth services

It is all too obvious today that young people have their own culture! Their clothes, their language, their music, their habits, their magazines all make them unmistakable! And they want it to be that way most of the time. One survey[6] called them 'Spoilt Brats' and said they were:

- More affluent than any youth generation in British history
- Brought up by the most divorced, least child-orientated parents ever
- Part forced, part encouraged to grow up earlier than before
- As sexually promiscuous as the last generation, despite the threat of AIDS
- Materialistic—looking after number one, having been brought up in the Thatcherite 80s
- Resentful of the increasing numbers of old people
- A tough generation to communicate with, requiring new thinking in marketing and advertising to do so.

In other words, almost a breed apart. If the secular commercial interests reckon on new thinking and marketing, so should the church. Churches which have experimented with specialist youth services, usually late on a Sunday evening, complete with their own music (with a beat), songs, video perhaps and different manners of worship, have been brilliantly successful, if popularity and large numbers are anything to go by. Such ensures that the words used are understood. Lines like 'consubstantial, co-eternal while all endless ages run' will *not* appear![7] Some churches are so desperate to reach their young people that they are willing to try anything! Well, try specialist youth services.

The young people we interviewed generally supported such services. Nothing commands universal support, but young people were enthusiastic about this possibility. It caters to their psychology, to where society (via the media) tells them they ought to be, it gives them freedom to experiment, it allows them the comfort of familiar music and speech idioms. So, go for it!

I believe it is important, however, that we do not make the mistake of having special youth services as we did initially with the Sunday School. The Sunday School was the children's church and in the beginning rarely integrated with the church. Youth Services might be seen as the contemporary equivalent of a Teenage Sunday School (upgraded to allow for cultural and age differences), and therefore advisable. They might be so seen, but all that does is to make them the Youth Church. By all means give youngsters special attention, but they are still part of the whole church. The methods of integration will be totally different from the Sunday School—the analogy is totally inept here—but they must be just as real. House groups, discussion groups, youth clubs are all possible, and all will be attended. But just normal contact with adults will do. Adults need to talk to young people the same as they talk to anyone else. For some years I've taken young people out for an evening dinner as occasion and opportunity allows. This is invariably appreciated. They may not look like adults (by the way they dress) but they like being treated as adults. Why not do so? They love, absolutely love, to talk and talk and talk. Well, let them! Show you're interested in them.

Mention was made earlier of the Dallas church which had a 400% increase in teenagers attending it in a year because adults in the church were encouraged to invite them to their homes for a weekend. They felt part of the church, integrated, and so stayed. They *belonged*.

Specialist Youth Services are an example at one end of a scale. The other end is simple, *participation* by young people in the work and worship of the church. It has been suggested this is one reason why the Roman Catholics and New/House Churches are especially able to retain teenagers. There is a tendency for churches run by adults simply to 'make provision for young people.'

Sydney Jones, Brigade Secretary of the Boys' Brigade wrote,

'They have much to contribute to the management of the church and adolescents are capable of being involved in decision making about worship, witness and sustaining fellowship. They are used to being involved in decision making at school and at home whereas at church they tend to be recipients of what others arrange. It takes courage to use those whose faith may be new and fragile but we have to get away from describing young people as the Church of tomorrow. They are the Church of today—it is theirs as much as it is anyone else's and they must be encouraged to take ownership of it. We do not have Old People's Councils so why have Youth Councils? In my view participation by young people in the whole life of the church, including its management, is an issue which must be addressed if we are to hold on to them.'

In his major book on nominal Christians, *Winning Them Back*[8] Professor Eddie Gibbs suggests 'Decentralise in order to impact the world more extensively', and he suggests the church provide support systems to facilitate witness, and develop contextualized approaches to witness. He is talking primarily of reaching nominal adults but these principles are equally relevant for reaching nominal teenagers. It should be noted that the surveys found relatively few atheist teenagers, but scores of nominal ones. Many teenagers have open minds. Giving them an opportunity of attending something relevant for them, such as their own youth service, is likely therefore to make very considerable impact. The churches which have already tried this route have proved it so. For those who like belonging, it gives them something to belong to.

## 3. Broaden their understanding

Surveys have shown a number of areas where teenagers feel genuinely confused. One of these is the area of creation and science. Teenagers believe that churchgoers must accept the account of a seven-day creation which many feel science disproves. It is the essential clash of evolution versus creation, and evolution is invariably taught as a fact in all the branches of science teenagers study. The church has ducked this issue for too long. There is one section of the church, the so-called 'creationists', who have published many books underlining Biblical and archaeological support for their viewpoint. There is undoubtedly considerable evidence to justify many of their statements and which threaten normal understanding of the evolutionary position. Unfortunately the way in which some of what is said irritates. The willingness to listen to objections, and to be less than totally dogmatic in their position does not come easily to those who have had to think through their beliefs the hard way. But to do so would make their teaching more acceptable. And that teaching still needs to be heard. However it is done, here is an urgent issue, requiring a language teenagers can understand, which needs to be tackled quickly.

Notwithstanding the illogicality that many more teenagers believe in God than go to church, teenagers tend to say 'Those who believe in God should go to church.' Being a Christian is seen as being primarily a system of beliefs, reflected through relationships. And yes, . . . it might issue in church attendance also! Few teenagers outside the church appreciate the spiritual dimension to life. This was very clear in one of Leslie Francis' major studies. Teenagers think, and teenagers certainly feel— mind and heart are active, over-active sometimes. But there is a whole new dimension of spirit which most teenagers need to realize is there. The way to God has to come through the gates that are already open—eargate and eyegate. They need therefore more knowledge on spiritual issues which is where so much RE teaching seems to fall down. What is faith? Who are people of faith? What did they do? Why did they do it? Answers to such questions need not only be in historical references but somehow also allow teenagers to meet people of faith today. Some years ago one Southampton school ran a series of assemblies—for a whole term—where each Wednesday a speaker spoke on 'My faith and my job'. Speakers ranged from an aeronautical engineer to an ambulance driver. The pupils really appreciated these talks, as spirituality was seen there in front of them.

The one area of close agreement between churchgoing and non-churchgoing teenagers is that of relationships. Both agree that good relationships are important, and a Christian naturally is expected to have and maintain good relationships. But what is a relationship? We are not using the word in the sense of a boy-girl relationship. Good relationships involve forgiveness of others' mistakes, being considerate towards other people's feelings, appreciating others' viewpoints, helping people when necessary, treating other people equally (and that does not just apply to racial issues), being friendly, being on good terms with others.

For a Christian all these are important, but non-churchgoers appreciate their importance too. How can one actually become a 'good' person? Primarily through the power of the transforming Holy Spirit. This then might be seen as just another part of the spirituality issue just described, but it is actually more specific. There is a woeful misunderstanding in nominal and notional Christians of the Person and Work of the Holy Spirit, and across the bridge of the need for making good relationships, it may be possible to help teenagers outside the church understand more of the work of this third person of the Trinity. Charismatic experience is powerful, but the work of the Holy Spirit is wider than just focusing on the 'charismatic' front, as teenagers would define it. Here also is an area where clearer understanding needs to develop.

### 4. Deepen their theology

This leads on to the question of keeping teenagers. How do we keep them? Not by marginalizing them. Some churches spend more on flowers than their young people. We keep them partly by deepening their theology.

It will have been obvious even to the most casual reader that the theology of many teenagers, even churchgoing teenagers, leaves a lot to be desired! Their perception, their language, their concepts of Christian things seem to have developed more from the world than the authorities behind the faith. This may be more true in non-evangelical churches than evangelical, but the findings make it apparent that all is not rosy in evangelical gardens either. Both communities have got work to do!

What does this mean in practice? More Bible knowledge, in a phrase; an apologetics framework, in another. But these phrases are too simplistic. RE syllabuses give less weight to Bible knowledge. And it is not knowledge per se that drives theology, though it may be a good part of it. Give 15 year olds (year 9) reasons why it is acceptable to believe Jesus rose from the dead. It is applied knowledge, which roots theory into life, which makes for effective life principles. So teenagers need the opportunity to discuss hard questions, and at length when required (that is, past midnight with umpteen cups of coffee!) The issues have to be argued, tossed about, and thought through. And they have to be the practical issues of the day for them—abortion, drugs, alcohol, sex, the environment, the elderly and the future (though not their future). Let's not be afraid of facing them with the truth for 'the truth shall set you free'.[9]

How can we teach them that theology? Only a small fraction of teenagers can be reached through the churches; all teenagers can theoretically be reached through the schools. Additional help in, and support for, RE work in schools is needed, so that the facts of Christian history, Christian people and Christian belief can be better known and understood, working alongside existing staff.

In reality adults have to realise what Winkie Pratney has long said, 'You were never their age.' Today's teenagers have grown up with total media exposure, with the possibility of no permanent job, maturing physically earlier, making major decisions sooner, possibly without an expected family structure, unsupervised free time, no moral clue in society, and often a sheer inability to cope.[10] This is their world, and leaders, adults, youth workers have both to relate to it and bring faith principles to impinge upon it. And it is not easy to find people with the aptitude, the willingness and the time. They will often also require training.

In addition, the methods by which many adults were taught are inappropriate for today's learning methods. GCSEs are about enquiry, teasing information out. It is not notes dictated by the teacher that today gets students through examinations. Those dedicated to helping teenagers need to be willing to be retaught themselves. Perhaps that's the most scary bit of the process and why so few get there.

## 5. Challenge them—but not too much

How do we keep our teenagers? By giving them 'a model for radical discipleship,' as Andy Hickford said when I interviewed him. Tony Campolo, the American sociologist, said, 'Young people leave the church because we don't challenge them enough.' I'm sure that's true. Let them get involved in the church, even before they join. Utilize their entrepreneurial spirit.[11]

Challenge is there aplenty. Society all round needs help. Part of the way the New/House Churches have built commitment into their young people is to challenge them—to help with evangelism, to lead with their music, to be involved in leadership. With one of my sons I attended a local Ichthus Fellowship meeting (having obtained permission from the overall leader, Roger Forster). My son told me it was 'a typical worship'. We sang, we prayed, we listened to a good sermon by someone I would judge to be in her mid-twenties, and we drank tea afterwards while we spoke to the pastor. He cared for this church of 70 members and was planning to plant another shortly. He had had one year's full-time training and spent a day a week with Roger Forster in a kind of day-release scheme. His age? 'I'm 22,' he told us. Let us not forget that

George Whitefield was an international evangelist at 26; Charles Simeon was inducted at Holy Trinity Church, Cambridge at 23 and Charles Spurgeon was drawing vast congregations to his church at 19.

Another of my sons is thinking of helping at a local hospice for a year. Another spent part of his holidays working with deprived youngsters. Is my family special? No—the needs are there, everywhere, and young people given the opportunity will respond.

Two teenagers in our church decided to take a year out between school and university. Both went overseas with missionary societies, one to do radio work in the Philippines, and the other to teach and administer in a French-speaking part of Africa. Both had an experience which will be with them for the rest of their lives. Operation Mobilisation has challenged thousands of youngsters through its Love Europe work, or evangelizing with literature and local meetings in Old Eastern Europe. Agapé, or Campus Crusade, works in dozens of countries. Youth With A Mission (YWAM) has an extensive programme worldwide. 'YWAM has played an important role in helping nascent charismatic communities among youth, (providing) discipleship training programmes not being supplied locally,' wrote a Catholic priest.[12] Such opportunities abound elsewhere too with many openings to help in Asia, America or Africa.

But while aimless young people might want challenge, we must be careful not to go over the top. Reasonable expectations is what they underlined in one survey reported earlier. Teenagers are not adult yet, they do not always react maturely, they sometimes take silly decisions, but to be able to make mistakes within a broad framework of acceptance encourages growth and deepens their development.

How do we keep our teenagers? By involving them from the start. Give them a safety net of relationships. Church attendance is only a part of the story. Give special attention at the critical transition period of 14 to 15—so many of the graphs dip here, and face them with the discipleship challenge at 17 to 18, when again so many experiment in so many ways.[13] Does this degree of challenge sound far too great? Perhaps your church isn't big enough to have such influence? It is true that churches with fewer than 26 adults often have difficulties in maintaining an effective young people's ministry[14]—often, but not always. You may just want to post up the following, which one Salvation Army Hall did.[15]

---

**The TEEN Commandments**

1) Stop and think before you drink
2) Don't let your parents down—remember they brought *you* up
3) Be humble enough to obey. You will be giving orders yourself some day
4) At the first moment turn away from unclean thinking
5) Don't show off when driving. If you want to show off, go to Brands Hatch
6) Choose friends on whom you can depend
7) Go to a place of worship regularly. God gives us the week, give Him back the hour
8) Choose your companions carefully. You will be judged by the company you keep
9) Avoid following the crowd. Be an engine not a carriage, a leader not a leaner
10) Even better, keep the original Ten Commandments

---

## 6. Make their faith special

How can we try and help our teenagers? 'Teenagers develop strong interests in ideals and ideologies as they search for personal identity,' writes a Christian psychologist.[16] Christianity may have bored them previously but notwithstanding they are often willing to make serious spiritual commitments, as the large numbers responding at Mission to London and Mission

England events in the mid-1980s made clear. 'They have a powerful need to strengthen their consciences and seek the meaning of life. They begin to integrate faith into their life system, making a pact with God.'[17] Jews have a special ceremony for their sons on their thirteenth birthday. Relatives and friends are invited, and on that occasion the 13 year old is declared a young adult, with increased responsibilities and freedoms. The parents make a verbal contract with their son. Indeed in some Conservative and Reformed Synagogues an analogous ceremony is now held for 13 year old girls.[18]

Christian parents could do something similar, writing a contract giving them new freedoms along with new responsibilities. For example, parents could agree in future to waive arbitrary bedtime rules (whilst necessary for children, it irritates teens). They could remind their children of spiritual responsibilities and encourage them to make some commitments, without parental pressure being applied. Relatives and friends could be invited to a 'covenant' signing ceremony, but guests should not bring gifts. 'Passage into adulthood has many emotional and spiritual implications which should not be confused with materialistic gain.'[19] Such a ceremony helps parents realize that their children are growing up and that they should treat them as reasoning adults, even if less mature. Subsequent communication with them needs to show especial love and respect. This concept is not identical to the Anglican service of Confirmation, a kind of equivalent to the Jewish Mizpah ceremony. That Confirmation was an important factor for subsequent church attendance for many underlines the value of something special for teenagers wanting to express a real commitment.

'If a child lives with security he learns faith'.[20]

We analysed all the school questionnaire answers by the marital status background of the parents of teenagers, about a fifth of whom came from homes without two married parents. Very few of the answers were significant because of this, showing the tremendous job most single parents are doing, often under extremely trying circumstances.

Making faith special for the child may have repercussions on the parents. 'Offspring frequently have a more profound effect on the spiritual development of their parents than does the pastor.'[21]

## 7. Love never ends[22]

I had been invited to preach one Sunday morning in the West country, and afterwards had lunch with the vicar and his family. One of his sons was present who had had an extremely emotional and stressful time at university which had mentally affected him. Communication with him, as I speedily found, was, to say the least, extraordinarily difficult. As I was driven to the station the vicar explained the situation and then simply said, 'In these circumstances, all we can do is to love and pray.' His solution is true—and not just for his son—but for all who would both seek to reach and to keep teenagers.

John Allen, the youth leader of Belmont Chapel in Exeter, a church with strong Christian Brethren connections, was asked what encourages young people to attend church in their teenage years. How, in effect, do you love them through? He replied, 'When you have a church which is observing discipline, teaching and the sacraments. Young people are integrated into the church when they feel a sense of belonging to the wider adult congregation. Young people learn and grow best in an environment where adults are also learning and growing'[23] (so they too have pencil and paper ready to take notes in a sermon). Following what the New/House Churches and Roman Catholics have learned, he went on, 'Sacraments and church disciplines are also important factors in helping teenagers to develop a lifelong commitment both to Christ and His Church.'[24] John Wimber said, 'People come when they have a job to do.'

Ian Vallance, a Scripture Union Schools worker, said,

'Churchgoers need to learn to accept and love teenagers for what they are, not for what they might become.' Mark Landreth-Smith, of the Coign Church, put it as 'teenagers require a loving and lively environment where they feel valued.' You love them by getting among them, not waiting for them to come to you. An attractive youth programme helps, but valuing them and welcoming them helps more. Nick Aiken of the Diocese of Guildford said, 'We need to appreciate them more.' 'Make them valued members of the Community,' urged Patrick Harrison of the Diocese of Arundel and Brighton, and added, 'give them opportunities to participate in the decision making in the parish.'

The transitions are important. A former Bishop of Southwark once said, 'We have moved from where Christianity is culture to where Christianity is choice.' We want young people both to choose Christianity and to stay with it. The teenage years are years of transition and we have to help in these periods. The glue which binds friends together is love, for love never fails. Not the cheap love of casual sex which is how so many teenagers translate the word, but a love which is 'patient and kind, not jealous or boastful, not arrogant or rude. Love does not insist on its own way; it is not irritable or resentful; it does not rejoice at wrong, but rejoices in the right. Love bears all things, believes all things, hopes all things, endures all things. Love never ends.'[25]

---

### Summary

- Use the Sunday School to reach as many as possible.
- Allow specific youth services, but integrate them.
- Answer teenagers' questions on creation, belief, the Spirit, thoroughly.
- Tackle relevant issues with realism.
- Challenge young people, but not overchallenge them.
- What about a formal but freely entered contract?
- What ever happens, keep on loving them!

## EPILOGUE

World Vision of Australia have been in the forefront of thinking through some of the principles and challenges in community development. In a recent listing they included the following item,[26] specifically looking at the concerns of the Third World. It is an astonishing list, and applies not only to needful aid programmes but also very readily to the development of Christian teenagers:

### The gift that releases

| IT'S NOT | IT IS |
|---|---|
| Money | Choice |
| Programmes | Solving a problem |
| Ready answers | Struggling together |
| Complexity | Simplicity |
| Speed | Process |
| Paternalism | Friendship |

# Appendix 1

# *Teenage Church Attendance by Different Categories*

In Chapter 3 figures were given for teenage (15–19 year old) church attendance in England in 1989. On average they were 7% of the total churchgoers, and an average of 9 teenagers per church. Similar analyses may be ascertained with other criteria, and are given in Table 68 with the figure in brackets denoting the average number of 15–19 year olds per church. 'Catholic' is in inverted commas since it includes some Anglicans and thus more than just the Roman Catholic church.

Other analyses have also been undertaken. The Salvation Army was 6% (6)[1], the Assemblies of God 9% (9)[2], and the Kent Baptist Association 6% (9)[3]. In West Yorkshire[4] the District figures were Bradford 6% (10), Caldersdale 5% (7), Kirklees 6% (8), Leeds 7% (14) and Wakefield 6% (8). In Surrey,[5] the district figures were Elmridge 8% (20), Epsom and Ewell 5% (11), Guildford 5% (8), Mole Valley 5% (7), Reigate and Banstead 5% (8), Runnymede 5% (8), Spelhorne 7% (11), Surrey Heath 8% (11), Tandridge 7% (9), Waverley 15% (an exceptional figure for unknown reasons) (21), Woking 5% (12). In London[6] the boroughs were Barking and Dagenham 8% (12), Barnet 7% (9), Bexley 7% (15), Brent 11% (36), Bromley 7% (15), Camden 5% (7), Croydon 6% (18), Ealing 5% (10), Enfield 9% (24), Greenwich 7% (10), Hackney 6% (6), Hammersmith and Fulham 5% (7), Haringey 9% (16), Harrow 9% (28), Havering 7% (14), Hillingdon 6% (12), Hounslow 7% (9), Islington 7% (7), Kensington and Chelsea

Table 68: Church attendance by 15–19 year olds by different categories

| Environment | | Churchmanship | | Denomination | |
|---|---|---|---|---|---|
| Towns | 8% (13) | 'Catholic' | 9% (29) | Independent | 16% (17) |
| Commuter rural | 8% ( 7) | Anglo-Catholic | 9% ( 8) | Pentecostal | 9% (12) |
| Mixed built-up areas | 8% (12) | Charismatic evangelical | 8% (12) | Afro-Caribbean | 9% (10) |
| Inner city | 7% (12) | Mainstream evangelical | 8% ( 5) | Roman Catholic | 8% (36) |
| City centre | 7% (11) | Broad evangelical | 6% (10) | Baptist | 7% ( 8) |
| Council estate | 7% (12) | Liberal | 6% ( 6) | Orthodox | 7% ( 8) |
| Suburban | 7% (14) | All others | 6% ( 6) | Other Free Churches | 6% ( 5) |
| Remote rural | 6% ( 3) | Broad | 5% ( 4) | Anglican | 5% ( 5) |
| | | Low Church | 5% ( 3) | Methodist | 5% ( 4) |
| | | | | United Reformed | 4% ( 4) |

| Church change | | When services held | | Congregation size | |
|---|---|---|---|---|---|
| Growing churches | 7% (10) | Morning only | 8% (16) | 50 or under | 5% ( 1) |
| Static churches | 7% ( 7) | Morning and evening | 7% ( 2) | 51–100 | 5% ( 3) |
| Declining churches | 6% ( 6) | Evening only | 4% (12) | 101–200 | 7% ( 9) |
| | | | | Over 200 | 10% (38) |

3% (9), Kingston-upon-Thames 9% (18), Lambeth 4% (5), Lewisham 7% (13), City of London 4% (6), Merton 10% (27), Newham 6% (9), Redbridge 8% (15), Richmond-upon-Thames 7% (17), Southwark 7% (10), Sutton 7% (15), Tower Hamlets 5% (5), Waltham Forest 6% (7), Wandsworth 6% (10), and Westminster 10% (23).

The denomination figures may be compared to a similar analysis by Leslie Francis in 1980[7] which gave the average number of teenagers (13–19, a slightly wider age group) per church as Roman Catholic (46), Ecumenical Centres (18), Church of England (16), Baptist (12), Methodist (10), United Reformed (10), Salvation Army (3), and Society of Friends (3).

These denominational figures for teenagers are based on the English Church Census results of numbers attending church for all age-groups. The actual figures per denomination were not published in *Prospects for the Nineties* but are given in Table 69 as basic reference data. The percentages by age-group (broken down by gender) were however given in the earlier volume.[8]

**Other recommended books**

Steve Chalke, *The Christian Youth Manual*, Kingsway, 1992
Mark Ashton, *Christian Youth Work*, Kingsway, 1986.
Roger Owen, *Parents Guide, 12–16*, Kingsway, 1988.
Pete Ward, *Youth Culture and the Gospel*, Marshall Pickering, 1992.
Pete Ward, *Worship and Youth Culture*, Marshall Pickering, 1993.

*Table 69: Church attenders by age and denomination 1989*

| Denomination | Under 15 | 15–19 | 20–29 | 30–44 | 45–64 | 65 or over | Total |
|---|---|---|---|---|---|---|---|
| Anglican | 348,000 | 73,600 | 126,200 | 250,300 | 359,500 | 334,300 | 1,491,900 |
| Baptist | 71,500 | 17,400 | 27,200 | 50,400 | 53,800 | 50,600 | 270,900 |
| Roman Catholic | 411,300 | 135,400 | 191,600 | 311,400 | 397,600 | 268,600 | 1,715,900 |
| Independent | 132,700 | 62,800 | 56,200 | 78,700 | 56,900 | 38,200 | 425,500 |
| Methodist | 116,200 | 23,600 | 36,700 | 64,300 | 118,700 | 152,800 | 512,300 |
| Orthodox | 2,900 | 900 | 1,500 | 1,700 | 3,100 | 2,200 | 12,300 |
| Other Churches | 30,600 | 6,200 | 9,300 | 16,400 | 24,100 | 27,000 | 113,600 |
| Pentecostal | 73,000 | 19,600 | 35,300 | 44,200 | 41,200 | 23,400 | 236,700 |
| URC | 35,300 | 5,500 | 9,200 | 20,400 | 34,500 | 44,400 | 149,300 |
| Total All Churches | 1,221,500 | 345,000 | 493,200 | 837,800 | 1,089,400 | 941,500 | 4,928,400 |
| *of which* free churches | 459,300 | 135,100 | 173,900 | 274,400 | 329,200 | 336,400 | 1,708,300 |

# Appendix 2
## *Methodology*

### 1. Questionnaires for church teenagers

In order to gauge the views of a wide range of teenage church attenders the sample of church teenagers was structured by denomination, churchmanship, environment and area. Seven denomination/churchmanship categories were used based on an analysis of current teenage church attendance from the English Church Census. The first six groups are approximately equal. The seventh was three times the size of the other groups.

1. Independent evangelical (including New/House Churches, Brethren and FIEC)
2. Baptist/Methodist evangelical
3. Other Free evangelical (including United Reformed Church, Afro-Caribbean churches, Salvation Army and Pentecostal)
4. Anglican evangelical
5. Free non-evangelical
6. Anglican non-evangelical
7. Roman Catholic

Churches in each of these categories were sampled in three areas (North, South and London). Within these areas churches were sampled in four environments (city centre, suburb, council estate and rural).

Churches were sampled from the MARC Europe computer

and were asked to participate in the survey. The table below shows the number of churches contacted in each area and the number which agreed to participate.

*Participating Churches*

| Number of churches contacted | Number agreeing to participate | Actual response | Response rate |
|---|---|---|---|
| North—248 | 71 | 48 | 68% |
| South—209 | 68 | 53 | 78% |
| London—159 | 53 | 37 | 70% |
| Total—616 | 192 | 138 | 72% |

Having agreed to take part in the survey, ministers were sent ten questionnaires to distribute to young people between the ages of 12 and 18 who regularly attended church.

The young people were provided with envelopes so that they could seal their reply in the envelope before returning it to their minister. They were assured that their questionnaire would not be looked at by their minister but would be returned directly to MARC Europe. Individual youngsters/churches could not be identified as the questionnaires were unmarked, ensuring confidentiality.

A total of 891 completed questionnaires were returned, an average of 6.5 per church. The response rate from city centre churches was 60%, suburb 78%, council estate 72% and rural 79%. The response rate from evangelical churches was 67% and 78% from non-evangelical. The response rate from Anglican churches was 94%, Baptist 91%, Roman Catholic 85%, Other Free churches 56%, Independent churches 52% and Methodist 40%.

## 2. Questionnaires for non-church teenagers

Teenagers who were not regular churchgoers were contacted through secondary schools. Schools which agreed to take part in the survey clustered in geographical areas close to responding churches. Schools in these areas were sampled and the head teachers were asked to allow their pupils to participate in the survey.

The table below shows the number of schools contacted in each area and the number which agreed to take part in the research project.

*Participating schools*

| Number of schools contacted | Number agreeing to participate | Actual response | Response rate |
|---|---|---|---|
| North— 28 | 15 | 10 | 66% |
| South— 43 | 20 | 16 | 80% |
| London— 52 | 11 | 5 | 45% |
| Total— 123 | 46 | 31 | 67% |

The participating schools were sent questionnaires to distribute across Years 7, 9, 11, and 13, ensuring that young people across the 12–18 age range participated. Questionnaires were distributed by teachers. Each pupil was given an envelope so that they could seal their reply before returning it to the teacher.

A total of 1,531 completed questionnaires were returned (an average of 49 per school), of which 1,131 were used for analysis purposes.

*Interviews with young people who do not attend church*

84 non-church attenders were interviewed in the three broad study areas (North, South and London).

A note was made of the geographical clustering of churches participating in the survey and interviews were conducted in the same areas, as follows:

North—Sheffield, Liverpool, Middlesbrough
South—Bristol, East Anglia, Southampton, Guildford, Kent
London

The majority of the interviewers were Frontier Youth Trust and Shaftesbury Society workers. Additional interviewers came from other Christian youth organizations and individual churches. Most received training from MARC Europe staff on conducting interviews.

The first question interviewees were asked concerned the frequency of their church attendance. The answer to this question was used to categorize them as either 'ex-church' or 'non-church'. 'Ex-church' teenagers were those who had attended church regularly in the past while 'non-church' teenagers were those who had never attended church regularly. 'Regular' church attendance was defined as at least once a month. A different interview schedule was used with the two groups of teenagers.

## Interviews with church attenders

Sixteen teenage church attenders were interviewed in the three broad study areas.

## Interviews with church leaders

To add further depth to the research project six 'key' youth leaders were interviewed, listed in the Acknowledgements. These people were chosen because of the breadth of their experience, covering local, regional and national youth work, and the range of denominations and organisations which they represent.

## Literature Search

In addition, studies undertaken by other people, surveys reported in the Christian or non-Christian press, articles, books written by teenage authorities were consulted and used as appropriate. The range of sources used is reflected in the Notes section, where full attribution is given.

## Census Analysis

The English Church Census data was specially analysed to pull out teenage information. This is incorporated where relevant, and is particularly seen in Appendix 1.

# Appendix 3
## *The Questionnaires*

## YOUNG PEOPLE'S SURVEY

This survey looks at how young people spend their spare time and what they think about religion and the church. Please help us by answering the following questions.

All your answers are confidential. Do not write your name on the questionnaire. Please put your completed questionnaire in the envelope provided and seal it. This will be returned straight to us. No one else will read your answers. Thank you for your help.

1. What do you do in your spare time? (Tick all boxes that apply)

| Play sport | Listen to music | Hang around with friends |
| Watch videos | Watch television | Spend time with boyfriend/girlfriend |
| Go to the pub | Go to a youth club | Go to church activities |
| Go to the cinema | Play arcade games | Go to disco/nightclubs |
| Do homework | Play home computer/electronic games | Other hobbies/interests |

2. What is your religion? (Circle one letter only) eg. (a.) Christian

a. Christian   b. Muslim   c. Jew   d. Sikh   e. Hindu
f. Buddhist   g. No religion   h. Other (please specify)

IF YOUR RELIGION IS NOT CHRISTIAN, PLEASE SUBSTITUTE TEMPLE/MOSQUE/SYNAGOGUE FOR 'CHURCH' IN THE REST OF THE QUESTIONNAIRE

3. Many teenagers do not go to church. Why do you think that is?

(Tick no more than five boxes)

They think it is boring
They think it is irrelevant
Going to church isn't the 'done' thing
They don't like the people who do go

They don't know what happens at church
None of their friends go
They've got better things to do on a Sunday
They don't like the moral teaching
They don't feel welcome

They don't know anyone at church
They don't like the minister/leader
They don't believe in God
Their parents don't encourage them to go
Other (please specify)

4. Do you ever think about whether or not God exists?   Yes [ ]   No [ ]

5. Do you believe in God?   Yes [ ]   No [ ]

6. Do you believe that we can know God personally?   Yes [ ]   No [ ]

7. Which of the following come into your picture of God? (Circle all that apply)

a. Love   b. Creator   c. Policeman   d. Spoilsport   e. Judge
f. Mother   g. Saviour   h. Father   i. Old man   j. Other (specify)

8. Who do you think Jesus Christ is/was? (Circle one letter only)

a. The Son of God   b. A very wise human being   c. An ordinary human being
d. A spaceman   e. Someone who never existed

9. Have you ever been involved in any of the following? (Tick all that apply)

| Reflexology | Hypnosis | Ouija boards |
| Tarot cards | Astrology | Using crystals |
| Channelling | I Ching | Meditation |

10. Have you had a religious experience?

Yes [ ]
No [ ]
Don't know [ ]

If Yes, was the experience.......?

(Tick one box on each line)

| | Yes | Not sure | No |
|---|---|---|---|
| A conversion experience | | | |
| To do with healing | | | |
| Visions/voices/dreams | | | |
| Beyond description | | | |
| Feeling as if somebody/something were trying to communicate with you | | | |
| A feeling of peace | | | |
| To do with nature | | | |
| Becoming a Christian | | | |
| The presence of God | | | |
| Some other spiritual/supernatural force | | | |
| Something else (please specify) | | | |

11. Have you ever attended church regularly, say at least once a month?   Yes [ ]   No [ ]

12. How often do you go to church now? (Circle one answer)

a. Nearly every week   b. At least once a month   c. Several times a year
d. Once or twice a year   e. Hardly ever

IF YOU USED TO ATTEND CHURCH AT LEAST ONCE A MONTH BUT NO LONGER DO SO, ANSWER QUESTIONS 13 - 20. OTHERWISE, GO STRAIGHT TO QUESTION 21.

13. For how long did you attend church on a regular basis? ____ years ____ months

14. What sort of church did you attend? (Tick one box only)

| Church of England | United Reformed Church | House church |
| Roman Catholic | Methodist | Brethren |
| Baptist | Pentecostal | Salvation Army |
| Other (specify) | Independent | Presbyterian |

15. Please use the boxes below to show who you usually went to church with and who you sat with.

| | Family | Friends | By yourself |
|---|---|---|---|
| Usually went to Sunday services with... | ☐ | ☐ | ☐ |
| Usually sat with... | ☐ | ☐ | ☐ |

16. Why did you go to church?

17. Did you attend any of the following church activities? (Circle all that apply)

a. Home group/Bible study group   b. Prayer group   c. Evangelistic group
d. Youth group   e. Music group   f. Other (please specify)

18. Did you do any of the following at church services at least once every six months?

(Tick all boxes that apply)

| | | | |
|---|---|---|---|
| Ring the bells ☐ | Teach in Sunday School ☐ |
| Sing in the choir ☐ | Play in the music group ☐ |
| Help with creche ☐ | Serve refreshments ☐ |
| Serve at altar ☐ | Read lesson/Bible reading ☐ |
| Lead worship ☐ | Did none of these things ☐ |
| Welcome visitors ☐ | |
| Preach ☐ | |
| Lead prayers ☐ | |
| Dance/drama ☐ | |
| Take collection ☐ | |

19. How old were you when you stopped attending church regularly? _____

20. Why did you stop attending church? Was it because.....?

The worship service was boring ☐
The congregation was not welcoming ☐
There were few other people there of your age ☐
There were no activities for young people ☐
You had serious doubts about the Christian religion ☐
The services were old-fashioned ☐
Some other reason (specify) ☐

21. Do you attend a church youth group now? Yes ☐ No ☐

22. Have you been to a Christian church within the last year for any of these services?

Wedding ☐   Christening/baptism ☐   Easter day/eve ☐
Funeral ☐   Carol service ☐   Harvest festival ☐
Christmas day/midnight ☐   Mothering Sunday ☐

23. What do you think of church services in general? Are they.......? (Tick all that apply)

Old-fashioned ☐   Modern ☐   Lively ☐
Friendly ☐   Challenging ☐   Boring ☐
Irrelevant ☐   Depressing ☐   Easy for a stranger to join in ☐
Enjoyable ☐   Difficult to understand ☐

24. Why do you think some young people go to church?

25. Did you regularly (at least once a month) attend Sunday School or a similar group at these ages? (Circle all that apply)

a. 5 - 6 years old   b. 9 - 10   c. 13 - 14   d. 15 plus

26. If you did regularly attend Sunday School, what did you think of it? (Circle all that apply)

a. Waste of time   b. Encouraged me to attend church   c. Learnt a lot
d. Enjoyable   e. Boring   f. Irrelevant

27. In your opinion, what makes a person a Christian? (Tick all that apply)

Being born in the UK ☐   Believing the Bible is true ☐
Believing in God ☐   Being baptised/christened ☐
Knowing Jesus as personal Saviour ☐   Leading a good life ☐
Something else (specify) ☐   Going to church ☐
Don't know ☐

28. Have you been.....? (Circle all that apply)

a. Baptised/christened   b. Confirmed/admitted to adult membership of a church

29. Which of the following statements best describes your present religious commitment? (Tick one box only)

I am a strongly committed Christian ☐
I am a Christian, but not very committed ☐
I am not sure whether or not I am a Christian ☐
I am no longer a Christian ☐
I have never been a Christian ☐

30. If you can think of a famous sportsman/woman, pop star or celebrity who is a Christian, please write their name(s).

31. Are you: Male ☐ Female ☐   32. How old are you? _____

32. Are your parents: Married ☐   Unmarried ☐
Divorced ☐   One has died ☐
Separated ☐   Both have died ☐

33. Who do you live with?

34. Does your father/guardian have a job? Yes ☐ No ☐   Retired ☐ Don't know ☐

If yes (or retired), what is his/her job?

Thank you very much for your help.

Now put the questionnaire in the envelope provided, seal it and return it to the person who gave it to you.

## YOUNG PEOPLE'S SURVEY

This survey looks at what young people think about the church and how they spend their spare time. National church leaders are keen to know what young people think about the church so that they can respond to your views. Please help us by answering the following questions.

All your answers are confidential. Do not write your name on the questionnaire. Please put your completed questionnaire in the envelope provided and seal it. This will be returned straight to us. No one in your church will read your answers.

Thank you for your help.

**1. What do you do in your spare time?** (Tick all boxes that apply)

| | |
|---|---|
| Play sport | Listen to music |
| Watch videos | Watch television |
| Go to the pub | Go to a youth club |
| Go to the cinema | Play arcade games |
| Do homework | Play home computer/ electronic games |

| | |
|---|---|
| Hang around with friends | |
| Spend time with boyfriend/ girlfriend | |
| Go to church activities | |
| Go to discos/nightclubs | |
| Other hobbies/interests | |

**2. How often do you go to church?** (Circle one answer) eg.(c) Never

a. Nearly every week    b. At least once a month    c. Several times a year
d. Once or twice a year    e. Hardly ever

**3. What sort of church do you attend?** (Tick one box only)

| | |
|---|---|
| Church of England | United Reformed Church |
| Roman Catholic | Methodist |
| Baptist | Pentecostal |
| Other (specify) | Independent |

| |
|---|
| House Church |
| Brethren |
| Salvation Army |
| Presbyterian |

**4. Please use the boxes below to show who you usually go to church with and who you sit with.**

| | Family | Friends | By yourself |
|---|---|---|---|
| Usually go to Sunday services with... | | | |
| Usually sit with... | | | |

**5. What do you think of your usual church service? Is it......?** (Tick all that apply)

| | |
|---|---|
| Old-fashioned | Modern |
| Friendly | Challenging |
| Irrelevant | Depressing |
| Enjoyable | Difficult to understand |

| |
|---|
| Lively |
| Boring |
| Easy for a stranger to join in |

**6. Which parts of the service do you enjoy most?** (Tick no more than three boxes)

| | |
|---|---|
| Singing traditional hymns | Prayers |
| Singing modern hymns/songs | Sermon |
| Other music items | Bible reading |
| Holy Communion/Mass/Eucharist | Personal testimony |

**7. Do you do any of the following at church services at least once every six months?**

| | |
|---|---|
| Ring the bells | Welcome visitors |
| Sing in the choir | Lead prayers |
| Help with creche | Dance/drama |
| Serve at altar | Take collection |
| Lead worship | |

| |
|---|
| Teach in Sunday School |
| Play in the music group |
| Serve refreshments |
| Read lesson/Bible reading |
| Do none of these things |

**8. Why do you go to church?**

**9. Do you attend any of the following church activities?** (Circle all that apply)

a. Home group/Bible study group    b. Prayer group    c. Evangelistic group
d. Youth group    e. Music group    f. Other (please specify)

**10a. Most teenagers do not go to church. Why do you think that is?**

| | |
|---|---|
| They think it is boring | |
| They think it is irrelevant | |
| Going to church isn't the 'done' thing | |
| They don't like the people who do go | |
| | (Tick no more than five boxes) |
| They don't know what happens at church | |
| None of their friends go | |
| They've got better things to do on a Sunday | |
| They don't like the moral teaching | |
| They don't feel welcome | |
| They don't know anyone at church | |
| They feel out of place | |
| They don't like the minister/leader | |
| They don't believe in God | |
| They don't encourage them to go | |
| Their parents don't (please specify) | |

**10b. Have you ever felt like not going to church any more?**    Yes [ ]    No [ ]

If Yes, why did you feel that way?

**11. Do you think you will stop attending church in the future?**    Yes [ ]    No [ ]
Why is that?

**12. Did you regularly (ie at least once a month) attend Sunday School or a similar group at these ages?** (Circle all that apply)

a. 5 - 6 years old    b. 9 - 10    c. 13 - 14    d. 15 plus

13. **If you did regularly attend Sunday School**, what did you think of it? (Circle **all** that apply)

a. Waste of time   b. Encouraged me to attend church   c. Learnt a lot
d. Enjoyable   e. Boring   f. Irrelevant

14. Did you regularly attend Sunday church services (ie at least once a month) at these ages? (Circle **all** that apply)

a. 5 - 6 years old   b. 9 - 10   c. 13 - 14   d. 15 plus

15. Have you had a religious experience?

Yes ☐   No ☐   Don't know ☐

If **yes**, was the experience......?

(Tick **one** box on each line)

| | Yes | Not sure | No |
|---|---|---|---|
| A conversion experience | ☐ | ☐ | ☐ |
| To do with healing | ☐ | ☐ | ☐ |
| Visions/voices/dreams | ☐ | ☐ | ☐ |
| Beyond description | ☐ | ☐ | ☐ |
| Feeling as if somebody/something were trying to communicate with you | ☐ | ☐ | ☐ |
| A feeling of peace | ☐ | ☐ | ☐ |
| To do with nature | ☐ | ☐ | ☐ |
| Becoming a Christian | ☐ | ☐ | ☐ |
| The presence of God | ☐ | ☐ | ☐ |
| Some other spiritual/supernatural force | ☐ | ☐ | ☐ |
| Something else (please specify) | ☐ | ☐ | ☐ |

16. Have you ever been involved in any of the following? (Tick **all** that apply)

Reflexology ☐   Hypnosis ☐   Ouija boards ☐
Tarot cards ☐   Astrology ☐   Using crystals ☐
Channelling ☐   I Ching ☐   Meditation ☐

17. Which of the following come into your picture of God? (Circle **all** that apply)

a. Love   b. Creator   c. Policeman   d. Spoilsport   e. Judge
f. Mother   g. Saviour   h. Father   i. Old man   j. Other (specify)

18. Who do you think Jesus Christ is/was? (Circle **one** letter only)

a. The Son of God   b. A very wise human being   c. An ordinary human being
d. A spaceman   e. Someone who never existed

19. In your opinion, what makes a person a Christian? (tick **all** that apply)

Being born in the UK ☐    Believing the Bible is true ☐
Believing in God ☐    Being baptised/christened ☐
Knowing Jesus as personal Saviour ☐    Leading a good life ☐
Something else (specify)    Going to church ☐
Don't know ☐

20. Have you been......? (Circle **all** that apply)

a. Baptised/christened   b. Confirmed/admitted to adult membership of a church

21. Which of the following statements best describes your present religious commitment? (tick **one** box only)

I am a strongly committed Christian ☐
I am a Christian, but not very committed ☐
I am not sure whether or not I am a Christian ☐
I am no longer a Christian ☐
I have never been a Christian ☐

22. If you can think of a famous sportsman/woman, pop star or celebrity who is a Christian, please write their name(s). _____

23. Are you: Male ☐   Female ☐    24. How old are you? _____

25. Are you still in full-time education? Yes ☐   No ☐

If **No**, do you have a job? Yes ☐   No ☐

What is your job? _____

26. Do you have any of the following qualifications? (Circle **all** that apply)

a. GSCEs/O levels   b. A levels   c. College diploma/certificate
d. Vocational qualifications

27. Are your parents: Married ☐   Unmarried ☐
Divorced ☐   One has died ☐
Separated ☐   Both have died ☐

28. Who do you live with? _____

29. Does your father/guardian have a job? Yes ☐   Retired ☐
No ☐   Don't know ☐

If **yes** (or **retired**), what is his/her job? _____

Thank you very much for your help.

Now put the questionnaire in the envelope provided, seal it and return it to the person who gave it to you.

CHURCH

YOUNG PEOPLE'S SURVEY

Hello, I'm doing a survey on what teenagers think about the church. National church leaders are keen to know what young people think about church services and activities so that they can respond to your views. All your answers will be confidential. Are you willing to take part in the survey?

1. Please use the cards to show me how often you go to church. (Show cards)

Nearly every week ☐  Once or twice a year ☐
At least once a month ☐  Hardly ever ☐
Several times a year ☐

2. How old were you when you started to attend church?

3. Why did you choose to come to this particular church?

4. What denomination is the church you attend? (Read out only if necessary)

Church of England ☐  United Reformed Church ☐  House church ☐
Roman Catholic ☐  Methodist ☐  Brethren ☐
Baptist ☐  Pentecostal ☐  Salvation Army ☐
Other (specify) ☐  Independent ☐  Presbyterian ☐

5. Is the denomination of the church especially important to you?  Yes ☐  No ☐

6. Why did you start to attend church?

7. Did your parents ever encourage you to attend church on a regular basis?

And what about Sunday School?

Have you ever attended Sunday School?

If Yes, what did you think of it?

8. Is this the only church you have attended on a regular basis?  Yes ☐  No ☐

If Yes, why is that?

If No, which denominations have you attended in the past?

Church of England ☐  United Reformed Church ☐  House church ☐
Roman Catholic ☐  Methodist ☐  Brethren ☐
Baptist ☐  Pentecostal ☐  Salvation Army ☐
Other (specify) ☐  Independent ☐  Presbyterian ☐

Why did you leave your last church?

9. If you moved to another part of the country, would you look for another church to attend?  Yes ☐  No ☐

If Yes, how would you decide which church to attend?

If No, why is that?

10. Please use the cards to show me who you usually go to Sunday services with.

(Show cards)  Family ☐  Friends ☐  Alone ☐

11. What do you like about attending church?

12. What do you dislike?

13. Do your friends know that you go to church?  Yes ☐  No ☐

If Yes, what do they think about it?

If No, what has stopped you from telling them?

14. Many young people don't go to church. Why do you think that is?

15. Which of the following do you believe in? Please say Yes or No for each word on the card. (Show card)

| | Yes | No | | Yes | No |
|---|---|---|---|---|---|
| God | | | Re-incarnation | | |
| Heaven | | | Jesus | | |
| Hell | | | | | |

16. Do you think Christianity is relevant to you?   Yes ☐   No ☐

Why do you say that?

17. Has there been a time in your life when you stopped going to church for one year or more?   Yes ☐   No ☐

If Yes, How old were you when this happened?

How long did you stay away from church?

Why did you stop attending church? Any other reasons?

18. Have you ever felt like not attending church any more?   Yes ☐   No ☐

If No, Why did you feel like this?

19. Have you....?

| | |
|---|---|
| Been baptised | ☐ |
| Been confirmed | ☐ |
| Taken communion | ☐ |
| Been admitted to adult membership of a church | ☐ |

20. Does your church have activities/groups especially for children and young people?

If No, Do you think it should?

If Yes, What activities/groups are organised?

Would you describe the youth activities as excellent, good, average or poor?

20. How could church services be made more attractive to young people?

21. How do the young people and the older people in your church get on together?

22. Are young people given any responsibility in your church?

If Yes, What do they do?

Do you think giving young people responsibility helps the church?   Yes ☐   No ☐

If Yes, How does it help?

23. Do you think churches should have services which are especially geared to young people?   Yes ☐   No ☐

Why do you think that?

If I could finish by asking you a few questions about yourself.

24. How old are you?

25. Gender (Interviewer to record)   Male ☐   Female ☐

26. Are you still in full-time education?   Yes ☐   No ☐

If No, Do you have a job?

What is your job?

**Thank you very much for your help.**

# YOUNG PEOPLE'S SURVEY

Hello. I'm conducting a survey on young people's attitudes towards the church. Please will you help me by answering some questions? All your answers will be confidential.

1. Have you ever attended church on a regular basis, say at least once a month?

Yes ☐   No ☐   IF YES, USE THIS FORM

2. What denomination was the church you attended? (Read out only if necessary)

Church of England ☐   United Reformed Church ☐   House church ☐
Roman Catholic ☐   Methodist ☐   Brethren ☐
Baptist ☐   Pentecostal ☐   Salvation Army ☐
Other (specify) ☐   Independent ☐   Presbyterian ☐

3. Why did you choose to go to that particular church?

4. Was the denomination of the church especially important to you? Yes ☐ No ☐

5. Please use the cards to show me who you usually went to Sunday services with.

(Show cards)   Family ☐   Friends ☐   Alone ☐

6. How old were you when you started to attend church?

7. What made you start to attend church?

8. Did your parents ever encourage you to attend church on a regular basis? Yes ☐ No ☐

And what about Sunday School? Yes ☐ No ☐

Have you ever attended Sunday School? Yes ☐ No ☐

If Yes, What did you think of it?

9. Did your church have activities/groups especially for children and teenagers?

Yes ☐ No ☐

If No, Do you think it should have done?

If Yes, What activities/groups were organised?

Would you describe the youth activities as excellent, good, average or poor?

10. What did you like about attending church?

11. What did you dislike?

12. How did the young people and the older people in your church get on together?

13. Were young people given any responsibility in your church? Yes ☐ No ☐

If Yes, What did they do?

Do you think giving young people responsibility helps the church? Yes ☐ No ☐

If Yes, How does it help?

14. For how long did you attend church regularly?

15. Why did you stop attending?

Any other reasons?

16. Please use the cards to show me how often you go to church now. (Show cards)

Nearly every week
At least once a month
Several times a year
Once or twice a year
Hardly ever

17. Many young people don't go to church. Why do you think that is?

18. Do you think churches should have services which are especially geared to young people?   Yes ☐   No ☐

Why do you think that?

19. How could church services be made more attractive to young people?

20. Do you think Christianity is relevant to you?   Yes ☐   No ☐

Why do you say that?

21. Which of the following do you believe in?  Please say Yes or No for each word on the card.  (Show cards)

| | Yes | No |
|---|---|---|
| God | | |
| Heaven | | |
| Hell | | |
| Re-incarnation | | |
| Jesus | | |

22. Have you....?

| | Yes | No |
|---|---|---|
| Been baptised | | |
| Been confirmed | | |
| Taken communion | | |
| Been admitted to adult membership of a church | | |

If I could finish by asking you a few questions about yourself.

23. How old are you?

24. Gender (Interviewer to record)   Male ☐   Female ☐

25. Are you still in full-time education?   Yes ☐   No ☐

If **No**, Do you have a job?   Yes ☐   No ☐

What is your job?

Thank you very much for your help.

## YOUNG PEOPLE'S SURVEY

Hello. I'm conducting a survey on young people's attitudes towards the church. Please will you help me by answering some questions? All your answers will be confidential.

Yes [ ]   No [ ]   **IF NO, USE THIS FORM**

1. Have you ever attended church on a regular basis, say at least once a month?
Yes [ ]   No [ ]

2. Do you ever think about whether or not God exists?   Yes [ ]   No [ ]

3. Which of the following do you believe in?   Please say Yes or No for each word on the card. (Show card)

| | Yes | No |
|---|---|---|
| God | | |
| Heaven | | |
| Hell | | |
| Re-incarnation | | |
| Jesus | | |

4. Would you say that you have had a religious experience?   Yes [ ]   No [ ]
If Yes, Can you describe it to me?

5. Do you think Christianity is relevant to you?   Yes [ ]   No [ ]
Why do you say that?

6. Do you know anyone of your own age who goes to church?   Yes [ ]   No [ ]
If Yes, how do they get on with others who don't go to church?
If No, Do you know anyone at all who goes to church?

7. Did your parents ever encourage you to attend church on a regular basis?   Yes [ ]   No [ ]
And what about Sunday School?   Yes [ ]   No [ ]
Have you ever attended Sunday School?   Yes [ ]   No [ ]
If Yes, What did you think of it?

8. Have you ever attended a church youth club or youth organisation?   Yes [ ]   No [ ]
If Yes, Did you enjoy it?

9. Apart from special occasions such as weddings and christenings, when was the last time you went to a church service?
If have attended a church service, what did you think of it?
How did you feel when you were inside a church?

10. Please use the cards to show me how often you go to church now?   (Show cards)
Nearly every week [ ]
At least once a month [ ]
Several times a year [ ]
Once or twice a year [ ]
Hardly ever [ ]

11. Many young people don't go to church. Why do you think that is?

12. Why do you think some people go to church?

13. Do you think churches should have services which are especially geared to young people?   Yes ☐   No ☐

Why do you think that?

_____

14. How could church services be made more attractive to young people?

_____

15. What, if anything, would encourage you to attend church?

_____

If I could finish by asking you a few questions about yourself.

16. How old are you?

_____

17. Gender (Interviewer to record)   Male ☐   Female ☐

18. Are you still in full-time education?   Yes ☐   No ☐

If No, Do you have a job?

What is your job?

Thank you very much for your help.

## YOUTH LEADER INTERVIEWS

Six Youth Officers were asked the following questions:

1. Could you start by telling me briefly about your experiences of working with teenagers.

2. Do you think teenagers have a certain image of the church and Christians? What is that image?

3. How important are RE lessons for:
a) teenagers and their image of the church?
b) teenagers and their image of Christianity?

4. What are the main pressures faced by today's teenagers?

5. Are different pressures faced by rural and urban teenagers?

6. How real is the sense of peer pressure?

7. Do you think teenagers are more influenced by the attitudes of their friends or parents regarding church?

8. In your experience, how evident is the role of New Age thinking and the occult in teenage circles?

9. In what ways do the pressures which we have discussed influence their attitude towards the church?

10. The English Church Census showed that many teenagers left the church during the 1980s. Has this been your experience?

11. Why do you think young people often leave the church in their teens?

12. How important do you think childhood Sunday School attendance is in encouraging teenagers to attend church regularly?

13. What factors or attitudes keep the majority of teenagers away from the church?

14. Many teenagers say church is boring. Is this fair? What could be done to change it?

15. Are the moral demands of Christianity a major factor in keeping young people away from the church?

16. In general, how do you think teenagers are viewed by the church? Are they welcomed by other church attenders?

17. Do evangelical and non-evangelical churches view young people differently?

18. Would you say that work with teenagers is seen as a priority by most churches?

19. In encouraging teenagers to attend church, how important is it that:
a) the minister relates well with this age group?
b) there are other teenagers in the church?

20. What are the main factors which encourage young people to continue to attend church throughout their teenage years, despite the many pressures they face?

21. Do you think it is important to give young church attenders responsibility?

22. Certain denominations, such as the Roman Catholic Church and House Churches, have been more successful at encouraging young people to attend church. Why do you think that is the case?

23. What, if anything, do you think other churches can learn from these denominations?

24. Which parts of church services do young people tend to enjoy most?

25. How could church services be made more attractive to young people?

26. Do you think churches should have services which are geared especially to young people?

27. Do our churches have something relevant to say to today's young people and, if so, are they saying it?

28. How do you think the church can encourage more young people to attend church?

29. How can we ensure that our young people continue in the church into their twenties?

30. Is there anything else which you would like to add? Any issues which you don't feel we have covered?

# *Notes*

## Introduction

1) L.J. Francis, 'Measurement reapplied: research into the child's attitude towards religion' in *British Journal of Religious Education*, Vol 1 1978, pages 45–51

2) L.J. Francis, 'Christianity and the child today' in *Occasional Papers: Farmington Institute for Christian Studies*, Vol 6 1980

3) L.J. Francis, 'Drift from the churches: secondary school pupils' attitudes towards Christianity' in *British Journal of Religious Education*, Vol 11 1989, pages 76–86

4) L.J. Francis, 'Monitoring attitude towards Christianity: the 1990 study' in *British Journal of Religious Education*, Vol 14 1992, pages 178–182

5) L.J. Francis and D.W. Lankshear, 'Church provision for pre-school children: impact on urban church life' in *Research in Education*, Vol 48 1992, pages 55–64

6) L.J. Francis and D.W. Lankshear, 'The impact of church schools on urban church life' in *School Effectiveness and School Improvement*, Vol 2 1991, pages 324–335

7) L.J. Francis and D.W. Lankshear, 'The impact of children's work on village church life' in *Spectrum*, Vol 21 1992, pages 35–45

8) L.J. Francis and D.W. Lankshear, 'The rural rectory: the impact of a resident priest on local church life' in *Journal of Rural Studies*, Vol 8 1992, pages 97–103

9) L.J. Francis and D.W. Lankshear, 'Ageing clergy and the rural church' in *PSIGNE Newsletter*, Vol 42 1992, pages 12–19

10) L.J. Francis, 'Denominational schools and pupil attitudes towards

Christianity' in *British Educational Research Journal*, Vol 12 1986, pages 145–152

11) L.J. Francis and A. Jewell, 'Shaping adolescent attitude towards the church: comparison between Church of England and county secondary schools' in *Evaluation and Research in Education*, Vol 6 1992, pages 13–21

12) L.J. Francis and J. Egan, 'The Catholic school as "faith community": an empirical enquiry' in *Religious Education*, Vol 85 1990, pages 588–603

13) L.J. Francis and H.M. Gibson, 'Parental influence and adolescent religiosity: a study of church attendance and attitude towards Christianity among 11–12 and 15–16 year olds' in *International Journal for the Psychology of Religion*, in press

14) L.J. Francis, 'The religious significance of denominational identity among eleven year old children in England' in *Journal of Christian Education*, Vol 97 1990, pages 23–28

15) L.J. Francis, H.M. Gibson and D.W. Lankshear, 'The influence of Protestant Sunday Schools on attitude towards Christianity among 11–15 year olds in Scotland' in *British Journal of Religious Education*, Vol 13 1991, pages 35–42

16) L.J. Francis and A. Montgomery, 'Personality and attitudes towards Christianity among eleven to sixteen year old girls in a single sex Catholic school' in *British Journal of Religious Education*, Vol 14 1992, pages 114–119

17) L.J. Francis, 'Religion, neuroticism and psychoticism' in J.F. Schumaker (ed.), *Religion and Mental Health*, Oxford University Press, New York 1992, pages 149–160

18) L.J. Francis, P.R. Pearson and D.W. Lankshear, 'The relationship between social class and attitude towards Christianity among ten and eleven year old children' in *Personality and Individual Differences*, Vol 11 1990, pages 1019–1027

19) L.J. Francis, P. Fulljames and H.M. Gibson, 'Does creationism commend the gospel? a developmental study among 11–17 year olds' in *Religious Education*, Vol 87 1992, pages 19–27

20) K.E. Hyde, *Religion in Childhood and Adolescence: a comprehensive review of the research*, Religious Education Press, Birmingham, Alabama 1990

21) Peter Brierley, *'Christian' England*, MARC Europe, London 1991

## 1) Teenagers' Social Environment

1) Peter Brierley, *'Christian' England*, results of 1989 English Church Census, MARC Europe, London 1991, Table 31, page 82

2) 'Young Britain', survey by Carrick James Market Research, reported in *Survey* Autumn 1990, page 18

3) Paul Meier et al, *Introduction to Psychology and Counselling*, Monarch, Tunbridge Wells 1991, page 201

4) Op cit (item 2), with figures increased by inflation factor

5) George Barna, *The Invisible Generation: Baby Busters*, Barna Research Group, Glendale, California 1992, page 20

6) Gary E Russell, 'Baby boomers and the Adventist Church' in *Ministry* July 1992, page 14

7) See for example Doug Murren, *The Baby Boomerang*, Regal Books, Ventura, California 1990

8) From *UK Christian Handbook* 1992/93 Edition, edited by Peter Brierley and David Longley, MARC Europe, London 1991, Table 7, page 208

9) *The NCH Factfile*, Children in Britain 1992, National Children's Home, London 1992, page 19

10) John Haskey in *Population Trends*, No 61 Autumn 1990, page 39

11) M P M Richards, 'Parental Divorce and Children' in *ESRC Data Archive Bulletin* No 51, September 1992, page 7

12) *Population Trends*, No 58 Winter 1989

13) Peter Brierley, *Act on the Facts*, MARC Europe, London 1992, page 41

14) A more detailed discussion may be found in *Families and Households: Divisions and Change*, edited by C Marsh and S Arber, Macmillan, London 1992. Quote op cit (item 11) page 34

15) National Council of Women study by Research International, and quoted in *Research*, January 1993, page 4

16) C Hohn, *Determinants of Fertility Trends*, Ordina 1983, page 263

17) *Population Trends*, No 69, Autumn 1992, OPCS, page 2

18) The rate for girls aged under 14 and under 20 are based on the population of girls aged 13 and 15–19 respectively

19) M Simms and C Smith, *Teenage Mothers and Their Partners, survey in England and Wales*, Research Report No 15, Department of Health and Social Security, HMSO, London 1988, page 1

20) Ibid, page 2
21) David Coleman and John Salt, *The British Population*, Patterns, Trends and Processes, Oxford University Press 1992, pages 131/2
22) Op cit (items 2 and 13), page 210
23) Ibid
24) Trustee Savings Bank survey by Research International in December 1992, reported in *Daily Telegraph* 31 December 1992
25) Ibid
26) *Students in Higher Education*, Statistical Bulletin, Department for Education, No 19/92 October 1992
27) Bullers Wood School for Girls, Chislehurst, Kent, School Assembly for Year 11, 5 November 1992
28) Trustee Savings Bank survey in April 1992, reported in the *Guardian* 23 May 1992
29) Op cit (item 5), page 98
30) *Reclaiming a Nation*, the challenge of re-evangelizing Canada by the year 2000, edited by Arnell Motz, Church Leadership Library, Richmond, Canada 1990, page 228/9
31) Report of Girl-child Conference, held by World Vision Australia, February 1992, Appendix B:3
32) Quoted by Roger Tredre in the *Independent on Sunday*, and reported in *Bookseller* 11 December 1992
33) George Barna, *The Barna Report 1992/93*, Regal Books, Ventura, California 1992, pages 236–247
34) Op cit (item 9), page 63
35) Op cit (item 9), page 64
36) Nicky Cruz, *A Final Warning*, Kingsway, Eastbourne 1992, pages 149/150
37) Bob Moffett, 'Living a Lie' in *Youthwork*, Issue 3 April 1992, page 3
38) Op cit (item 9), page 69
39) World Christian News, edited by Paul Filidis, YWAM, Colorado Springs, November 1992, page 9
40) Personal letter to Mr Gordon Holloway of the Shaftesbury Society, December 1991 but also used on the cover of the Crusader's video 'The Challenge of Change'
41) OPCS *Monitor*, 'Deaths by cause: 1991 registration', July 1992, page 6
42) News item in *Young People Now*, National Youth Agency, London, Issue 38, June 1992, page 6

43) Op cit (item 2)
44) Winkie Pratney, *Devil take the Youngest, The War on Childhood*, Huntingdon House Publishers, Lafayette, Louisiana 1985. Extensive quotations have been taken from this book
45) Leviticus 18:21
46) Matthew Henry, *People's Bible Dictionary*, quoted in op cit (item 44), page 58
47) 2 Kings 16:3; 23:10, Jeremiah 32:35
48) 1 Kings 11:7
49) Op cit (item 44), page 61
50) Op cit (item 44), pages 63–65, 85
51) Revelation 12:4,5
52) Op cit (item 44), page 122
53) Op cit (item 9), page 54
54) *The Times* 14 December 1984
55) Op cit (item 44), page 125
56) *Daily Telegraph* 24 April 1992
57) Op cit (item 44), page 173
58) Figures taken from appropriate editions of *Social Trends*, HMSO, Norwich
59) Rev David Winter, 'The Outsiders' in *Youthwork*, No 2 February 1992
60) John Finney, *Finding Faith Today*, How does it happen? Bible Society, Swindon, Wiltshire 1992, Figure 10, page 14

## 2) Teenager's Leisure Activities

1) BBC West *News Feature* spokesman, 28 February 1992
2) Gallup Survey of sample 518 fourth and fifth year school pupils, reported in *Daily Telegraph*, 2 October 1991
3) Boyd Myers, *Young People's Relationships, Lifestyle and Sexual Attitudes*, report on 1,729 questionnaires returned from 150 church youth groups for Agapé, Birmingham, April 1991. Private circulation. The *Christian Initiative on Teenage Sexuality* was founded by Agapé, Care for the Family and Oasis after this survey. Dave and Anne Carlos co-ordinate this work and publish a quarterly newsletter, available on request, to all those in church or youth leadership roles. CITS, 46 Green Road, Hall Green, Birmingham B28 8DD–021 777 8957

4) Revd Dr Harry Gibson and Revd Dr Leslie J Francis, A profile of television vision and programme preferences amongst secondary school pupils in Scotland, a sample of 5,432 11–15 year olds attending state secondary schools in Dundee 1987 in *Collected Original Resources in Education* Vol 16, Part 1, Fiche 2, FO9, 1992,

5) M Schofield, *Sexual Behaviour of Young People*, Longmans, London 1965

6) Elmer Towns, *Encyclopedia on Sunday School*, Tyndale House Publishers, 1992 and quoted in 'Reaching the Buster Generation' in *Church Growth Today* Vol 7 No 2 1992, page 3

7) Ibid, page 4

8) Ibid

9) David Toma, et al, *A Straight Word to Kids and Parents*, Help for Teen Problems, edited by Hutterian Brethren, Plough Publishing House, New York 1987, page 11

10) Ibid, page 13 (Daniel Moody)

11) Op cit (item 5)

12) Op cit (item 3), page 43

13) Op cit (item 6), page 2

14) Reported in 'Children's Book News' in the *Bookseller*, 13 November 1992, page 1499

15) Op cit (item 3), Table 34, page 29

16) Report in *Daily Telegraph* 24 April 1992

17) George Barna, *The Barna Report 1992/93*, Regal Books, Ventura, California 1992, page 285

18) *Planning for More Growth*, Above Bar Church Attendance Survey, MARC Europe 1987

19) Robert J Wybrow, *Britain speaks out 1937–87*, A social history as seen through the Gallup data, Macmillan, Basingstoke, Hampshire 1989, page 140

20) John Buckeridge, 'Teen Mags Survey' in *Youthwork* Issue 3, April 1992, pages 12/13

21) Op cit (item 5)

22) Op cit (item 6), pages 3,4

23) 'Young People and Sex' in *Youthwork* in *Alpha* magazine No 1, December 1991

24) Op cit (item 23) NOP poll for *Independent on Sunday*

25) Op cit (item 23) Exeter University survey of 4,000 young people 15–24 years old

26) Op cit (item 23) Agapé survey of 1,700 young people, 84% claiming to be Christian (item 3)
27) Op cit (item 23) Major British Survey, November 1989
28) Op cit (item 23) Time magazine
29) Op cit (item 23) OPCS Monitor 1990, and Table 2
30) Op cit (item 5)
31) Op cit (item 3), based on Table 36
32) Report in the *Independent*, 21 July 1992
33) Dr Maureen Blake, 'The Young Person and Sex' in the *Presbyterian Herald Family Magazine*, No 557, October 1992, Belfast, page 18
34) *Christian Initiative on Teenage Sexuality*, Agapé, Birmingham, Issue 1, Summer 1992, page 4
35) Terry Mattingly, 'Wholly holy—living by whose standards' in *Alpha* December 1992, page 34
36) Revd Edward Pratt, *Living in Sin?, A response to cohabitation*, St Simon's Church, Southsea, Hampshire 1992, pages 16–19
37) Op cit (item 2)
38) *Sweet Dreams?, Research into 'Major's children'* by Trustee Savings Bank PLC, Birmingham, April 1992
39) *Labour Force Survey*, Quarterly Bulletin, No 1 September 1992, page 7
40) Dr Leslie J Francis, *Young and Unemployed*, Costello, London 1984, page 94
41) Article by Helen Gibson in *Readers' Digest*, May 1990, page 102
42) Ibid
43) John Smith, 'Cults of violence and healing tribes' in *Alpha* magazine, July 1992, page 30
44) Bob and Gretchen Pasantino, *When the Devil Dares Your Kids*, Eagle Books, Guildford, Surrey 1991, page 59
45) Luke 11:24–26 (Revised Standard Version)
46) Article in *Religion Today* Vol 7 No 2 Spring 1992, Page 3
47) Dr David Burnett, *Dawning of the Pagan Moon*, MARC, Eastbourne, East Sussex 1991, and quoted in Act on the Facts, MARC Europe, London 1992, page 205. Emphasis mine.

## 3) Teenagers and the Church

1) Genesis 17:25
2) Genesis 37:2

3) 2 Kings 14:21
4) 2 Chronicles 26:16
5) 2 Kings 24:8
6) 2 Chronicles 33:1
7) Luke 2:42
8) Luke 5:42
9) Peter Brierley, *Prospects for the Nineties*, MARC Europe, London 1991, page 21
10) Peter Brierley and Byron Evans, *Prospects for Wales*, Bible Society and MARC Europe, London 1983, page 28
11) Peter Brierley and Fergus MacDonald, *Prospects for Scotland*, National Bible Society of Scotland and MARC Europe, London 1985, page 60
12) Rev Nick Aiken, 'Signs of the Times', in *Twenty First Century Christian* January 1990, page 15
13) Peter Brierley, *Church Nominalism in the 1990s*, based on survey by Professor Eddie Gibbs, MARC Monograph No 40, MARC Europe, London 1992
14) Peter Brierley, *'Christian' England*, MARC Europe, London 1991, Table 60, pages 162/3
15) 'Multi-church affiliations' in *Ministry Currents*, Barna Research Group, Glendale, California, Vol 1 No 1, April 1991, page 6
16) George Barna, *The Barna Report 1992–93*, Regal Books, Ventura, California, 1992, Table 95, page 278
17) Op cit (item 13)
18) Boyd Myers, *Scottish Church and Social Concerns Survey*, study by MARC Europe for National Bible Society of Scotland, Church of Scotland and Roman Catholic Church, 1992
19) News item in *Alpha* magazine, November 1992, page 9
20) Op cit (item 18)
21) Boyd Myers, *Young People's Relationships, Lifestyle and Sexual Attitudes*, report on 1,729 questionnaires from 150 church youth groups for Agapé, Birmingham, April 1991. Private circulation. See further comments on item 3 in Chapter 2
22) Peter Brierley, *Mission to London, Phase I: Who Responded?* MARC Europe, London 1984
23) Patricia Hannan, *Report from DES Funded Research Project into the Spiritual Dimension of Young People's Experience*, YWCA, July 1991, page 16

## 4) Motivations for Church Attendance

1) Peter Bentley, 'Tricia Blombery and Philip Hughes, *Faith without the Church?, Nominalism in Australian Christianity*, Christian Research Association, Victoria, Australia 1992, pages 62, 63, 88, 90, 93

2) *Young People in the 80's*, HMSO, London 1983

3) *Views from the Pews, Lent 86 and local ecumenism*, British Council of Churches/Catholic Truth Society, London 1986

4) Review in *Third Way*, March 1987, page 30

5) David G Bromley (editor), *Falling from the Faith*, Causes and consequences of Religious Apostasy, Sage, London 1988, Table 5.1, page 94

6) Ibid, page 14

7) Tom Sine, *Wild Hope*, Monarch, Tunbridge Wells, Kent, 1991, page 184

8) Leslie J Francis, Harry M Gibson and Peter Fulljames, 'Attitude towards Christianity, Creationism, Scientism and Interest in Science among 11–15 year olds' in *British Journal of Religious Education*, Vol 13 No 1, September 1990

9) Report in the *Independent*, 11 September 1990

10) Peter Fulljames, Harry M Gibson and Leslie J Francis, 'Creationism, Scientism, Christianity and Science : a study in adolescent attitudes' in *British Educational Research Journal* Vol 17 No2, 1991

11) Helmut Reich, 'Between Religion and Science : Complementarity in the Religious Thinking of Young People' in *British Journal of Religious Education* Vol 11, 1989

12) Jeff Astley and David Day (editors), *The Contours of Christian Education*, McCrimmon Publishing, Great Wakering, Essex, 1992, Chapter 23 'Christianity Today : The Teenage Experience', Leslie J Francis, pages 364/5

13) *Background to the Task*, supplement to *On the Other Side*, the Report of the Evangelical Alliance Commission on Evangelism, Scripture Union, London, 1968. A synopsis of the study may also be found in *Entering the Kingdom—a fresh look at conversion*, edited by Monica Hill, British Church Growth Association and MARC Europe, London, 1988

14) Canon John Finney, *Finding Faith Today, How does it happen?* British and Foreign Bible Society, Swindon, Wiltshire 1992, page 24

15) Ibid, Figure 13, page 24
16) Keith Hinton, *Growing Churches Singapore Style*, Ministry in an urban context, Overseas Missionary Fellowship, Sevenoaks, Kent 1985, page 119
17) Op cit (item 14) Figures 15 and 16, pages 36/37
18) 'Beyond sheep stealing', leader in *Church of England Newspaper*, 2 October 1992
19) Reported in *Ambassador*, General Synod Board of Mission and Unity, London and quoted in Church of England Newspaper 1 May 1992
20) Laurence R Iannaccone, 'Religious Practice : A Human Capital Approach' in *Journal for the Scientific Study of Religion* Vol 29, 1990, page 301
21) Peter Brierley, *Mission to London Part 1*, MARC Europe, London 1984
22) Peter Brierley, *Who goes to Church?*, Mission to London Part 2, MARC Europe, London 1985
23) Phil Back, *Mission England, What really happened?*, MARC Europe, London 1986
24) Matt Vanderzahn, 'Teenagers have no hope' in *Decision* magazine January 1992, page 9
25) Arnell Motz (editor), *Reclaiming a Nation, the challenge of Re-evangelizing* Canada by the year 2000, Church Leadership Library, Richmond, British Columbia 1990, pages 142/3
26) Mrs Anne Adams, *Did it rain the day you were saved?*, Project work conducted for Workshop on 'Foundations in Christian Leadership' under Director Noel Moules, Sheffield 1989, private circulation
27) Peter Brierley, *A Century of British Christianity*, Historical statistics 1900–1985, with projections to 2000, MARC Monograph No 14, MARC Europe, London 1989, Figure 23, page 38
28) Jeff Astley and Leslie J Francis (editors), *Christian Perspectives on Faith Development*, Gracewing Fowler Wright Books, Leominster, Herefordshire 1992, page 15/16
29) *How Faith Grows*, Faith Development and Christian Education, edited by Dr Jeff Astley, National Society/Church House Publishing, London 1992, pages 20, 21, 24, 27, 30 and 33
30) Op cit (item 28), pages 16–18
31) Op cit (item 28), Table 1, page 17

32) Reginald Bibby, *Fragmented Gods, the poverty and potential of religion in Canada*, Irwin Publishing, Toronto, Canada 1987, page 54

33) Ibid, page 99

34) S Harding, D Phillips and M Fogarty, *Contrasting Values in Western Europe, Unity, diversity and change*, Macmillan, London in association with the European Value Systems Study Group 1986, pages 68, 69

35) Jane Burton in *Daily Telegraph* 20 December 1991

36) Damian Thompson in *Daily Telegraph* 20 December 1991

37) Report in *Alpha* magazine November 1992, page 23

38) Appeared in *Daily Express* 17 September 1992, and reproduced with permission

39) Report in *Sarum Link* May 1992, page 12

40) Sandra Kimber, *Tomorrow's Potential—and Today's!*, survey of British Missionary Societies on missionary education of children and young people, 1985

41) Nick Aiken (editor), *Creative Ideas for Youth Evangelism, Helping your youth group to grow*, Marshall Pickering, London 1993

## 5) The Influence of School, Sunday School and Home

1) Figures from *UK Christian Handbook, 1992/93 edition*, edited by Peter Brierley and David Longley, MARC Europe, London 1991, Table 48, page 656

2) Leslie Francis, *Religion in the Primary School: Partnership between Church and State*, Collins, London, 1987, page 194

3) J Rust and Leslie J Francis, *Curriculum Influence on the Attitudes of School Children in Religious Education*, SSRC Research Report, HR 5580, October 1979

4) Michael Svennevig, Ian Haldane, Sharon Spiers and Barrie Gunter, *Godwatching, Viewers, Religion and Television*, John Libbey, London and IBA, 1988, Table 4.6, page 25

5) Leslie J Francis, 'Reliability and validity of a short measure of attitude towards Christianity among 9–11 year old pupils in England' in *CORE*, Vol 16, Part 1, Fiche 2 AO2 1992

6) Op cit (item 4) , page 25

7) Leslie J Francis, David W Lankshear and Paul R Pearson, 'The Relationship between religiosity and the short form JEPQ (JEPQ-S) indices of E, N, L and P among 11 year olds' in *Personality and Individual Differences* Vol 10 No 7 1989, pages 763–769

8) Leslie J Francis, 'Measuring attitude towards Christianity during childhood and adolescence' in *Personality and Individual Differences* Vol 10 No 6 1989, pages 695–698

9) See references listed in 'Monitoring Attitudes towards Christianity: the 1990 Study' by Leslie J Francis in *British Journal of Religious Education*, Vol 14 No 3, Summer 1992

10) Ibid

11) John E Greer and Leslie J Francis, 'Religious Experience and Attitude Toward Christianity among Secondary School Children in Northern Ireland' in *The Journal of Social Psychology* Vol 132 No 2 1991, pages 277–79

12) Leslie J Francis and Alan Jewell, 'Shaping adolescent attitude towards the church : comparison between Church of England and County Secondary Schools' in *Evaluation and Research in Education*, Vol 6 No 1 1992, pages 13–21

13) Canon John Finney, *Finding Faith Today, How does it happen?* British and Foreign Bible Society, Swindon, Wiltshire 1992, page 17

14) Op cit (item 7). See also Leslie J Francis and Alice Montgomery, 'Personality and Attitudes towards Christianity among 11–16 year old girls in a single sex Catholic School' in *British Journal of Religious Education*, Vol 14 No 2 Spring 1992, pages 114–19

15) T J Mark, 'A study of cognitive and affective elements in the religious development of adolescents', unpublished doctoral thesis, 1979, reviewed by William Kay in the *Digest* May 1981

16) Leslie J Francis and Laurence B Brown, 'The Influence of home, church and school on prayer among 16 year old adolescents in England' in *Review of Religious Research* Vol 33 No 2 December 1991, pages 112–122

17) Leslie J Francis, *The significance of Denominational Membership for young people*, Culham College Institute for Church related Education, 1983, page 14

18) Leslie J Francis, 'The Influence of Religion, Gender and Social Class on Attitudes toward School among 11 year olds in England'

in the *Journal of Experimental Education* Vol 60 No 4 Summer 1992, pages 339– 48

19) Michael P Hornsby-Smith and Raymond M Lee, *Roman Catholic Opinion, A study of Roman Catholics in England and Wales in the 1970s*, Department of Sociology, University of Surrey 1979, Page 76

20) Ibid, Table 6.1, page 212

21) Ibid, Table 6.6, page 213 excluding 'Don't knows'

22) Ibid, Table 6.8, page 216

23) Ibid, Figure 1, page 222

24) Peter Brierley, *Prospects for the Nineties*, MARC Europe, London 1991, page 45

25) Leslie J Francis and John E Greer, 'Measuring Christian Moral Values among Catholic and Protestant Adolescents in Northern Ireland' in *Journal of Moral Education*, Vol 21 No 1 1992, pages 59–65

26) J E Greer and L J Francis, 'The Religious Profile of Pupils in Northern Ireland' in *Journal of Empirical Theology*, Vol 3 No 2 1990, pages 35–50

27) Revd Dr John E Greer and Revd Dr Leslie J Francis, 'Measuring attitudes towards Christianity among pupils in Catholic Secondary Schools in Northern Ireland' in *Educational Research*, Vol 33 No 1 Spring 1991, pages 70–73

28) Op cit (item 5)

29) Op cit (item 16)

30) Leslie J Francis and Josephine Egan, 'The Catholic School as 'Faith Community'—an empirical inquiry' in *Religious Education* Vol 85 No 4 Fall 1990, pages 588–603

31) Peter L Sissons, *The Social Significance of Church Membership in the Borough of Falkirk*, report to Hope Trust and Church Ministry Department, Church of Scotland, 1973

32) Leslie J Francis and David W Lankshear, 'The Impact of Church Schools in Village Church Life' in *Educational Studies* Vol 16 No 2 1990, pages 117–129

33) Leslie J Francis and David W Lankshear, 'The Impact of Church Schools on Urban Church Life' in *School Effectiveness and School Improvements* Vol 2 No 4 1991, pages 324–335

34) Leslie J Francis and David W Lankshear, 'Urban Church Schools: Their Effect on Local Church Life' in *Cross Current, a Christian Voice in Education*, No 38 Summer 1992, pages 11–13

35) Op cit (item 17), page 5

36) Introductory chapter on 'Perspective on Religious Disaffiliation in *Falling from the Faith, Causes and Consequences of Religious Apostesy*, David G Bromley (Editor), Sage, London 1988, page 15

37) Op cit (item 17), page 16

38) Op cit (item 24), page 20

39) Thomas W Laquer, *Religion and Respectability : Sunday Schools and Working Class Culture 1780–1850*, Yale University Press 1976, but graph reproduced in op cit (item 41), page 22

40) David Martin, *A Sociology of English Religion*, New York 1967, page 42

41) Peter Brierley, *Children and the Church*, MARC monograph No 16, MARC Europe, London 1989, page 24

42) Op cit (item 41), page 25

43) Peter Brierley, *'Christian' England*, MARC Europe, London 1991, Table 41, page 102

44) Leslie J Francis, *Rural Anglicanism, a future for young Christians?* Collins 1985

45) Interview in *Alpha* magazine August 1991, page 17

46) Leslie J Francis, Harry M Gibson and David W Lankshear, 'Influence of Protestant Sunday Schools on attitudes towards Christianity' in *British Journal of Religious Education*, Vol 14 No 1 Autumn 1991, pages 35–42

47) Article 'Chalke Talk . . . Danger Zones!' in *Alpha* magazine March 1992, page 28

48) Shirley Jackson, *Christian Youth Work in Newham*, report on Newham Youth for Christ Survey, Newham YFC 1986, page 7

49) Brian Clews, *March for Jesus Roadshow* Report, Sunbury-on-Thames, Middlesex, May 1992, opinion poll results

50) Boyd Myers, *Young People's Relationships, Lifestyle and Sexual Attitudes*, Report for Agapé, Birmingham, MARC Europe, London 1991, private circulation. For further details see item 3 Chapter 2

51) Donald Postenski and Reginald Bibby, *Canada's Youth 'Ready for Today'*, comprehensive survey of 15–24 year olds, Canadian Youth Foundation 1988, page 18

52) John Smith, 'Cults of violence and healing tribes' in *Alpha* magazine July 1992, pages 30/31

53) Op cit (item 50), Tables 11 and 16, pages 10 and 14

54) Op cit (item 50) Table 21, page 19

55) Op cit (item 50) Table 24, page 21

56) Op cit (item 50) Table 20, page 17

57) *Children—the Influencing Factor*, Mintel Report 1991, reported in Daily Telegraph 25 October 1991

58) Robyn Richardson, *Parenting, a Reading Guide*, Zadok Institute for Christianity and Society, Bouton, ACT, Australia, No R27, March 1992

59) 'Passing on values that count' in *Context, Research to make religion relevant*, MARC Canada, Vol 3 No 1 January 1993, page 1

60) Ibid, page 2

61) Reginald W Bibby and Donald C Posterski, *Teen Trends, A Nation in Motion*, Stoddart, Toronto, Canada 1992, page 205

62) Ibid, page 213

63) Ibid, page 214

64) Corry Azzi and Ronald Ehrenberg, 'Household Allocation of Time and Church Attendance' in *Journal of Political Economy*, Vol 83 Part 1 1975, pages 27–56

65) Ronald G Ehrenberg, 'Household Allocation of Time and Religiosity : Replication and Extension' in *Journal of Political Economy*, Vol 85 1977, pages 413–423

66) Op cit (item 50), Table 38, page 32

67) *Background to the Task*, Scripture Union, London 1968. For more details see Chapter 4 (item 13)

68) Op cit (item 13), page 11

69) Paul D Meier, Frank B Minirth, Frank B Wichern and Donald E Ratcliff, *Introduction to Psychology and Counselling*, Christian Perspectives and Applications, Monarch, Tunbridge Wells, Kent, second edition 1991, page 254

70) Ibid

71) Proverbs 22:6

72) Op cit (item 61), pages 221/2

73) Tom Sine, *Wild Hope, A wake-up call to the Challenges and Opportunities of the 21st Century*, Monarch, Tunbridge Wells, Kent 1992, page 278

74) 'Faithful Parenting—ideas for shaping a new generation' in *Decision* magazine October 1991, page 17

75) Op cit (item 61), page 199

76) John 15:15

77) *Young People and Values in Western Europe*, Pro Mundi Vita Dossiers No 4, 1984 but fuller details than given in the text here are included in *What are Churchgoers Like?* Peter Brierley, MARC Monograph No 6, MARC Europe, London, May 1986, pages 28–31

## 6) Teenage Beliefs and Values

1) Quoted in *Reclaiming a Nation, the Challenge of Re-evangelizing Canada by the year 2000*, edited by Arnel Motz, Church Leadership Library, Richmond, BC 1990, page 35

2) Mick Byrne reported in *Survey*, Market Research Society, London Autumn 1990, page 14

3) *Young People's Relationships, Lifestyle and Sexual Attitudes*, survey report by Boyd Myers for Agapé, Birmingham, MARC Europe, London 1991, private circulation, page 23. For further details see item 3 Chapter 2

4) Jeff Astley and David Day (editors), *The Contours of Christian Education*, McCrimmon Publishing, Great Wakering, Essex 1992, Chapter 22 in *What is a Christian? Investigating the understanding of 16–19 year olds* by Leslie J Francis, Carolyn Wilcox and Jeff Astley

5) 2 Corinthians 4:4

6) Peter Brierley, *Act on the Facts*, MARC Europe, London 1992, page 158

7) Peter Bentley, 'Tricia Blombery and Philip Hughes, *Faith Without the Church?, Nominalism in Australian Christianity*, Christian Research Association, Victoria, Australia 1992, page 59

8) Proverbs 18:24

9) Phil Moon, *Finding a Youth Evangelism Strategy that Fits*, Grove Booklets on Evangelism, No 18, Nottingham 1992, page 19

10) 'Tricia Blombery, *Tomorrow's Church Today*, Christian Research Association, Victoria, Australia 1989, page 35

11) Leslie J Francis, *Believing without belonging : the teenage experience*, interim findings from 'Young People, Religion and Values Today' project, private circulation, page 8

12) George Barna, *The Barna Report 1992–93*, Regal Books, Ventura, California 1992, Table 73, page 255

13) Op cit (item 6)

14) *Christian Perspective on Faith Development*, edited by Jeff Astley and Leslie J Francis, Gracewing, Leominster, Hertfordshire 1992, page 252

15) Leslie J Francis, *Youth in Transit*, Gower, Aldershot, Hampshire 1982, page 55

16) Arkle L Bell, *Beliefs and Values—the Conflict between young people, Christian Youth Workers and local Christian organizations*, MA dissertation, Brunel University, May 1991, private circulation, page 72

17) Peter Brierley, *'Christian' England*, MARC Europe, London 1991, Figure 42, page 203

18) Bishop Lesslie Newbigin, 'The Gospel and our Culture' Consultation, 300+ delegates at Swanwick, July 1992, *Report of the Proceedings*, page 4

19) Ibid, page 51

20) David Day and Philip May, *Teenage Beliefs*, Lion Publishing, Oxford 1991

21) *British Social Attitudes*, Annual Report, Gower Publishing, (now Dartmouth Publishing), Aldershot, Hants with Social and Community Planning Research, London. Example quoted published in 1989, page 11

22) Op cit (item 15), page 54

23) Op cit (item 16), page 72

24) John Benington, *Culture, Class and Christian Beliefs*, Scripture Union, London 1973

25) Roger Mitchell, *Searching for Values*, Frontier Youth Trust, London 1976

26) Trustee Savings Bank survey by Research Business among 600 young people, reported in *Daily Telegraph* 18 May 1992

27) Gallup survey of 518 fourth and fifth year school pupils, reported in *Daily Telegraph* 2 October 1991

28) Op cit (item 26)

29) Reginald W Bibby and Donald C Postenski, *Teen Trends, A Nation in Motion*, Stoddart, Toronto, Canada 1992

30) 'Teen Trends' in *Context*, Vol 2 Issue 2 July 1992, MARC Canada, page 6

31) Op cit (item 12), Tables 61, 62, 64, 65, 68, 69 and 67 respectively

## 7) Reaching and Keeping Teenagers

1) Letter to *The Times* 9 May 1988

2) See for example Leslie J Francis and David Lankshear 'Church Provision for pre-school children : impact on urban church life' in *Research in Education*, No 48, November 1992, pages 55–64

3) Doreen Irvine, *From Witchcraft to Christ*, Concordia, London 1973

4) Revelation 12:4

5) Winkie Pratney 'Obstacles to Youth Work' in *Youthwork* No 1 December 1991 in *Alpha* magazine

6) Report *Spoilt Brats*, an extensive survey of teenagers and children of 1980s, Gold Greenlees Trott, advertising agency, 1989, and described in *Alpha* magazine November 1991, pages 30/31

7) Boys' Brigade England and Wales Committee, *Conference/ Consultation with Ministers*, November 1992, Summary, page 7

8) Eddie Gibbs, *Winning Them Back*, Monarch, Tunbridge Wells, Kent 1993

9) John 8:32

10) Winkie Pratney, *Welcome to the Nightmare*, notes of a talk, private circulation

11) Truman Brown Jr, 'Twenty-one keys for Reaching Baby Boomers' in *Growing Churches* magazine April-June 1991, page 17

12) Rev Peter Hockey, 'A story of Para-church Ecumenism' in *Religion Today*, Centre for New Religions, Kings College, London, Vol 8 No 1 Autumn/Winter 1992, page 16

13) So Andy Hickford, Youth Minister at Stopsley Baptist Church, Stopsley, Luton, Bedfordshire

14) Leslie J Francis and David W Lankshear, 'Do Small Churches hold a future for children and young people?' *MC*, Vol 33 No 1 1992, pages 15–19

15) Salvation Army Hall poster, Letchworth, September 1987
16) Paul D Meier, Frank B Minirth, Frank B Wichern, and Donald E Ratcliff, *Introduction to Psychology and Counselling, Christian Perspectives and Applications*, Monarch, Tunbridge Wells, Kent, second edition 1991, page 254
17) Ibid
18) Ibid
19) Ibid
20) Anon
21) George Barna, *Successful Churches*, report of Barna Research Group, Glendale, California 1990, reproduced with permission as MARC Monograph No 33, MARC Europe, London 1991, page 9
22) 1 Corinthians 13:8
23) Communicated via Andy Hickford
24) Ibid
25) 1 Corinthians 13:4–8
26) John Steward, World Vision of Australia, Melbourne, Australia

## Appendix 1

1) Peter Brierley, *The Salvation Army : What do its members say*? MARC Europe, private report London 1992, page 77
2) Boyd Myers, *Churchgoing changes in the Assemblies of God 1991–1992*, MARC Europe, private report, London 1992, page 10,
3) Boyd Myers, *Towards the Future of the Kent Baptist Association, Volume 1: The Main Report*, MARC Europe, private report, London 1992, page 6
4) Peter Brierley, *Prospects for the Nineties : West Yorkshire*, MARC Europe, London 1991
5) Peter Brierley, *Surrey, District by District*, MARC Europe, London 1992
6) Peter Brierley, *London, Borough by Borough*, MARC Europe, London 1992
7) Leslie J Francis, *Teenagers and the Church*, a profile of church-going youth in the 1980s, Collins Liturgical Publications, London 1984, Table 2.2, page 170
8) Peter Brierley, *Prospects for the Nineties*, Trends and Tables from the English Church Census, MARC Europe 1989, pages 20–47

# Index

## Christian Research Association

The vision of the Christian Research Association (CRA) is that by the year 2000, the use of relevant research by Christian leaders in strategic planning will be common place. *Reaching and Keeping Teenagers* is one such example.

The CRA publishes the *UK Christian Handbook* (UKCH) every two years. It is a mine of information on British Christianity, a one-volume reference library giving 17 pieces on information for over 5,000 organisations in the United Kingdom. It is not just bought in Britain. Ted Limpio, of Sepal in Brazil, wrote, "I couldn't help but be impressed by the quality and thoroughness of your work."

Corporate members of the CRA get a hardback copy of the UKCH *free*, and individual members are able to buy it at a substantial discount. Members also get the information bulletin, *Quadrant*, five times a year, are able to access the CRA Resources Library gratis, and are entitled to discounts on research work and training seminars.

Ask for more details of the CRA **today** by writing to the Christian Research Association, Vision Building, 4 Footscray Road, Eltham, London SE9 2TZ, or phone us on 081–294 1989. We look forward to hearing from you.

## British Church Growth Association

The British Church Growth Association was formed in September 1981 to help and encourage the church in Britain to move into growth in every dimension. The Association endeavours to offer practical help as well as encouraging and initiating church growth thinking and research.

Membership of the BCGA is open to both individuals and organisations interested in or involved in the theory or practice of church growth. Members receive the *Church Growth Digest* (the Association's journal) four times a year, information about activities through the Newsletters, special discounts and links with other researchers, teachers, practitioners, and consultants as well as help or advice on allied matters.

Further information is available from the Secretary, British Church Growth Association, 3a Newnham Street, Bedford, MK4 2JR, Tel: 0234 327905.